COMPUTER SCIENCE, TECHNOLOGY AND APPLICATIONS

LOGIC OF ANALOG AND DIGITAL MACHINES

COMPUTER SCIENCE, TECHNOLOGY AND APPLICATIONS

Additional books in this series can be found on Nova's website under the Series tab.

Additional E-books in this series can be found on Nova's website under the E-books tab.

COMPUTER SCIENCE, TECHNOLOGY AND APPLICATIONS

LOGIC OF ANALOG AND DIGITAL MACHINES

PAOLO ROCCHI

Nova Science Publishers, Inc.
New York

Copyright © 2012 by Nova Science Publishers, Inc.

All rights reserved. No part of this book may be reproduced, stored in a retrieval system or transmitted in any form or by any means: electronic, electrostatic, magnetic, tape, mechanical photocopying, recording or otherwise without the written permission of the Publisher.

For permission to use material from this book please contact us:
Telephone 631-231-7269; Fax 631-231-8175
Web Site: http://www.novapublishers.com

NOTICE TO THE READER

The Publisher has taken reasonable care in the preparation of this book, but makes no expressed or implied warranty of any kind and assumes no responsibility for any errors or omissions. No liability is assumed for incidental or consequential damages in connection with or arising out of information contained in this book. The Publisher shall not be liable for any special, consequential, or exemplary damages resulting, in whole or in part, from the readers' use of, or reliance upon, this material. Any parts of this book based on government reports are so indicated and copyright is claimed for those parts to the extent applicable to compilations of such works.

Independent verification should be sought for any data, advice or recommendations contained in this book. In addition, no responsibility is assumed by the publisher for any injury and/or damage to persons or property arising from any methods, products, instructions, ideas or otherwise contained in this publication.

This publication is designed to provide accurate and authoritative information with regard to the subject matter covered herein. It is sold with the clear understanding that the Publisher is not engaged in rendering legal or any other professional services. If legal or any other expert assistance is required, the services of a competent person should be sought. FROM A DECLARATION OF PARTICIPANTS JOINTLY ADOPTED BY A COMMITTEE OF THE AMERICAN BAR ASSOCIATION AND A COMMITTEE OF PUBLISHERS.

Additional color graphics may be available in the e-book version of this book.

LIBRARY OF CONGRESS CATALOGING-IN-PUBLICATION DATA
Rocchi, Paolo.
Logic of analog and digital machines / author, Paolo Rocchi.
p. cm.
Includes bibliographical references and index.
ISBN 978-1-62100-754-8 (softcover)
1. Computer logic--Popular works. 2. Logic design--Popular works. I. Title.
QA76.9.L63R63 2009
005.101'5113--dc22
2010012213

Published by Nova Science Publishers, Inc. ✚ *New York*

Contents

Foreword ix
Peter J. Denning

Introduction xiii

Symbols and Acronyms xv

Part 1

Chapter 1	A Rock Amid the Route	**1**
	1. A Chameleon	*2*
	2. Practical Perspective	*8*
	3. Sharpness	*14*
	4. Information Relativism	*22*
	5. Anarchic Issue	*30*
	6. Instrumental Acquisition of Information	*37*
	7. Complete Catalogue	*40*
	8. Concluding Remarks	*40*
	Bibliography	*42*
Chapter 2	Two Courses of Action	**47**
	1. Natural and Artificial	*47*
	2. Analog is Close to Nature	*48*
	3. Sharpness First	*54*
	4. After the First Stage	*57*
	5. Encoding	*64*
	6. Concluding Remarks	*72*
	Bibliography	*73*
Chapter 3	The Extravagant Realm	**75**
	1. Eclectic Profile	*75*
	2. Various Mathematical Theories	*85*
	3. Meticulous Designers	*90*
	4. Paradigms and Technologies	*93*
	5. Concluding Remarks	*100*
	Bibliography	*103*

Part 2		**105**
Chapter 4	System Architecture	**107**
	1. From Information to Units	108
	2. Two Models for a Digital System	116
	3. Concluding Remarks	118
	Bibliography	121
Chapter 5	Nets and Spots	**123**
	1. Analog Components	123
	2. Channels	124
	3. Systems for Transmission	128
	4. Control of Computer Nets	132
	5. Concluding remarks	135
	Bibliography	137
Chapter 6	Storage	**139**
	1. Efficient Logistics	139
	2. Digital Memories	140
	3. Files	141
	4. Databases	144
	5. Design of Data Organizations	146
	6. Concluding Remarks	149
	Bibliography	151
Chapter 7	Efficient Strategy	**153**
	1. Compression	154
	2. Encryption	155
	3. Redundancy	157
	4. Concluding Remarks	163
	Bibliography	164
Chapter 8	Adapt for Survival	**167**
	1. Software Programming	167
	2. Adaptation	169
	3. Work Organizations	176
	4. Programmable Systems	181
	4. Concluding Remarks	184
	Bibliography	186
Chapter 9	The Galaxy of Programs	**189**
	1. Variable Influence of the Context	189
	2. Spectrum of Possibilities	192
	3. Concluding remarks	195
	Bibliography	202

Part 3		**205**
Chapter 10	People Like to Communicate	**207**
	1. Human Work	*207*
	2. Poor and Rich Languages	*208*
	3. No Worry for Information Techniques	*211*
	4. One Sign One Sound	*213*
	5. Hybrid Appliances	*220*
	6. Concluding remarks	*221*
	Bibliography	*222*
Index		**225**

FOREWORD

By Peter J. Denning

Computer Science is a very young discipline compared to most others. Alan Turing published the seminal paper of the field in 1936. Around the same time, the militaries in Germany, UK, and US commissioned the first digital electronic computer projects. One of these, the Colossus at Bletchley Park in the UK, was used to break the German Enigma code and help turn the tide of World War II; its existence was not made public until the 1970s. The other projects reached completion after the war: the ENIAC at University of Pennsylvania in 1946 and EDSAC at University of Cambridge in 1949 are prominent examples. The first academic degree in computing was University of Pennsylvania's program in computing in 1959. The first academic computer science departments were Purdue and Stanford in 1962.

For many years, people in the other fields were not sure what to make of computer science. Depending on their background, they saw computer science as an outgrowth of mathematics, science, or electrical engineering. Although many people were delighted with the advances enabled in many fields by computing technologies, they did not see anything fundamental about computing to warrant a permanent seat at the table of science. It became a standing joke that any field using the name "science" in its title could not be a real science based on deep, universal principles. In reaction, many people in the field today called it the "computing field", a shorthand for "computer and information science and engineering".

Through the mid 1980s, when most computer scientists were focused on building computer systems and networks, an engineering perspective dominated the field. Many observers believed that in due course, once the infatuation with the newness of computing wore off, computer science would be absorbed back into electrical engineering. Other observers believed that the only part of computer science that worked with fundamental principles was the mathematics part; they believed that in due course, computer science would be absorbed back into mathematics.

In the mid 1980s, a new development threw a wrench into these beliefs. A growing number of scientists declared that computational science was a new paradigm of science, a new way to approach scientific discovery, experiment, and validation. The computational science movement gained momentum when physicist Ken Wilson was awarded a Nobel Prize for his discovery of fundamental principles for phase changes in materials, using computational methods with renormalization groups. Under pressure from Wilson and other well-known scientists, the US government formed an interagency high performance computing coordination committee and established a major research program to tackle "grand challenge problems in science". In 1991, the US Congress recognized all this with the High Performance Computing and Communications Act. Computer scientists became major players, cooperating with scientists in many other fields.

Starting in the middle 1980s, the nascent Internet began expanding exponentially, bringing the results of computer science research into millions of homes and businesses. A decade later, the World Wide Web burst on the scene; another result of computer science research, the Web gave birth to new ways of sharing information and the e-commerce revolution. In this context, new and amazing wonders began to appear including interactive multimedia graphics, virtual reality games, massive multiplayer online games, web science, social networking, digital libraries, distance learning, public-key cryptography, quantum computing, and much more.

Thus, by 2000, it was clear that this odd field was not going to be "absorbed" into any of its predecessor fields. Its staying power was the result of its tapping into deep and fundamental principles that could bring value to millions of people.

I myself was among the first who graduated with academic degrees in the new field. I was not beholden to a background in mathematics, science, or electrical engineering as were many of my teachers and founders of the field. I identified completely with the new field and made it my life's work.

In 1969, a year after receiving my PhD, the leaders of an NSF project called "computer science in engineering" invited me to put together a team to develop a core course in operating system principles. The notion that computer operating systems relied on fundamental scientific principles was radical at the time. My team had no difficulty identifying fundamental principles for concurrency, memory management, name management, protection of data, and design of complex software systems. These principles became the core of operating systems textbooks since that time. I joined with Ed Coffman to write a book, *Operating Systems Theory* (Prentice-Hall, 1973) that laid out all the resulting analytical models for operating systems and showed how to use them for prediction and design.

Many other areas of computer science established conferences and journals about their fundamental principles. Operating systems were not alone in being principles-based.

Thus, from the earliest days of my career, I was a firm believer that computer science rested on fundamental principles that were not known in other fields. It was always a puzzle to me that others thought, instead, that the fundamental principles of computing came from mathematics, physics, and electrical engineering. I saw many principles that mathematicians, physicists, and electrical engineers did not know. In 1985-1993 I wrote 47 installments of the "science of computing" column for *American Scientist* magazine, where I devoted myself to showing these principles to the scientists from many fields.

By the 1990s, the standard way of describing the computing field was to list its key technologies -- for example, algorithms, data structures, programming languages, networks, operating systems, graphics, and artificial intelligence. In the mid 1990s, I concluded that this way formulation obscured the fundamental principles. I began to ask whether there might be a way to reformulate computer science so that it did not seem like a technology field. This led me to found the Great Principles of Computing Project (greatprinciples.org), which offered an alternative framework for the field. The framework offers the fundamental principles of the field in the seven categories computation, communication, coordination, recollection, automation, evaluation, and design.

This framework calls immediate attention to the principles, which are then manifested in technologies. The framework distinguished permanent principles from fast-changing technologies that incorporated them. The seven categories are unique to computing.

This framework reopened old questions that were investigated at the beginning of the field and lapsed during the giant technology push from 1955 through 1985. These questions include: what is information? What is computation? What are the limits of computation? What can we know through computation? What can't we know? Although there may be no final, definitive answers to these questions, the process of asking them can produce major new insights, discoveries, and inventions.

In this context comes Paolo Rocchi with his deep and penetrating inquiry into the nature of information. In this book he takes great strides with the first great question, "what is information?"

Two things become immediately clear from Rocchi's inquiry. First, information pervades most, if not all, fields at their deepest levels. That includes the natural sciences. Second, no other field studies information as a pervasive, natural phenomenon. He concludes that computer science, which focuses on the universal principles of information, is unique and is performing a service not done by any other field. This conclusion echoes Paul Rosenbloom of USC, who claims computing as the fourth great domain of science, along with the physical, life, and social sciences.

The founders of the computing field frequently said that the new field was devoted to the study of information processes. However, faced with the difficulty of defining information, and with the skepticism that computing deals with fundamental issues, many in the field retreated to the term "data processing". They used "data" to refer to the symbol-sequences that controlled the machine and defined its input and output, and they left "information" to be the assignment of meaning to data. With this distinction, information was pushed outside the machine, and the machine only had to deal with the precise rules of symbol manipulation. The same distinction was a hallmark of Claude Shannon's information theory, which by design did not address the "semantics" of data and signals.

But this distinction always left many people feeling unsatisfied. If information is the assignment of meaning, does it not then become subjective? There can be no guarantee that one person will assign the same meaning as another. How can we have scientific reproducibility when the fundamental phenomenon is a matter of individual assessment?

Rocchi's conclusion is that information consists of (1) a *sign*, which is a physical manifestation or inscription, (2) a *relationship*, which is the association between the sign and what it stands for, and (3) an *observer*, who learns the relationship from community and holds on to it. This package incorporates all the previous notions of information. The observer as a member of a social community gives uniformity of interpretation and continuity over time. Rocchi explores how this notion applies to analog and digital representations in processing, interpreting, storing, retrieving, and transmitting information.

It is a rich exploration, well worth reading and reflecting on.

Peter Denning
Salinas, California

November 2009

INTRODUCTION

Computer systems shine in the limelight long since. Electronic businesses have demonstrated uninterrupted innovation and have acquired enduring success. Researchers contrived a wealth of solutions that have produced and are still producing brilliant earnings. Hardware and software products have changed our lifestyle and this exciting context has left little time for scientists to analyze the inner nature of Computing. Cultural progress in Computer Science is lagging behind the progress of technology.

There is in human beings a surge of curiosity about the significance of Computing which expects answers but some significant references appear outdated. I quote the Turing machine, an indisputable cornerstone in the field devised in the thirties, which basically exhibits a static image of computing. The pressing changes of software programs which practitioners manage in the living environment call Turing's model into question. Take the information theory defined by Claude Shannon when computers looked like huge cupboards. His seminal work has kept the same profile for over half a century and theorists toil after the inquiries on quantum information. John von Neumann transplanted the mathematical concept of algorithm into the software in the fifties. Nowadays multimedia applications and objects programming apply communicative criteria rather than abstract syllogisms and the mathematical approach appears somewhat outdated in the new context.

The works by Turing, Shannon and von Neumann proved to be adequate to understand the early systems built by pioneers, but are not up to comprehending the present-day evolved systems. Theorists should enhance our understanding of technologies. Various solicitations have emerged in journals and books[1,2] in the attempt to promote the culture in the field. Practitioners need thorough models as a basis to surmount professional difficulties and even it is necessary to provide computer users with help.

I accepted these challenging invitations and in a special manner I was involved in examining the profile of computing systems. I delved into the conundrum of what really the analog and the digital logic consists.

The approach to follow together with the subject matter puzzled me. "There are two fundamental modes of study – wrote Thomas C. Chamberlain[3] – The one is an attempt to follow by close imitation the processes of previous thinkers and to acquire the results of their investigations by memorizing. It is the study of a merely secondary, imitative or acquisitive

---

[1] Wegner P., Goldin D. (2003) - Computation beyond Turing Machines- *Communications of the ACM*, 46(4).

[2] Wing J.M. (2008) - Five Deep Questions in Computing - *Communications of the ACM*, 51(1).

[3] Chamberlain T.C. (1890) - The Method of Multiple Working Hypotheses - *Science* 15, 92.

nature. In the other mode the effort is to think independently, or at least individually. It is primary or creative study." The innovative flavor of computing pushed me toward the second course. I looked for an original pathway and made an attempt to see computer systems by using new glasses. I directed my efforts from an independent viewpoint and took a research-course that was as demanding as a mountain trek at high altitude. The quest covered decades, and the route crossed very remote areas on rough and desert terrains.

Matthew Arnold holds that culture is the ultimate authority in society, although high-culture classes sometimes take a conservative tendency. What is different may be viewed as a threat, and what is unconventional is often associated with an occasion to waste time. The risks entailed by unexpected replies appear evident to me.

But many people trust that what is different may be better than what we currently know, and the presentation of my findings is a challenge worth accepting.

SYMBOLS AND ACRONYMS

ACM	Association for Computing Machinery
CPU	Central Processing Unit
DES	Data Encryption Standard
DNA	Deoxyribonucleic Acid
E	Signifier
EM	Electromagnetic
EN	Signified
ERD	Entity Relationship Diagram
EV	Environment
FSM	Finite State Machine
GN	Geographic Network
GP	General Purpose
H	Entropy
ICT	Information and Communication Technology
IEEE	Inst. of Electrical and Electronic Engineers
IFIP	Intl. Federation for Information Processing
IS	Information System
LAN	Local Area Network
OP-AMP	Operational Amplifier
OR	Operations Research
OS	Operating System
R (normal)	Observer
R (italic)	Redundancy
S	General System
SDM	Software Development and Maintenance
STT	State Transition Table
V	Volt

Part 1

Chapter 1

A ROCK AMID THE ROUTE

An ample circle of scholars is open to gain deeper insights into computer technologies and hopes that explanatory theories will be brought up to date. Alvin Schrader (1986) has analyzed various conceptualizations that appeared in the literature over the past 80 years and underlines the needs of universal definitions and concepts in information science. Edsger W. Dijkstra authored several papers on fundamental topics of programming from the sixties up to the year of his death in 2002. Peter J. Denning is intensely concerned about appropriate principles on Computing and is perhaps the most active living advocate for the conceptual development of this field. "*Computing as a Discipline*" – the preliminary report of the ACM task force on the core of Computer Science (Denning et al 1989) – captured the intensive interest of researchers and gave rise to ample debates within the scientific community.

I absolutely share the feeling and the aims pursued by those scholars. My investigations addressed topics close to the principles of Computer Science but the starting point of my way is rather new with respect to current literature.

As a physicist I am inclined to see the *principle of causality* as a solid ontological principle which provides the basis to modern sciences (Hübner et al 1983). Any material event has a practical origin and the correspondence between causes and effects regulates the logic of machines in addition to the logic of natural phenomena. The principle of causality sustains engineering besides theoretical sciences, in particular this principle makes clear that the product w, carried on by S, is the cause of the system S in that the outcome w determines the components of S and the entire logic of S. Manufacturers install S and this in turn outputs w. First comes S and later w on the operational time table; instead things go the opposite way in the intellectual sphere due to the principle of causality. The examination of w precedes the scrutiny of S since this product determines the features of the machine. The principle of causality yields the natural method of study which may be found in many sectors: as first one becomes aware of w and later of S. For ease an engineer-to-be takes lessons on Chemistry and Organic Chemistry, and then can comprehend the plant that refines raw petroleum. He/she masters the refinery processes only when familiar with oil and derivatives that result in the refinery operations.

Nobody has ever disputed this rational approach but no author has applied this mode to the computer sector so far. The computing machine S manipulates information, and one should examine information first and computer technologies later. But to the best of my knowledge, commentators introduce the hardware components and the software programs on the *as-is* basis. They usually describe analog and digital solutions just created and are not inclined to discuss what makes those solutions happen, to explicate the great principles that guide – or should guide – computer experts.

The reasons for this odd behavior may be easily assessed.

Huge obstacles impair the efforts of thinkers to clarify what is information. The course that looks to be the most natural on paper actually involves a lot of argument in reality. The analysis of technical solutions grounded on the concept of information is an open challenge and I mean to proceed in stages along this trying way.

1. A Chameleon

Various scientists are unraveling the nature of information in numerous areas. Experts in Neurosciences, Linguistics, Cognitive Sciences, Sociology, Education and Communication besides Informatics search for the solid definition of what is information. Different scientific theories have been put forward to explain what is information but none has reached universal consensus. Ritchie (1986) observes:

"Confusion has also arisen from confounding the precise technical and statistical usage of words such as 'uncertainty', 'information' and 'communication' with the more common, everyday usage of these words".

The classification of those theories is challenging too. The ensuing partial list can give an idea about the variety of schools of thought:

- The *algorithmic* theory of information by Solomonoff, Kolmogorov (1965), and Chaitin (1977);
- The *autopoietic* theory of information by Maturana, Varela (1980);
- The *biological* information theory by Jablonka (2002);
- The *cybernetic* information theory by Nauta jr. (1970);
- The *dynamic* theory of information by Chernavsky (1990);
- The *economic* theory of information by Marschak (1971);
- The *Fisherian* theory of information by Fisher (1950);
- The *general* information theory by Klir (1991);
- The *general* theory of information by Burgin (2009);
- The *hierarchical* information theory by Brookes (1980);
- The *independent* theory of information by Losee (1997);
- The *living system* information theory by Miller (1978);
- The *logical* theory of information by Tarski (1983);
- The *organizational* information theory by Stonier (1994);
- The *philosophy* of information by Floridi (1999);
- The *physical* theory of information by Mityugov (1976), Levitin (1992);
- The *pragmatic* theory of information by von Weizsäcker (1974), von Lucadou (1987);
- The *qualitative* theory of information by Mazur (1974);

- The *semantic* theory of information by Carnap, Bar Hillel (1953);
- The *social* theory of information by Goguen (1997);
- The *sociological* theory of information by Garfinkel (2008);
- The *statistical* theory of information by Shannon (1949);
- The *statistical* theory of information by Wiener (1961);
- The *systemic* theory of information by Luhmann (1990);
- The *utility* theory of information by Harkevich (1960).

Electrical engineers began using the term '*information*' to describe data transmission during the first half of the twentieth century. Those engineers were involved in down-to-earth questions; and made efforts to maximize the amount of transmitted data and to minimize noise (Hartley 1928). Claude Shannon was the first to devise a formal conceptualization of information in the engineering field. Shortly afterward his work stimulated investigations directed toward several directions. The diverging intents and purposes of the various theories appear apparent. The above listed adjectives: *semantic*, *algorithmic*, *autopoietic*, etc. can aid the reader's intuition. K. E. Pettigrew and Lynne McKechnie (2001) conducted a survey on the use of theories in information science and conclude how the examined theories often stand without the least explicit relationship to each other. A circle of Shannon followers – such as Marschak, Kolmogorov, Brookes, and Miller – considers the master's theory good but insufficient and refines it or enriches it with new contributions. The rest of the cited writers propose a variety of more or less original alternative definitions of information. A group of authors – see Burgin and Klir – searches for a comprehensive conceptualization; others give up holistic aspirations. Carnap's view on information revolves around on Semantics; instead Shannon deliberately ignores the aspects of Semantics. Kolmogorov reasons at the pure technical level, whereas Bateson, Maturana and Varela aim at unifying the view of the mind with the world out there and have inaugurated the '*second order cybernetics*', an original cultural movement. Norman Wiener rejects the idea that information is physical, and Tom Stonier sees information as much a part of the physical universe as energy and matter. Whilst to Shannon information is inversely proportional to probability, to Wiener it is directly proportional to probability: the one is simply the negative of the other.

Theorists do not converge even on the nature of the problem; a circle sees information as a quantity to measure – e.g. Shannon, Kolmogorov, Fisher and Klir – other thinkers – e.g. Floridi – are convinced of the prismatic constitution of information which one can scrutinize only from the philosophical stance. The former are prone to attack the problems using analytical methods, the latter rejects any analytical approach and claims that pure philosophy can enlighten the argument.

All these efforts yield a lot of papers and books. There is no lack of scientific contributions on the table however those proposals have not led to a generally recognized definition. Complaints about the misunderstandings and misuses of the very idea of information are frequently expressed (Sayre 1976). Schrader (1986) holds:

> "The proliferation of notions of what information means staggers the mind: 134 variant notions have been documented in the present research. This proliferation demonstrates the conceptual chaos issuing from the definitional literature of information science."

There are so many irreconcilable issues that I am prone to conclude with René Thom (1975):

"Information is a semantic chameleon"

I am intimately positive and am convinced that the wealth of theories is a sign of vitality and liveliness of thought. The scientific community begets ideas and projects, and advances even when the works seem to fail the intended targets. In fact multiple views mature the minds of researchers who derive the definitive solutions through debates and confrontation.

Unfortunately this is not the case of the information area since authors develop clashing viewpoints and rarely show a collaborative attitude. They even squabble and take a strike at one another. They often deny any validity to their opponents and – there is something worst – do not accept confrontation. For example Shannon's followers interpret this statement in a very radical mode:

"These semantic aspects of communication are irrelevant to the engineering problem."
(Shannon 1949)

And in practice refuse a dialogue with semioticians and linguists who methodically focus on the meanings of signs. On the other side a circle of humanists plunges into literary genres and does not bother about the *information and communication technology* (ICT). Uncommunicative thinkers do not facilitate progress in the field which presently shows a rather sorry state.

Strong divisions, incomplete and generic outcomes do not seem to support my cultural project, that is, to go deep into the computer technologies starting from the notion of information. The lack of solid theoretical references looks like an immense rock amid the route that obstructs my progress.

I have just taken to the road with the ambitious purpose of proceeding along a challenging route and I cannot go onward.

A. Odd Opponents and True Friends

Some decades ago I got distressed by this barrier. I felt unhappy of course and had a strong desire to circumvent this obstacle. I investigated all over the literature in the hope of coming up with a better idea. At last this exploration paid its dividends and bore evidence that my initial bleak sensation was partially incorrect.

When a reader explores works involved in the various aspects of information, or crosses the borders erected amongst the numerous sectors dealing with communication, he/she meets with a pleasant discovery: the vast majority of scientists do not dissent completely.

Authors conflict upon the abstract idea of information, but agree on what a piece of information consists. A piece of information is a *sign*, also named *signal, message, piece of news* etc. Signs take the form of *words, images, numbers, music, sounds, gestures* and *objects* and different schools of thought achieve common conclusions. The comprehension of a piece of information surprisingly proves to be rather uniform. Scholars – including Shannon whom we shall see next – are prone to deem that a piece of information has a material basis and fulfils a semantic function. They tend to converge upon the idea that a sign has a physical origin and stands for something.

In accordance to the most popular terminology deriving from Ferdinand De Saussure, we shall call the body of a sign as the *signifier* (= E); and the represented entity as the *signified* (= NE). The distinction between signifier and signified has sometimes been equated to the familiar dualism of *form* and *content*. Small bodies of ink on paper, electric impulses along wires, sonorous waves in the air, and pixels on the display screen are familiar examples of signifiers in the computer sector. By contrast the signified does not need to be a real object but is some referent to which the signifier refers. By way of illustration take:

New York

This film of ink is the signifier E and the large American town considered the centre of the world is the signified $NE1$. I can also use this item of ink to denote the idea of New York that I have in mind (= $NE2$) and thus I handle an immaterial signified.

When we examine closely the Shannon paper (1949), we find that he calculates signals conveyed in a channel which are physical quantities and carry on a message. He recognizes that – for example – four voltage values **1001** make a flow of electric impulses and symbolize the alphabet letter A, **1100** does B etc. Søren Brier (2008) remarks:

The Shannon theory "presumes that signals are meaningful codes established in a system of signs, such as the Morse code for the alphabet, that makes sense for humans".

Shannon accepts that an electric impulse (= E) signifies something like a letter (= NE) or a figure despite the fact that he considers Semantics to be irrelevant from the theoretical view.

The abstract interpretation of information lies beyond the horizon. Nobody can say when the definitive solution will be established; in the meanwhile scientists subscribe to conceptualization on what a sign consists in. The shared contents may be expressed by this concise issue:

A sign has a physical origin (= E) and stands for something in the world (= NE).   [1.1]

The material and semantic properties of signs summed up in [1.1] did not follow the same way in literature, they had far different provenance and fortune during the centuries.

The semantics of signs was recognized since a long time. Very early on the naïf idea of meaning saw the light in Western culture. Aristotle, the genius involved in all the known disciplines of his era, also found the time to bother about human communication. In "*De Interpretatione* (On Interpretation)", a short treatise dealing with language and logic, he writes:

"Spoken words are the symbols of mental experience and written words are the symbols of spoken words. Just as all men have not the same writing, so all men have not the same speech sounds, but the mental experiences, which these directly symbolize, are the same for all, as also are those things of which our experiences are the images." (Aristotle 2004).

Whilst the semantic nature of signs appeared evident early on and was developed through a lot of discussion, the physical side of information was muddy up to recent decades. Ancient writers marked the basis of linguistic signs using the Latin term '*vox (voice)*' which vaguely alludes to a psychological constitution. Ferdinand De Saussure (1983) presumed the *form* of a sign is immaterial and added the language itself is "a form, not a substance".

In the last century the progress of ICT helped thinkers to become gradually aware of the concrete body of information, and finally authors tended to converge toward the material interpretation of E. Even Gottlob Frege (1892), Tadeusz Kotarbinski (1968) and other followers of the logical schools, who sustain the most abstract stance, partake of the concrete origin of information. Charles Morris (1964) and Doede Nauta coined the clause *information carrier* and we even find the terms *sign vehicle* to highlight the physicism of a symbol. The base E looks like a cart loading goods: a very practical perspective indeed!

Regardless of which interpretation one gives to the tenet of information, I find general consensus on [1.1] which I rewrite in the following pair of points:

(1) *A signifier has a physical basis,*
(2) *A signifier stands for something.*

B. The Semantic Triangle

Pleasant discoveries in literature did not come to an end for me.

A large number of specialists agree that a third element is necessary to complete the interpretation of signs. The semantic processes do not have mechanical-artificial origins and authors come into accord that the connection between the signified and the signifier does not operate in the world out there; an *intellectual sense-maker* or *interpreter* links the signifier to the signified.

A great number of thinkers made the semantic elements progressively intelligible in the arch of centuries. Sextus Empiricus, Severinus Boethius, Thomas Aquinas up to De Saussure analyzed the components of a sign according to the fine reconstruction made by François Rastier (1990). In the late nineteenth century the American philosopher and logician Charles Sanders Peirce formulated the triadic model (Hartshorne et al. 1931-66). In 1923 C. K. Ogden and I. A. Richards (1989) drew a geometrical diagram to clarify the semantic processes and fixed the *thought* as the sense-maker.

The concept of *thought* has a reasonable degree of generalness for the present work. The intellect recognizes/ interprets/ invents the meanings of signs and brings about the entire semantic processes. Saussure wrote that E and E^* are "intimately linked" "by an associative link" in the mind and "each triggers the other". This is enough for us to conclude that the *thought* or the *mind ME* bridges E with NE.

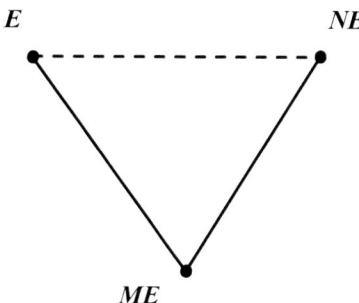

Figure 1.1. The semantic triangle.

One cannot deny that the semantic triangle raises a lot of serious questions.

Whilst commentators' positions tend to converge around the concepts of signifier and signified, the functions of the sense-maker raise a lot of discussion and lie far from unified conclusions. Terms such as: *interpretant, sense, signification, semiosis, significate, thought* and *reference*, connote the vertices of the triangle, and this varied terminology mirrors the contrasting philosophical perspectives and pinpoints the misaligned interpretations of the semantic processes. What meanings exactly signify is still rather mysterious. Bertrand Russell and G. Frege believe meaning is a nominated subject (Wolfgang, 1994); A. Tarskij assumes meaning is an interrelation between a sign and a significate; L. Wittgenstein says that a meaning is a relation between a sign and people's behavior. Ogden and Richards mention 23 different definitions of the term '*meaning*' in their monograph (Ogden et al. 1989).

The recourse to the public character of words begs the question of how the mind is supposed to gain access to the extra-mental world. Some thinkers posited that there must be a realm of concepts in the mind as bearers of meaning, but Wittgenstein and others have brought suspicion on treating thoughts as '*mental representations*'. Man's intellect executes a wealth of functions: it recognizes the significance of a sign; it extends the meanings or updates the coverage of the signifier etc. The importance of the sense-maker has a particular appeal for communication and media theorists who stress the value of its active process, while others highlight the receptive aspect of the intellect. The psychological and sociological features of significance cast light upon the human arbitrariness that prove to be not trivial. On the other hand, logicians focus on the truth and the falsity of intellectual reasoning, and highlight the determinism of the semantic relationships.

Alan Turing, John von Neumann and other modern thinkers on Artificial Intelligence (AI) are convinced of direct connections extant between the computer and the human mind. The brain can be found to be performing something like computational processing. One can read the intriguing history of the efforts of scientists to develop a machine able to think like a human being in (Pratt 1987). The bonds between natural intelligence and artificial devices make it even more intricate to interpret what is significance and enhance the attraction of the semantic triad for commentators.

The semantic triangle encapsulates very important arguments deeply bound up with philosophical topics and even with unresolved questions concerning the logic and essence of human life. The intellectual nucleus of signs epitomizes the formation of human knowledge and raises debates upon the origin of the mind, upon its unpredictable and free nature, upon learning, memory, will, consciousness and many other knotty arguments.

Endless debates are taking place and any synopsis of current works risks being reductive and incomplete. These arguments go beyond the scopes of the present book addressing the computer technologies. I also overlook the prismatic facets of meaning such as denotation, connotation, articulation and intentionality. Far be it from me to comment the various positions emerging in the scientific community.

I am prone to accept the diagram in Figure 1.1 that will be enough for the purposes which I declare in the inception of this book. I mean to complete statement [1.1] in the following manner:

A sign is equipped with three elements in all: the signifier E, the signified NE and the mental function ME which relates the former to the latter. [1.2]

All those components which take place at the corners of the semantic triangle are necessary to create cognition, information, and communication. Two solid lines in Figure 1.1 link the signifier and the signified with *ME* in order to picture the substantial intervention of thought in the semantic process. The dotted line between *E* and *NE* will be commented later.

The lack of universal consensus upon what is information enables me to use the word '*information*' as a generic term henceforward.

2. PRACTICAL PERSPECTIVE

A number of thinkers define signifiers as the *surface structure* of a language, others mark a signifier as a *shape* of information. The terms *surface* and *shape* puts the signifier close to a suit whose appearance does not influence the personality of the man wearing it. This terminology echoes the difficulties of experts who did not arrive at a satisfactory definition of *E* for centuries, and hints the idea that signifiers play an ancillary role.

In my opinion this idea sounds rather dated in the face of the enormous amount of applied works dealing with the physical properties of information. A wealth of pragmatic quests pores over the material nature of signs. Computer scientists are the first of the class that amounts to a large number of members. Researchers coming from a variety of experimental fields analyze the structure and the properties of signifiers used in the world.

A. A Large Group of Disciplines

Fundamental qualities of communication derive from the material substance of signs, and linguists categorize languages depending on the material essence of languages. This classification, which is prerequisite to further studies includes for instance:

- *Textual languages* i.e. signifiers are words printed on paper,
- *Vocal languages* i.e. signifiers are sonorous words,
- *Gestural languages* i.e. signifiers are motions of limbs,
- *Pictorial languages* i.e. signifiers are colored pigments,
- *Musical languages* i.e. signifiers are sounds.

Physical features determine the nature of each language and cannot swap. Nobody can switch from one material medium to another medium without losses and modifications. For ease in 1725 Antonio Vivaldi published *"The Four Seasons"*, a violin concerto that recreates scenes located in spring, summer, fall and winter respectively. Each of the four parts is illustrated by a sonnet – presumably written by the composer – full of allusions ripe for sonic depiction. Concertos and sonnets recount the same scenes; they depict the same vistas and are very akin but the melodious language gives rise to sensations that the sonnets cannot stir. Ink and music convey untranslatable contents. One cannot exchange the feelings evoked by the poems with the sensations of the concertos because of their different material nature.

Word Order	Languages Number	%
SOV	497	41
SVO	436	35
VSO	85	7
VOS	26	2
OVS	9	1<
OSV	4	1<<
No dominant order	171	14
TOTAL	1228	

Figure 1.2. Popularity of word order (Source: Dryer op.cit.).

Typology, an entire and ever-increasing sub-field in linguistics, spells out the order of the words (Whaley 1996). Authors recognize six basic types of declarative sentences in all: SOV, SVO, VSO, VOS, OVS and OSV, where S marks the *subject*, O the *object* and V the *verb*. By way of illustration:

- English is a SVO language
  e.g. *"Tom* (=subject) *met* (=verb) *Sally* (=object)";
- Japanese is SOV
  e.g. *"Gakusei-ga hon-o yonda* (= *student book read*)";
- Welsh is VSO
  e.g. *"LLaddodd y ddraig y dyn* (= *killed the dragon the man*)".

The disposition of subject, verb and object is a physical property which leads to important classification of languages. SOV (subject-object-verb) is preferred by the largest number of modern languages. SVO (subject-verb-object) is the second group, but has the greatest number of speakers because this group includes the most popular idioms such as English, Chinese, French, Spanish, Portuguese, Russian, the Germanic languages, many languages of Africa and of Southeast Asia, including Khmer, Vietnamese, Thai, and Malay.

There are words in a language indicating the relation of the substantive to a verb, an adjective, or another substantive. These words are members of closed classes named as *prepositions* and *postpositions*. A preposition is placed before the intended substantive X, the postposition is located behind X. For example 'with' comes before 'me' in English sentences and is classified as preposition. Take: "Bob speaks with me"; the clause 'with me' is translated in Turkish as 'benim ile' (literary 'me with'), namely 'with' is a preposition and 'ile' is a postposition. It is evident how prepositions and postpositions regulate time-space properties of languages.

Linguists go on with their materialistic approach and discuss whether the disposition *adjective-noun* (AN) or otherwise *noun-adjective* (NA) emerges as the prevalent order in a phrase. For instance the English expression "Good morning!" is AN; the Italian clause "piogge sparse" is a NA form.

Experts even go into the displacement of the atomic parts in a word. They inquire into *prefixes, suffixes*, and *infixes* and how these parts changed position during the centuries and influenced the grammar rules.

Linguists dedicate a fair amount of attention to the *order* of words and word components which is a material characteristic. In fact the order regulates the spatial place of written words and the temporal priority of spoken words: order is a time-space property. It is not exaggerated to use the designation 'physical linguistics' for typology.

Marshall McLuhan (1965) masterfully explains how tiny physical details which belong to a communication system and which appear trivial at first glance, provoke broad and astonishing social phenomena. The medium has a profound influence on human thought of which the user may not always be conscious. McLuhan's famous aphorism:

"The medium is the message"

Summarizes how the construction of a medium adds contents to the mere message transmitted. The concrete constitution of a signifier and the way it is delivered has deep effects on the human soul; it alters human perception and affects human consciousness. The make-up of a medium delivers specific contents so that it directs listeners' attention, and influences the behavior of social groups.

The physical structure of a medium leads McLuhan to the distinction of *hot* and *cool media*. A hot medium enhances only one single sense and accordingly is rich in detail – note how the richness and poorness of details do not refer to the *content* but to the *form* in which this content is necessarily communicated due to the composition of the medium – the focus on one sense caused by a hot medium makes the recipient refer to his inwardness and thus separates him from the outside world. A cold medium in contrast lacks detail whilst it demands active attendance and a multi-sensory participation from the recipient.

Two examples illustrate this distinction: the radio is a hot medium and the television is cold. In actual fact the radio only enhances the acoustic sense and stimulates receivers' self-suggestion. By the way McLuhan remarks upon how the radio reinforced the excitement of the Nazi propaganda. Television stimulates visual, acoustic and also collective participation and should be considered a cold medium. The multi-sensory structure of TV provokes little involvement and, for example, conditions children into becoming passive observers.

Nowadays McLuhan followers such as Derrick de Kerckhove (1997) analyze the communicative structure of network systems which enhance and even deform our understanding of the world.

Internet's temperature gauges the fever of the world!

Paleographers and librarians are aware that a vegetal ink runs the risk of bleaching as time passes, and also the paper on which a historical document is written may deteriorate.

Experts take care of and preserve old writings that become darker and unreadable (Cunha et al. 1967). The physical state of ancient writing attracts the paleographers' attention and one concludes that even those researchers are massively sensitive to the empirical form of information.

Our bodies are complex systems and when something is wrong, our bodies inform us through special warning signs e.g. pain, fever, sweat, vomit, tremors, weight loss, shortness of breath, headache etc. The physical essence of those special signifiers – called *symptoms* – is evident to everybody and does not want further elucidations. *Semiotics*, a branch of medical science, teaches physicians how to recognize symptoms and how to diagnose correctly a disease (Gray et al. 2001).

Essential symptoms are those that are necessary to recognize the illness. One could have no conception of the existence of the disease X without the essential symptoms of X. These signs are so important to the disease that the latter cannot be present without them. There are *pathognonomic* symptoms that give the definitive indications of a certain disease or condition. For example the yellowness of the skin, of the sclerotica and of the nails is the pathognomic of jaundice. A doctor is sure that the patient has jaundice without making any further inquiry. Essential symptoms are judged as the necessary elements for a diagnosis, pathognonomic symptoms are defined as necessary and sufficient signs. A doctor takes into consideration any circumstance of the case to make the correct diagnosis, he also analyses the *accidental symptoms* that are not at all specific to the disease. Often it is up to a feeble symptom to determine the survival of a patient. In fact some diseases are *asymptomatic*: these diseases do not create any signifier and the patient is unconscious of his state. Cancer is a well known silent illness, namely cancer does not emit any symptom for a long while and when the signals come to light the possibilities of successful intervention become more difficult.

In sum, the material nature of symptoms intensely involves doctors and patients alike.

Gestures and facial expressions are important vectors of communication which make up the so-called *language of signs*. Through look behaviors, facial expressions, and head movements, people convey information on not only a person's emotional state but also on discursive and syntactic elements. The body organs moving with varying degrees of motion, gentleness or force exhibit different meanings and make evident the concept of signifier (Fernandez et al. 1997).

The language of signs may be found even in the animal kingdom. This territory has been explored by Thomas A. Sebeok, father of Zoosemiotics, by ethologists such as D. Griffin (1985), C. Heyes and others. Researchers decipher the system of signs used by animals to communicate: postures, gestures, cries, excrements, movements, which clearly are material signifiers. Experts subdivide the communication between senders and receivers belonging to the same species (*intraspecies comm.*) or belonging to different species (*interspecies comm.*). For example the signals for mating belong to the first class, and the signals exchanged between predators and preys pertain to interspecies communication.

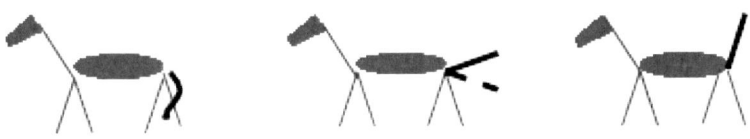

Figure 1.3.

Efforts have been concentrated on whether a common alphabet is possible on the basis of animal behaviors. E.g. a quadruped makes use of its tail to communicate. It keeps the tail between its legs to denote fear. If it wags its tail, it signifies happiness and devotion. The quadruped is antagonistic and aggressive when it raises its tail. The waving tail may be seen as the basic element of a code shared by various species of mammals: horses, wolves, dogs and so forth (Hailman 2008)

Since millennia people rather ignorant of the brain's physiology imagined human thought as being an airy entity. Plato, the early philosopher on idealism, placed ideas in the empyrean heaven. He developed a vision of two worlds: a world of unchanging ideas and a world of changing physical objects where we are living.

In the nineteenth century the scientific exploration of the brain processes initiated. In 1861 Paul Broca first described the section of the brain – close to the frontal lobe in the left hemisphere – which is involved in speech production. Later experts discovered how perceptual information from the eyes, ears, and rest of the body is sent to the right zone of the brain. Other specialized areas were found in the course of later investigations (see also the beginning of Paragraph 4 in the present chapter) (MacInteyer 2004). Modern techniques keeps up the physical origin of mental ideas in a factual manner. I quote *positron emission tomography* (PET), a nuclear medicine system which produces a three-dimensional image of the brain's activities; *magnetic resonance imaging* (MRI) is an effective tool that visualizes the inside of the brain (Vlaardingerbroek et al. 2003).

Chemical-electrical reactions embody intellectual activities and the cure of psychological diseases by means of drugs reinforces the awareness about the material origin of information within the brain. Neurological and Psychiatric studies corroborate the materialistic perspective on mental signifiers.

A court of justice gives judgment against an accused or otherwise acquits him after the accurate consideration of *evidences*. Scientists accept a theory supported by experimental *evidences* or else deny that theory. A manager chooses to follow a strategy in accordance to positive *evidences*. Crucial decisions are taken on the basic strength of *evidence*. Evidence is a sign or better still *evidence is a signifier* which plays a fundamental role in forming a conclusion or judgment. For instance, a broken window – an evident material object – is the proof that a burglary has taken place.

Current literature concentrates attention on several material particulars of evidences. Commentators focus on the physical properties pertaining to those signs due to the valuable role which a tiny part can play. E.g. tests sustain the supreme criterion to validate a scientific theory and the scientific method requires that evidences should be obtained through rigorous procedures (Wilson 1952). E.g. legal doctrines determine how objects may be submitted to a jury and how those objects enable a judge to decide upon the questions in dispute. Also verbal testimony cannot be generic but is physically bound to a real individual, who is officially admitted as a witness (Blazey et al. 1996).

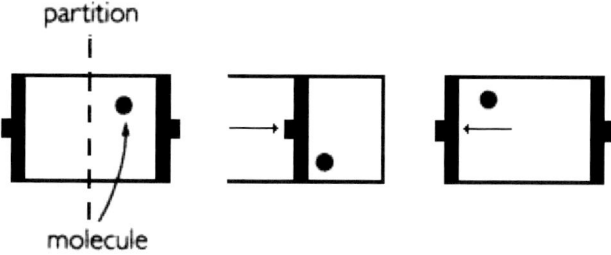

Figure 1.4.

An intriguing vein of studies seeks out the minimal signifiers in classical physics. In 1929 Leo Szilard, inspired by the thermodynamical system elaborated by Maxwell, envisioned a theoretical engine that consists of a cylinder with a single-molecule working fluid.

An operator observes a molecule in the chamber on the right and pushes the piston on the left toward the center partition. The molecule in motion impinges on the piston sliding it back to the left. This creates useful work and the cycle can begin anew. Szilard found that the amount of useful work per cycle is

$$W_C = k_B T \ln(2)$$

Where T is the absolute temperature of the system and k_B the constant of Boltzmann. The second principle of thermodynamics holds that energy cannot be created by nothing, thus Szilard supposed W_C is the energy absorbed to acquire information from the single molecule (Leff et al. 1990). Eminent physicists, say Bennett, Penrose, Zurek, Brillouin, Feynman, discussed this argument and lastly converged toward the illustration of Rolf Landauer (1961) who explained how the Slizard engine cannot work unless an operator takes energy to erase acquired information. In substance a sole molecule is the tiniest signifier in classical physics and absorbs energy W_C to be restored at the initial conditions.

Information has material origin, and demands physical power to be collected, erased, thrown away and so forth in the tiniest systems too. We can but agree with the gibe by E.T. Jaynes:

"The old adage 'knowledge is power' is a very cogent truth, both in human relations and in thermodynamics."

This short survey is an attempt to consider the material side of information on the basis of technical and non-technical investigations. Linguists, paleographers, physicians, ethologists, doctors, magistrates, experts in mass media and in cognitive sciences, and many others share the idea that information is tied to some substance and is not airy. They delve into the astonishing world of signifiers and benefit from their physical properties.

3. Sharpness

Technicians calculate and process signifiers all the day long and their perspective inevitably drifts apart from the stance assumed by the rest of the scientific community which is non-technical. In particular engineers describe their objects using the mathematical idiom: a method that does not tolerate any exception. Things are to be standardized, quantified, and measured using formal expressions.

One understands how demanding the process of rendering signifiers in grades is; however we can but regard this task as an unavoidable practice to discuss the digital and analog machines.

A. Toward a Principle

We have seen how a broad circle of scientists are familiar with the physical concept of information. Issue (1) is solid but sounds rather vague from the engineering stance. One wonders: When may a generic body be a sign?

What are the properties that determine a signifier?

How could those properties be formalized?

Three different groups of writers provide an answer and seem to go toward the same direction.

- I briefly quote experimentalists who scrutinize phenomena in biological and mechanical systems.
    - Physiologists bring evidence that nerve endings do not sense stimuli but *differences of stimuli*. Sense organs and internal receptors are solely capable of detecting contrasting pulses (Somjen 1983).
    - We learn from Neurology that a nerve impulse consists of a self-propagating series of polarizations and depolarizations. The spike reaches the *action-potential* +40 mV (millivolt) whose value is far away from the *resting-potential* located at − 70 mV. The nervous signifiers − about 110 mV apart − prove to be absolutely distinct (Partridge 2003).
    - Electronic engineers calculate the distance that makes any two signals distinguishable. They recognize this quality as essential for handling signals (Smirnov 1999).
    - Nature long ago learned to encode information about organisms in Deoxyribonucleic Acid (DNA). When a cell receives a biological material with different DNA, the cell rejects this biological material, notably a DNA code contrasts with another genetic code and has the evident property of being distinguishable (Loewenstein 1999).

- Since the classical age philosophers recognize that clear-headedness is a necessary requisite for humans namely sense data and non-sense data alike are to be neat. I mean to quote logicians who follow the reflections of Wilhelm Gottfried Leibniz and argue upon the *indiscernibility of identicals* and the *identity of indiscernibles*. They place great importance on the special properties of becoming distinct which render indiscernibles clear to the mind (O'Leary 1995). In substance the ideas developed by Man can be elaborated as long as those pieces of information are neat. Fuzzy tenets impair correct reasoning and it is natural to conclude that even mental ideas are to be definite signifiers.

- A principle of communication and art refers to the arrangement of opposite elements in a piece so as to create visual interest, excitement and drama. Authors adopt a wide set of contrasting items to arouse strong feeling e.g. light vs. dark colors; rough vs. smooth textures; large vs. small shapes. An artist can employ contrast as a tool to direct the viewer's attention to a particular point of interest within the piece.

It is recognized in the linguistic domain that a sign is an element capable of causing a contrast. Linguists highlight the distinctiveness of forms and Saussure (1983) says in explicit terms:

> Sign's "most precise characteristic is to be what the others are not".

And John Arthur Passmore (1985) offers a charming compendium:

> "Languages differ by differentiating differently".

Mark Burgin (2009) places the concept of change at the base of his general theory. He assumes that information causes changes either in the whole system that receives information or in a part of the system. A measure of information is some measure of provoked diversities.

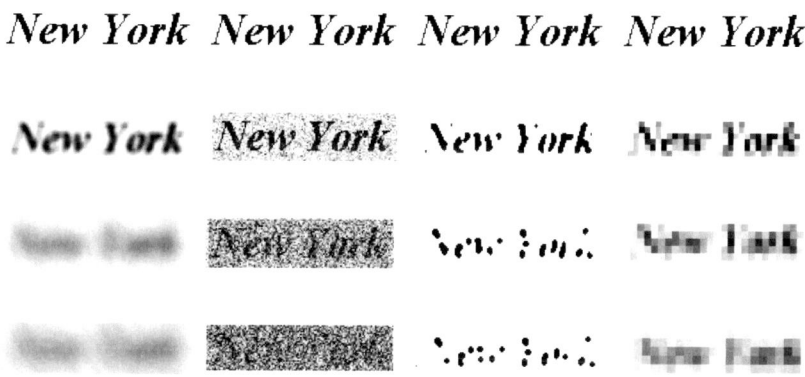

Figure 1.5. Four different deterioration processes (from left to right: blurring, noise, erosion, granulation) cause progressive loss of information.

Gregory Bateson (2000) broadly develops this view since he conceives the "elementary unit of information" as "a difference which makes a difference". Bateson argues that the term *'idea'* in its most elementary sense is synonymous with difference. Bateson underlines the contrast extant between the world as seen from the perspective of the mechanical sciences — a world in which effects are caused by rather concrete conditions or events, impacts, forces, etc. — and the world of communication, that is the psychological world in which effects are brought about by differences. In the effort to clarify this conception he holds that in any thing, say a piece of chalk, one can potentially see an infinite number of diversities around and within it, differences between the chalk and any other thing in the universe. It is precisely because of this infinite, Bateson argues that an observer selects and filters out a limited number of differences around and within the piece of chalk, which "become information".

Three groups of authors – experimentalists, philosophers and experts on communication – spell out the idea that *sharpness* is an essential requisite to information. Distinctness influences the existence of whatsoever piece of information and one can reasonably conclude that a signifier must be neat in order to work properly.

However the concept of sharpness sounds like an airy characteristic unless one establishes the conditions to verify this property. The discussion of operational features is of great significance to arrive to a formal conceptualization. I mean to delve into some practical aspects of distinctness and I pinpoint the following factors:

- Human speech, animals' signals, mass media messages, symptoms of sickness, mental ideas, and impulses in electric devices are to be sharp. Missing this characteristic, a signifier inevitably vanishes and cannot be employed. A generic entity is capable of informing due to the essential property of being distinct in a manner. If a signifier becomes fuzzy, it no longer carries on any content namely *sharpness establishes the condition of existence for signs*.
- Secondly distinctness does not appear as a yes/no property but *distinctness presents different degrees of quality*. Take the following object of ink which conveys information provided that the ink film contrasts with the white sheet:

New York

Instead when this signifier has a blurred outline, or it bleaches, or it thins out etc. (Figure 1.5), this film of ink works less and less, until it finally ceases to exist as a piece of information.

- As a matter of fact, *a signifier contrasts a close element with respect to the observer* R. The dissimilarity between any two signals makes a difference in R which acquires information. The agent R may be natural or artificial: a sense organ, a biological receptor, and a mechanical device. In practice R gives effect to the property of E which is distinct using an adjacent comparison term E^*.

The above written remarks lead to the following statement which I call *principle of sharpness*:

The entity E is a signifier if E differs from an adjacent entity E^* with respect to the reference R [1.3]

The verb *differs* can be translated into the symbol 'NOT=' (literally 'not equal') and principle [1.3] becomes with the mathematical language

$$E \text{ NOT=}_R E^* \quad (1.1)$$

Where E and E^* are elements of the algebraic space E_a.

Given the object E, if at least there is another element E^* that verifies (1.1) respect to an observer, than E is a signifier. Dissimilarity is the condition of existence for signs and is prerequisite to any subsequent study. In fact a sign can convey information provided that E is extant. If a signifier does not contrast in a way, E does not exist, neither can it represent NE. Discussion on the material nature of signs precedes the semantic study in point of logic and I shall develop the calculation of distinction.

B. Various Measures

Attempts have been made to quantify the differences existing between any two items, but the *calculus of diversities* applied to *complex items* has not produced conclusive outcomes so far. Similarities and dissimilarities amongst compounds cannot be measured using manageable approaches – see the classical work (Gordon 1999) – in that an aggregate exhibits a variety of facets which resist linear methods of comparison.

Happily the dissimilarities of *elementary items* can be quantified through easy criteria. I subdivide this calculation into two subsections: the first works out *single elementary signifiers*, the second *multiple elementary signifiers*.

Figure 1.6. Separated subsets and overlapping subsets.

1. Single Elementary Signifiers

A) - Let E and E^* be subsets in the set space E_s. From (1.1) one concludes that the signifier E is distinct if the subsets do not overlap namely the *intersection set* is empty

$$I = \{E \cap E^*\} = \emptyset \tag{1.2}$$

Instead the signifier becomes a blur when I is not empty

$$I \neq \emptyset \tag{1.3}$$

As an example take the letter **J** of ink as a signifier and the white sheet all around as E^*. The letter is fuzzy due to the grey zone including black and white spots as well. The letter **J** becomes sharp when verifies (1.2) and the grey zone disappears.

Figure 1.7.

B) - Let $\vec{E}$ and $\vec{E}*$ are applied vectors in the vector space E_v. $\vec{E}$ is distinct from $\vec{E}*$ when the application-points P_E and P_{E*} lie apart, namely the module of the *distance-vector* does not equal zero

$$|\vec{v}| \neq 0 \tag{1.4}$$

When (1.4) is false in the world, the vectors $\vec{E}$ and $\vec{E}*$ add up and automatically produce the resultant vector $\vec{G}$. The original vectors cannot be individually detected because $\vec{G}$ takes their place. The resultant vector $\vec{G}$ may be subdivided into two or more vectors at will, but there is no general rule to go back to the original vectors $\vec{E}$ and $\vec{E}*$ once they have been summed up and fused.

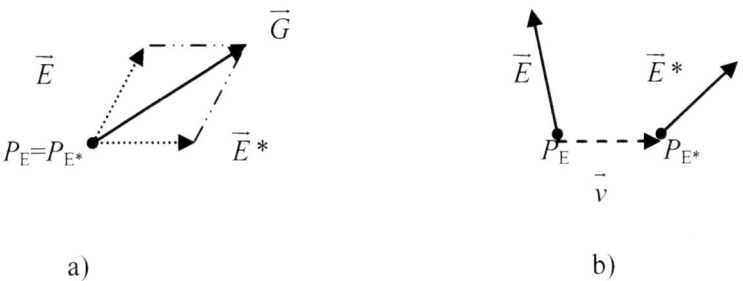

a) b)

Figure 1.8.

C) – Suppose E and $E*$ are points in the continuous metric space E_m. The signifier E is distinct if the points do not occupy the same place. The signifier disappears when E and $E*$ overlap. The following inequality derives directly from (1.1)

$$E \neq E^* \tag{1.5}$$

And leads to the *separation s* greater than zero

$$s = |E - E^*| \neq 0 \tag{1.6}$$

Digital experts measure the voltage gap s that ensures the separation between two bits. Even if the high-value and the low-value fluctuate, the bits remain distinct thanks to prudent size of s.

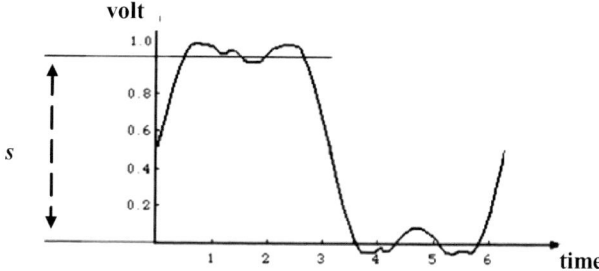

Figure 1.9. Electric square-wave.

Note how the measures above introduced have different meanings and purposes: the intersection set I depicts the low quality of a signifier; the size of the distance-vector and the separation give the margin that guarantees the distinctiveness of a signifier.

2. Multiple Elementary Signifiers

Sometimes R does not detect a unique signifier. When R perceives a set of scores which belong to the metric space ε_m, Statistics indicates the suitable course to follow:

"The object of statistics is information. The objective of statistics is the understanding of information contained in [a wealth of] data". (Miller et al 1994)

The observer detects a set of signifiers instead of only one, and it is necessary to locate the signifier capable of representing the whole data set. Statisticians search for the relevant information and identify the center of a set of scores applying different criteria. The most widely used measure of central tendency is the *mean* $\overline{E}$.

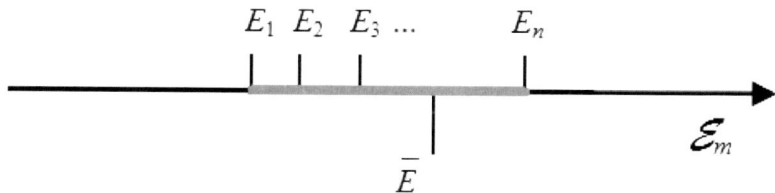

Figure 1.10.

The background space ε_m is the term of contrast for each signifier and the fuzziness of the mean is given by the spread of the data. The variability of the scores is the overall quality of $\overline{E}$ over ε_m. The *range* of the distribution namely the mere difference between the largest value and the smallest value of the data set, gives a rough idea of the quality of $\overline{E}$. More accurate measures for the spread are the *variance* and the *standard deviation*. The standard deviation is an appropriate measure when the score distribution is reasonably symmetric and does not exhibit multiple concentrations of scores.

D) – Suppose you are working with a set of discrete values $E_1, E_2, E_3,... E_N$ belonging to the metric space E_m, the arithmetic mean is computed simply by adding the values together and dividing by the number of values

$$\bar{E} = \frac{1}{N} \sum_{i}^{N} E_i \qquad (1.7)$$

The mean (1.7) yields the following standard deviation

$$\sigma = \sqrt{\frac{1}{N} \sum_{i}^{N} (E_i - \bar{E})^2} \qquad (1.8)$$

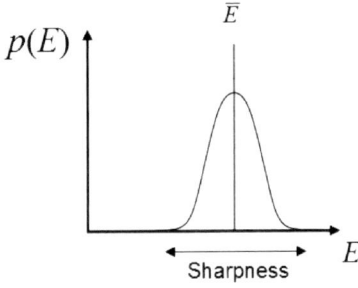

Figure 1.11.

E) – When the signifier is a continuous parameter with probability density function $p(E)$, the mean is obtained in this way

$$\bar{E} = \int E \cdot p(E) \, dE \qquad (1.9)$$

And the standard deviation is calculated in the ensuing manner

$$\sigma = \sqrt{\int (E - \bar{E})^2 \, p(E) \, dE} \qquad (1.10)$$

Where the integrals are definite integrals taken for E ranging over its field of observation.

When all the scores coincide with $\bar{E}$, the standard deviation is null and one has valuable information in hand

$$\sigma = 0 \qquad (1.11)$$

Conversely the more ample is σ and the more $\bar{E}$ becomes dim. When the scores scatter all over the axis E_m, the standard deviation tends to infinity and the calculated mean does not make sense

$$\sigma \to \infty \qquad (1.12)$$

F) When there are two or more statistical distributions, experts find an appropriate measure of *divergence* or *discrimination* between those distributions. A number of divergence measures for this purpose have been proposed and extensively studied by Jeffreys, Kullback, Leibler, Renyi, Kapur, Sharma and others. Some measures are specific cases of the divergence devised by Csiszfá (1967). His works consist with the sharpness principle but I refrain from expanding the discussion of this theory.

3. *Complex Signifiers*

Complex signals cannot be treated by mathematical tools in an easy manner, but diffracted images make an exception. *Diffraction* is a physical phenomenon resulting in the light waves that change in direction and intensity after passing through a small medium whose size is approximately the same as the wavelength of the light. By way of illustration suppose a beam of light passes through a single thin slit, the produced pattern is a central bright spot, surrounded by dark/light/dark/light spots. The spots become fainter and less distinct the farther away from the center they are.

Figure 1.12. Diffraction pattern.

G) Diffraction has the effect of turning a sharp beam of light into fuzzy images. This loss of detail leads to an inability to discern two sources of light which are very close together. In particular two sources of light produce two diffraction patterns E_j and E_k when they shine through the same slit. If the light sources are somewhat distant, the patterns are still distinguishable. When the two sources get close, the patterns E_j and E_k start to overlap and become dazed. Lord Rayleigh established the minimal distance between two diffraction patterns so that (1.1) is still true (Longhurst 1974). He found that two close images are distinct when the first diffraction minimum of the pattern E_j coincides with the maximum of the pattern E_k

The ensuing equation determines the parameters for the minimal distance between two sources of light according to the Rayleigh's criterion

$$\theta \approx \frac{\lambda}{w} \qquad (1.13)$$

Where θ is the apparent angle between the light sources E_j and E_k, λ is the wave length and w is the width of the slit.

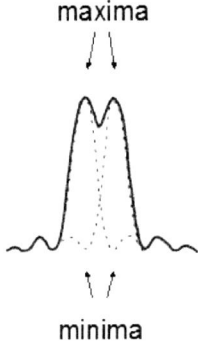

Figure 1.13. The criterion of Rayleigh.

H) Laymen appreciate the ability of an optical device – say a microscope or a telescope – to magnify an image which can be scarcely seen with the naked eye. Experts explicate this property of optical systems in rigorous terms and conclude that an optical device should be capable of separating two close spots of light. Roughly speaking a device is very good when it allows us to see two very close spots as distinct points.

Because diffraction deforms images, experts adopt the Rayleigh criterion and calculate the smallest angle between close objects that can be seen clearly to be separate. The *angular resolution* ϕ or *separation* of two object points is

$$\phi \approx 1.22 \frac{\lambda}{D} \qquad (1.14)$$

Where λ is the wave length of light and D is the diameter of the lens of the optical device.

Concluding, statement [1.3] expresses the principle of sharpness, and the calculus of diversities itemizes the features of signifiers. Symbolic formula (1.1) gives *the condition of existence of information* in absolute terms – namely yes/no – instead the mathematical equations illustrated from A) to H) quantify the degrees of quality reached by signifiers depending on their distance, fuzziness etc. The results derived from the principle of sharpness consist with the mathematical expressions obtained through empirical quests. It may be said that eqn. (1.1) tends to unify the view in the field and this will facilitate the analysis of the analog and digital appliances.

4. INFORMATION RELATIVISM

The perception of signs described by the principle of sharpness causes the birth of information but many thinkers mistrust the generality and reliance of perception. Things do not always turn out actually to be as they seem to human sense. There is ample reason to wonder about the epistemological reliability of perception, and theories of perception offer a variety of responses (Hirst 1992), (Dretske 2000), (Robinson 2001). Also Maturana and Varela (1980) argue over the illusory nature of human capabilities which plays a significant role in their theory of information

A wealth of evidences gives support to skeptics. I restrict myself to the literature on human eyesight which shows how the eye is not camera-like as initially believed but the eye and the brain build up images (Landy et al. 1995). The visual cortex covers five areas from V1 to V5 which achieve different operations, at different times and with differing organizations. Visual operations sometimes provide unfaithful outcomes. To exemplify the area V2 of the brain computes the visual contours in absence of light or color gradient, and offers a case of *visual illusion* which triggered the curiosity of Gaetano Kanizsa, Matthew Schmolesky and others (Seckel 2002). Phenomena of perception raise questions such as:

Is perception true or fallacious?
Does the perceiver create the perceived world?
Does information cause distinction or otherwise does distinction depend on the receiver?

The present account offers support to discussion. The principle of sharpness [1.3] holds that the perception of a sign relies on the confrontation term and presumes an observer who accomplishes the detection process. The intervention of E^* and R causes double relativism of necessity and one is obliged to conclude that information is not an absolute quantity in the present framework. I call *couple relativity* the impact of the touchstone E^* on the existence of E, and *reference relativity* the influence caused by the receiver R.

Figure 1.14. Kanizsa triangle.

Let us see three paradoxical effects resultant from the information relativism.

A. Reference Relativity – A Paradox

Universal experience shows that a sign dies as soon as it is no longer seen, a signifier does not work unless one discovers it. For example a lot of documents were sealed by the Allies at the end of the Second World War. Those items disappeared for decades until the end of the Cold War. In the nineties those secret documents became available and then information forgotten by everybody came into existence once again.

This phenomenon may be summed up in this way

A sign does not exist whenever it is not perceived by somebody, and all over again a sign disappears when it cannot be examined. [1.4]

An observer can kill information and can even revive it. This miraculous intervention sounds paradoxical since the decease of a signifier and its resurrection seems to deny the material nature of signs. Matter exists due to its inner essence and does not need any support to be in the real world, hence one could conclude: "Information disappears whenever we close our eyes or forget about it; therefore the physical origin of information has no foundation". The observer should not be capable of destroying and recalling to life a message if information is physical.

I try an answer to the above mentioned objections which sound like a refutation of the entire semantic triad.

I go back to inequality (1.1) which particularizes the conditions for the factual determination of a sign and holds that any object is a potential piece of information but its capability becomes effective provided that R intervenes.

$$E \text{ NOT=}_R E^*$$ (1.15)

The agent R allows a signifier to pass from the potential state to the real information state. An object goes on living as a sign when R keeps it alive and E disappears for as long as that object is no longer available to an observer. In conclusion, equation (1.15) assigns a special operational role to R which does not impact on the physical essence of signifiers. The observer does not modify the body E but merely its information state.

The interference of an observer denies the physical existence of information as long as one argues from the abstract stance. Inevitably one infers radical conclusions and finds out irreconcilable statements if he/she reasons on the metaphysical plane. Instead detection is a physical event in the present frame and does not constitute a philosophical argument.

Principle [1.3] suggests adopting the *operational perspective* to interpret the perception of information, and scientific experience sustains this view. Technicians prove to be able to step in and to surmount a number of obstacles using appropriate countermeasures. Engineers teach us how reference relativity may be tackled using practical tools. I quote four cases to exemplify this argument.

- In a number of circumstances the human senses are incompatible with E, the subsidiary probe $R^\wedge$ is sandwiched and the operator R controls the readout of $R^\wedge$. People face the impossibility of direct perception and amend through *indirect perception*.
- Cascade detectors make a complex arrangement and augment risks of distortion. Indirect perception makes even more evident how the properties of E may diverge from those possessed at the process outset. For example detection takes time and one should accept that all the events we perceive are to some extent in the past. In extreme cases the objects in the world may no longer exist at the moment when the process of perception occurs. As a case assume n is a positive number and light takes n years to travel from a star to us. Astronomers

are aware of perceiving the star as it was *n* years ago. Nowadays perhaps that star is no longer extant.

- Sometimes R has a physical contact with the signifier which does not remain the same afterward the detection process. A sensor is capable of modifying the form of information and scientists accurately care that *a measurement be not invasive* and the interference be negligible.
- Observer's actions result in critical consequences when *E* is *a quantum particle*. In fact the Schrödinger equation tells the possible positions of a quantum particle. The Schrödinger equation provides the probabilistic distribution of a quantum particle's possible positions. This distribution keeps true until a measurement is made. At this point an event known as the *collapse of the wavefunction* occurs, and the Schrödinger equation no longer exists. The probabilistic wave collapses to a single point after a measurement of position. The particle *E* that has a generic place in advance of measurement, occupies a precise points after the intervention of the observer R.

Inequality (1.15) is consistent with the idea that perception is not absolute and counsels to dissect the perception mechanisms from the operational stance, and provides flexible and analytic answers to paradox [1.4]. In fact observer's actions may be modified, corrected, optimized, reduced and so forth.

The wavefunction collapse was established on the theoretical plane, that is to say R causes systematic alteration in Quantum Mechanics (QM). Quantum theorists found out the wave collapse in the early twenty century and feared this phenomenon could involve the downfall of the cornerstone in modern positive sciences: the tests. Vivid debates arose within the scientific community. Reams have been written upon a number of thought experiments including *Schrödinger's Cat*, *Wigner's Friend*, and *Heisenberg's Microscope*. Profound theories have been proposed to clarify the weight of the observer over a quantum particle e.g. the *Copenhagen interpretation* (Petersen 1968), and the *hidden variables theory* (Hooft 1999). Under the influence of philosophical contributions the scientist David Bohm (1993) proposed ontological interpretations of Quantum Mechanics. Also extravagant theories came to light such as the *many-worlds interpretation* (Everett 1957).

The measurement problem in QM raises broader issues and debates from which two major philosophical positions emerge. On one hand, one sees Cartesian and Lockean accounts of observation as the creation of inner reflections and, on the other hand, neo-Kantean conceptions of observation as a quasi-externalized physiological process. The interpretation of quantum measurement is still a conundrum that becomes even more intricate when experts address those phenomena from the philosophical stance. I am not sure that the metaphysical approach which yields an all-embracing view and is not analytic is the better way to follow.

B. Couple Relativity – First Paradox

Neurologists hold that the sensory neurons once stimulated respond immediately, but then respond less and less until they may not respond at all (Bullock et al. 2001). To exemplify, if you press a digital pulp for a short while, the tactile receptors are no longer able to transmit this single sensation. The mechanical signal vanishes and you feel no pressure. A sense receptor detects stimuli if and only if the input varies, and cannot perceive a constant stimulus, that is to say *a sensory neuron cannot perceive only one stimulus*. The so-called *sensory adaptation effect* causes a receptor to detect differing stimuli whereas a single stimulus declines through time and disappears.

Norbert Wiener (1961) discovered how one elementary signal cannot be handled during his work on the automatic aiming and firing of anti-aircraft guns in the Second World War. He describes an evident experiment to summarize this astonishing property of information:

"If people always get the same signal, this becomes inessential and nothing may be transmitted with the same result".

Shannon illustrates the phenomenon quoted by Wiener through refined formalism. He introduces the entropy of a source conveying m signals with probabilities $p_1, p_2, p_3,.. p_m$

$$H = \sum_i^m 1/p_i \log_a(p_i) \qquad a, m \geq 2 \qquad (1.16)$$

Shannon infers that the entropy H tends to zero when the probability of one signal is unit and the remaining probabilities are null. Suppose $m=2$ we obtain

$$\lim_{p_1 \to 1}\left[1/p_1 \log_a(p_1) + 1/p_2 \log_a(p_2)\right] = $$
$$= \lim_{p_1 \to 1}\left[1/p_1 \log_a(p_1) + 1/(1-p_1)\log_a(1-p_1)\right] = 0 \qquad (1.17)$$

This result means that information is null when a source emits a unique signal.

One can summarize the phenomena described in literature through the following rather paradoxical sentence

A single elementary sign cannot exist. [1.5]

This issue can be justified by inequality

$$E \text{ NOT}=_R E^* \qquad (1.18)$$

This mathematical expression minutely relates how an observer is capable of seeing a sign as long as this sign contrasts with an adequate term of comparison. The inequality has no less than two terms and property [1.5] appears as a natural consequence of (1.18). The existence of a piece of information relies upon the adjacent element and one sole entity cannot work.

One can see something like [1.5] in a variety of situations. Psychologists remark how a repeated message annoys and diverts the attention; conversely the variety of the news attracts the consideration of humans. Novel and sudden events arouse curiosity which is particularly evident in babies whose brain immediately responds to novelties.

Pedagogues confirm the advantages of teaching two opposite concepts: good/evil; love/hate; youth/senility etc. instead of one single concept. A student can grasp a sole tenet with difficulty, instead the tenet E appears far more evident to a student if he gets the opposite notion E^*.

C. Couple Relativity – Second Paradox

Mr. A purchased ticket #99 and Mr. B purchased ticket #87 of the Lottery and later they have checked the Lottery results on newspapers. Ticket number #99 printed on a newspaper notifies A is a winner, but also number #87 missing on the newspaper conveys information; the absent number tells: "Mr. B is not a winner". This event spells out that a printed number is a sign and even a lacking number signifies something.

People often communicate by their voice and gestures. People notify their mind even through silence, namely nothing is enough to communicate. People use no sign to present a precise content or a state of the soul. The ability to effectively communicate with others relies on the use of words, pauses and interruptions too (Morrison et al. 2003).

Doctors analyze the symptoms of a patient and consider the presence of a symptom and even the absence of a symptom alike to diagnose the sickness suffered by a patient. The former are called *positive symptoms* and the latter *negative symptoms*. For example if a sick person has vomit, high fever and stomach pains, there are three positive symptoms and the disease is X. If a sick person has vomit and stomach pains but no fever – the fever is a negative symptom in this case – he suffers the disease Y. If a sick person has stomach pains but no fever and vomit – two symptoms are negative – he has the disease Z. Medical Semiotics confirms that a missing sign is a sign all the same.

Stylometry is the field of linguistics that recognizes and measures the distinctive, unique aspects of a writer. Experts assume that the essence of the individual style of an author can be captured with reference to a number of quantitative values. As an example, "*The Federalist Papers*", a series of articles published in 1787-88 with the aim of promoting the ratification of the new US constitution, were originally written under the anonymous *nom de plume* Publius, but are now known to have been written by James Madison, Alexander Hamilton, and John Jay (Hamilton et al. 2007). The authors of most papers were recognized except twelve papers for which there were persistent doubts between either Madison or Hamilton authorship. Stylometric analysis provided an answer in this way.

One particular stylometric technique includes measuring the frequency of usage of different words. One particular example of this is based on the choice between 'while' and 'whilst', two English function-words with the same meaning but with two alternate forms. The papers authored by Hamilton for sure include 36 instances of the word 'while' and only one instance of the word 'whilst', while the papers known to have been written by Madison include no instances of the word 'while', and twelve instances of the word 'whilst'. The Federalist Papers of unknown authorship include no instances of the word 'while', and nine instances of the word 'whilst', thereby analysts are prone to credit the authorship of the last Papers to Madison. This research spells out that the word 'while' is a sign even when this word is absent.

In conclusion it may be said:

A nonexistent sign proves to be a sign. [1.6]

This remarkable proposition seems to be the self-evident disproof of the material origin of information and Wiener (1961) sanctions:

"Information is information, not matter or energy. No materialism which does not admit this can survive at the present day."

The paradoxical phenomena described by [1.4] and [1.6] played a significant role in the history of information science. These effects appear so serious as to contradict the physical nature of information, and a number of authors searched and still search for a special quantity which should be called *information*. A circle of theorists is prone to believe that paradoxes [1.4] and [1.6] should be solved through abstraction and the conspicuous production of theories on information presented in the inception of this book is not alien to the problem we are presently discussing.

The question is still open since statement [1.6] poses an extremely knotty problem in point of logic. This statement has a contradiction in terms.

If a sign is no longer extant, how can be it a sign?
How can this sign be transmitted or perceived whether it does not exist?

A logician very likely cannot accept the evidence of facts in that [1.6] is an absurd proposition. Thus I mean to follow a different way. I recall eqn. (1.1) that is symmetrical and may be inverted

$$E^* \text{ NOT}=_R E \qquad (1.19)$$

This entails that even E^* is a signifier and can convey information provided that E^* contrasts with E that is given. In general the adjacent term of E is any, and we assume E^* null

$$E^* = 0 \qquad (1.20)$$

We obtain that the null element can inform people as long as this special signifier contrasts with another signifier

$$0 \text{ NOT}=_R E \qquad (1.21)$$

This equation spells out that nothing is a potential vehicle of information. Normally a signifier has a body, and by exception a signifier may be body-less. People communicate with the signifier (1.20) when they employ silence instead of sound to transmit positive feeling or personal disagreement. Vacuum is in use instead of matter; darkness in place of light; blank instead of a black form and so forth.

Eqn. (1.21) does not deny the physical essence of signs since silence, vacuum, blank and other body-less signifiers are real entities, and should not be understood as ethereal entities. E.g. the interstellar vacuum is not an abstract entity instead vacuum is the real place where we are living. E.g. silence is a sonorous wave with zero energy namely the silence owns precise physical properties.

Concluding the analysis of [1.3] provides formal answers to vexed questions that have resisted deep inquiries so far. The principle of sharpness sustains the skeptical feelings of thinkers about the process of perception, but does not sustain abstract or metaphysical conclusions. The definition $E \text{ NOT}=_R E^*$ yields answers to paradoxes [1.4], [1.5] and [1.6] consistent with practical experience whereas philosophical reasoning yields drastic and conflicting conclusions from which one cannot see the way out.

D. Information Relativity – Other Equations

Subsections from A) to I) show how the quality of a generic signifier is calculated through its comparison term. Further mathematical expressions – obtained after empirical researches – correlate the features of E, E^* and R and cast further light upon information relativism. Let us see a few of them.

1. Contrast

The act of distinguishing by comparing differences turns out to be of universal use. A popular measure of *contrast* is the ratio of two signifiers in opposition. There are many empirical measures of contrast that call up the couple relativism introduced in these pages. I quote a few forms.

- *Luminance contrast* – The simplest form relates the luminance of E with the luminance of E^*

$$C_L = \frac{L_E}{L_{E^*}} \qquad (1.22)$$

The *factor of contrast* calculates the difference of the *luminance* of the object and the *luminance* of the background, divided by the luminance of E (Hendee et al 1997)

$$C_F = \frac{|L_E - L_{E^*}|}{L_E} \qquad (1.23)$$

- *Color contrast* is the relation of two items measured in a suitable chromaticity system.
- *Dark-room contrast* is gauged with no ambient illumination.
- *Ambient contrast* is gauged in the presence of environmental illumination.
- *Successive contrast* is established between two optical states that are perceived or measured one after the other.

2. Perceived Signals

About the middle of the nineteenth century physiologists inquired the relationship between the physical magnitudes of a stimulus and the perceived intensity of that stimulus. They tested whether persons could notice a difference between a couple of stimuli. On the basis of experiments it was found that the smallest noticeable difference was roughly proportional to the intensity of the stimulus. For example when a person consistently feels that a 110 g weight is heavier than a 100 g weight, he can also feel that 1100 g is more than 1000 g. Since a constant relative difference, the Weber-Fechner law was established

$$P_{org} = \log\left(\frac{E}{E_0}\right) \qquad (1.24)$$

Where P_{org} is the stimulus perceived by the organ e.g. tactile sense, sight, hearing. E is the stimulus and E_0 is the threshold of the intended organ.

A formula symmetrical to (1.24) is used to calculate the signal emitted by a source. Engineers work out the intensity I_{source} of sound emitters using this empirical equation

$$I_{source} = 10\log\left(\frac{E}{E_0}\right) \qquad (1.25)$$

Where E is the acoustic power of the sound and E_0 is the minimal acoustic threshold equal to 10^{-12} watt/m². The quantity I is measured in *decibel*, in practice E_0 corresponds to 0 decibel: an individual does not perceive any sound.

Each receptor has the minimum threshold and the maximum threshold as well. For instance, physiologists find that 134 decibel is the maximum threshold E_m for human ears, which is usually called *threshold of pain* since a man suffers intolerable pain with such an intense sound.

In sum a sense organ, a device, a signal conveyor, or a probe does not handle an infinite set of signals but solely those varying from the maximum threshold E_m to the minimum threshold E_0 which are typical of R. Eqn. (1.24) and (1.25) include the variable E_0 and corroborate the reference relativity with precision.

5. ANARCHIC ISSUE

Let us turn our attention to the semantic triangle and run into the intriguing territory of Semantics.

A. Arbitrariness

There are more than 10,000 different languages and dialects currently in use world wide. The variety of the entries in multilingual dictionaries shows how meanings do not comply with general rules and individuals can denote an object using whatsoever symbol or sound. Meanings are not controlled by obligations. This idea emerged since the classical philosophy, Hermogenes claims in Plato's "*Cratylus*" (2004):

"Any name which you give, in my opinion, is the right one, and if you change that and give another, the new name is as correct as the old. We frequently change the names of our slaves, and the newly imposed name is as good as the old; for there is no name given to anything by nature; all is convention and habit of the users".

Saussure (1983), perhaps the most authoritative advocate of semantic freedom, holds:

The first principle of linguistics "refers to the fact that the forms of linguistic sign bear no natural relationship to their meaning".

Saussure points out that the traditional use of a word to designate an entity is not obliged by internal rules. He fixes *the principle of arbitrariness* which may be expressed in the following terms:

There is no necessary, intrinsic, direct or inevitable relationship between the signifier and the signified. [1.7]

In a language a form is not determined by what it signifies. No specific symbol is naturally more suited to an object than any other symbol. In general *E* does not result in *NE* neither is *E* motivated by the represented entity.

A circle of linguists inquiries the special properties of each language. Scholars delve around the unrepeatable connections of a language with the human group, his culture, and his historical evolutions. *Linguistic relativism* originated in German national romantic thought in the early 19th century was later developed by Sapir and Whorf (Gumperz et al 1996). Authors hold that the semantic structures of different languages should be fundamentally incommensurable, with consequences for the way in which speakers of specific languages might think and act. Language, thought, and culture are deeply interlocked, so that each language exhibits a distinctive profile. It may be said that the supporters of the linguistic relativism expound the principle of arbitrariness in a very pragmatic, accurate manner.

B. Universal Principle?

Authors, such as Lévi-Strauss, John Lechte, and others, deny or streamline the arbitrariness principle because of the large number of exceptions which seem to disprove [1.7]. *Linguistic universals* highlight common rules crossing languages and appear as solid negation of the human arbitrariness. For example, all languages have nouns and verbs; all vocal languages have vowels and consonants. Other phenomena such as the morphology of nouns, adjectives, and verbs motivate to a certain extent in a language. Significance is in part determined by imagination and in part is fixed by norms so that contemporary linguists wonder whether the arbitrariness principle is to be abrogated or to be expressed in a feebler way.

Saussure derives the principle of arbitrariness from the analysis of languages. He chiefly deduces his issue on the basis of empirical observations, and this is the vulnerable side of his method in my opinion. Solely the experimental and complete survey upon all the parts of a language – morphemes, lemmas etc. – could establish whether motivated significance is prevailing or does not prevail.

But the complete analysis on arbitrariness should be conducted into all the languages of the world. This workload is simply enormous and the statistical project cannot be put into practice. The immense set of linguistic elements makes unviable the exact determination of linguistic arbitrariness. In addition this inquiry would result in insecure conclusions since novel expressions which will be defined in the future could deny the outcomes just obtained.

In conclusion the rigorous experimental approach appears unworkable and unreliable; and I am inclined to follow another direction.

The semantic triangle just seen offers an aid.

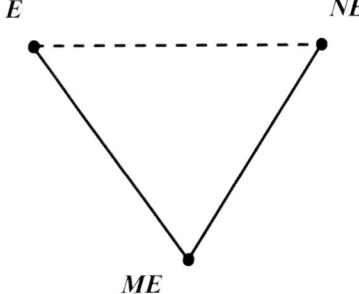

Figure 1.15. The semantic triangle.

The triad makes clear that the mind assigns the significance notably *ME* brings forth a variety of semantic activities, *ME* creates/ recognizes/ modifies etc. The lower vertex of the triangle plays a crucial role in *constructing reality*. In fact the brain does not merely label the objects of the world existing out there, but organizes the reality which is divided up into arbitrary categories by every language. The conceptual world with which each of us is familiar could have been divided up very differently using another language and this reinforces our convictions on human creativity.

An individual or a group determines the correspondence *E-NE* and resolves to follow imagination, an impulse of the soul, or otherwise a logical reasoning. Creative thought operates in unpredictable ways and has a conduct which by and large cannot be foreseen. *The essential freedom of ME should lead us to conclude that in principle no intrinsic property connects the signifier to the signified* and statement [1.7] should be assumed true.

A number of motives such as *reasons of convenience* encourage *ME* to correlate *E* and *NE* by means of a logical rule, of an analogy or another standard. For example icons imitate the signified objects and the meaning of an icon is easily recognized.

The arbitrariness principle does not exclude the possibility to fix motivated connections, but individuals' creativity never retires and repeatedly modifies a linguistic discipline. The rules established by the human mind vary by time passing and the diachronic studies upon a language bring to light how the principle of arbitrariness dominates the linguistic territory.

In conclusion people determine significance at absolute liberty and also linguistic motivations fall under the variable and unpredictable habit of the creative mind in accordance to [1.7].

C. Anarchy to Delimit

Hominids who lived in groups discovered a shared code was necessary to coordinate individual actions. People cannot reach common goals without communicating with one another. The members of a community pursue common purposes provided they cooperate; in turn it is necessary to talk in order to cooperate. Also animals which hunt together – such as wolves, hyenas and lions – establish a system of signs to avoid misunderstandings. Language is the prerequisite to the success of any social initiative.

The principle of arbitrariness complies with individuals' liberty but generates a lot of difficulties on the practical plane. The free nature of *E-NE* in the mind of the perceiver/observer/communicator muddies any issue and wastes the communication necessary for individuals to survive. Unpredictable meanings oppose the discipline which must be established for dialogues.

A community is based upon converging wills and collaborative behaviors, whereas principle [1.7] does not support human harmony. Arbitrariness is absolutely an anti-social precept since it does not sustain any rule to impart knowledge and to operate. People cannot have any interchange because of the impossibility of treating significance in a systematic manner. The principle of arbitrariness proves to be a non-positive principle and leads people to self-destruction.

Happily the origin of arbitrariness offers an aid to delimitate semantic anarchy. When one agrees on the idea that the principle of arbitrariness is originated by the human mind *ME*, one naturally concludes that [1.7] may be mitigated provided that individuals spontaneously relinquish or limit their own intellectual freedom. If the arbitrariness principle takes origin from the liberty of man, the obvious solution consists in the voluntary restriction of liberty.

As a matter of fact a solid *linguistic agreement* sustains the dialogues of men/women belonging to a social group. People learn how to communicate very early in the life and accept a set of common rules during childhood and in this way refrain from their absolute license. Social conventions govern the arbitrariness of signs and make the laws which bring Semantics under control.

A group of individuals generates a language as long as those individuals accept the law which confines their liberty within limits. In exchange the restriction of freedom allows them to cooperate and to live a more satisfactory life.

A vast circle of linguists is concerned with the social side of languages. Even those who inquire the universal aspects of language – e.g. see Chomsky (1980) and Davidson (1984) – recognize the importance of linguistic conventions. Other researchers plunge into the linguistic concords and search for deeper understanding of this matter. David Lewis treats the social nature of language in a systematic theory (Lewis, 1969). Lewis' conventionalism dissects the relation between the communicator and the listener and defines the language as a function that assigns truth conditions to sentences.

It is worth mentioning the *theory of speaker's meaning* by Herbert Paul Grice (1957) from which some theories on the social nature of language descend.

D. Formalized Agreement

The broken line on top of the semantic triangle (Figure 1.15) is intended to indicate that there is not necessarily any observable or direct relationship between the signifier and the signified.

$$E \text{ ----------- } NE \qquad (1.26)$$

A solid line formalizes the social convention settled by a semantic rule. The elements become fixed on the inter-subjective plane, significance becomes objective in a way.

$$E \longrightarrow NE \qquad (1.27)$$

The dotted line spells out the profound freedom of individuals in semantic affairs and the arrow (1.27) details how this freedom is commonly restricted to ensure mutual communication and collaboration. A language towers as the fundamental pact for people who live in common and have the same interests, all the operations have dependence on this linguistic pact. Semantic agreements are preliminary to any other collaborative accord (Wardhaugh 2002) and I append a few comments on (1.27).

1. Types of Signs and Types of Agreements

A broad variety of criteria intervenes in the linguistic accord symbolized by (1.27). Contrasting movements of the human soul determine a linguistic covenant. Imagination and rigid logic, intuition and facts, fantasy and historical tradition contribute to define a language, and modify a language without a pause. Different norms guide the social conventions and ensure the meanings of signs. It is rather impossible to condense this argument which thousands of specialists scrutinize from the *synchronic* and the *diachronic* perspectives.

In search of a compendium I find support in Peirce's *typology of signs* (Hartshorne et al, 1931-66), in fact he catalogues signs according to the ways in which a signifier refers to the signified. In substance Peirce recognizes three principal types of semantic relations.

i) *Symbol* – Symbols are purely conventional and fundamentally arbitrary, so that *the semantic relationship E-NE must be learnt*. Peirce holds that "A symbol is defined as a sign which becomes such by virtue of the fact that it is interpreted as such".

ii) *Icon* - The appearance of the icon E resembles the aspect of NE and *the semantic relationship evokes NE in ME*. In other words the signifier recalls the signified to the mind of the members of the community in a way. An icon is symmetrical to its model, and the linguistic agreement sometimes is suggested by psychological emotions.

iii) *Index* - The significance of an index reflects the reasons that connect the cause to the effect, the antecedent to the consequent. *The bond between E and NE is fixed on the strength of a precise logic* which cannot be modified by an individual's will. The logic of an index frequently is a part of an entire logical framework. For example a doctor recognizes the fever is an index of the sickness X in that the interpretation of symptoms pertains to the medical science.

Natural languages include signs belonging to the groups i, ii and iii, and one finds words and parts of words that are justified in a way.

Linguists have discovered an assortment of linguistic motivations of which I give a succinct account within this small list:

- *Phonetic motivation* e.g. onomatopoeic words: the naming of a thing or action is fixed by a vocal imitation of the sound associated with it.

- *Morphological motivations* e.g. abbreviations, analogies, and metaphors.
- *Semantic motivations* e.g. metonymy which is a word substituted by another closely associated figure.
- *Etymological motivations* given by historical linguistic evolution.

2. Small and Large Communities

The social origins of languages entail that each language is to be put in relation to the community which uses or used that language, the dimension of that community, the covered geographic area, the history of that community and so forth (Lehmann, 1992).

The language popularity scores the importance of a language. *Dialects, slang* and *jargons* rank the lower levels because they give body to smaller social phenomena with respect to the *natural languages* from which the dialects derive (Berns et al 2002). The diffusion of a language reflects convergence and harmony amongst people. For example the scientific community currently uses English as a universal medium, while some decades ago scientists also resorted to French and sometimes Russian and German for international reporting. Current uniformity shows how the inclination to separatism is regressing. On the other hand the emergence of a dialect shows the opposite tendency toward segregation or anyway toward the closure of a social group. Cities often contain a variety of ethnic groups which tend to underline specific identities. Lower social classes and even upper classes who do not want to mix with others, create slang.

Enlargement or restriction of linguistic covenants brings evidence of movements toward social union or separation. These phenomena embody social dynamics that even influence the digital machines' market. In broad strokes it may be said that aggregation recompenses mass production, conversely disaggregation should cause several small scale productions to serve little niches of markets.

At present semantic confluences benefit standard models. Globalization renders the computer market tempting, massive production rewards the inventor of an ICT solution with high profits.

3. Flexible and Rigid Conventions

It is obvious that also mathematicians communicate on the basis of social conventions. The largest part of the human community adopts the decimal figures to count: **0, 1, 2, 3, 4, 5, 6, 7, 8** and **9** took origin in India and were progressively accepted in the rest of the world during the course of the centuries. Pragmatic convergence gave origin to the writing of numbers; however mathematical agreements differ from the other linguistic agreements due to three significant reasons. Mathematicians deal with topics far less influenced by every-day living and not subjected to personal feeling. Secondly mathematical conventions cross the boundaries of nations and continents. For ease no written alphabet is as popular as the decimal base. Thirdly the mathematical contents are very precise and analytical. For example the number **19** is an exact value, by contrast the word '***young***' sounds generic and one wonders: What age does the adjective 'young' denote?

Universality and *precision* emerge as fundamental qualities of the mathematical language, and make the mathematical language far more stable than a natural language. It is a matter of fact, not an opinion. Real events show how updating a mathematical convention in use runs the risk of provoking a burdensome task. I illustrate an historical case to clarify the consequences provoked by mathematical universalism and precision.

From the mathematical viewpoint the friendliest base to write numbers is not decimal but is duodecimal. Twelve can be divided by 2, 3, 4, and 6, whereas ten is divisible only by 2 and 5. The hours of the day and the months of the year are organized on the duodecimal base and everybody goes through the easy way to divide daytime by regular intervals. For instance a sick man can take medicines once a day, twice, three, four, six, eight, twelve or twenty-four times a day and can easily infer the relative hour intervals.

Because the figures **0, 1, 2, 3, 4, 5, 6, 7, 8, 9** are already in use, it should be sufficient to append whichever couple of symbols to the decimal base and the duodecimal base is handy. This obvious suggestion, put forward during the French revolution when scientists revisited and unified the most important scientific conventions, was rejected. The migration from decimal to duodecimal, absolutely easy on paper, is impracticable due to the enormous social consequences and very heavy risks which may happen in everyday life. Think how many people may be swindled using a base in the place of the other base when they pay or collect money.

As a counter-example I quote numerous upgrades of the Latin alphabet achieved during the centuries. The original Latin alphabet included 21 letters and expanded up to 26 letters to the joy of the writers. E.g. the Anglo-Saxons appended the letter **w** (double u) that was not considered by the ancient Romans. Further regional extensions were created by adding *diacritics* to existing letters, by joining multiple letters together to make *ligatures*, by inventing completely new forms, or by assigning a special function to *pairs* or *triplets of letters*. For example the Germans use the symbol β in the place of **ss** (double s). All these changes were made in a natural manner and writers did not suffer any trouble or impostures.

4. Abstract and Concrete

I append a note on the Semantics of numbers that forestalls an important argument which will be treated in Chapter 4.

A noun in natural language refers indifferently to a physical entity or to a mental-abstract entity. Take the noun **Rome** that symbolizes the capital of Italy or otherwise the abstract idea of Rome that one has in mind. Also the mathematical language signifies practical entities and abstract entities alike, but the mathematical idiom excludes any confusion between these groups.

The semantic analysis of number leads us toward two precise classes. *Abstract numbers* are pure values used without connection to any particular object; abstract numbers are coded by digits such as **3, 41** and **782** and represent ideas included within the brain. A *concrete number* is the counterpart of determined physical entities and is qualified by a word or a symbol that associates the number to the intended physical entities in explicit manner. A writing rule discriminates the concrete number **3 eggs** that means something real, from the abstract number **3** that is a mental idea unrelated to practical specified entities. The pure number **3** has no direct reference with the objects in the world out there.

6. INSTRUMENTAL ACQUISITION OF INFORMATION

Engineers deal with exact forms of information, independent from human feelings. I feel myself obliged to examine the automatic acquisition of information: a necessary step toward the logic of analog and digital machines.

A. When is an Object a Sign or a Thing?

The sharpness principle includes E and E^* which are *algebraic elements*
$$E \text{ NOT}=_R E^* \tag{1.28}$$

No constraint confines the use of an algebraic element, and the present conceptualization holds that all the entities in the world are permanent possibilities of information. Each object which makes a difference with respect to an observer is an information item. E.g. the beer you are drinking, your hat, a tree in the garden and the Moon are common signifiers. The principle of sharpness may be rewritten such as:

Whatsoever object is a signifier if it is distinct with respect to an observer.   [1.8]

This conclusion agrees with the position of several commentators who share the idea that every object in the physical reality is a potential form of information. Umberto Eco (1979) goes so far as to extend the notion of sign to anything material which can be seen, heard, touched, smelt or tasted.

Not only is everything in the world considered information, moreover – I underline – *natural information* ensures the essentials to survive for an individual. A man/woman is capable of staying alive thanks to what he/she sees, listens to, smells and touches in the real world. Basically people are able to subsist thanks to the support of spontaneous information. Men/women eat, work, move etc. with the primary aid of spontaneous information, sometimes quoted as *sense data* in literature.

1. Special Significance

A spontaneous signifier has the possibility of representing anything and conforming to the types of signs devised by Peirce, for example a lion symbolizes power, and smoke is the index of fire. In addition each ordinary signifier is capable of making a special sense: natural E is the counterpart of itself; notably the Sun represents the Sun, a chair signifies a chair; a table represents a table, the lamp symbolizes the lamp and so forth. All the physical items fulfill this extraordinary semantic function

Each physical item represents itself.   [1.9]

This objective and rather obvious semantic function has fundamental importance and plays an essential role in favor of the human survival. An individual can live thanks to the entities extant all around him/her, and an individual recognizes the objects in the world because *each object symbolizes itself*. The ensuing formal expression makes explicit how the natural signifier coincides with the signified

$$E \equiv NE \qquad (1.29)$$

The *semantic relationship is said reflexive* with the mathematical language. The extremes overlap and the graph (1.27) assumes the ensuing shape

$$E \equiv NE \qquad (1.30)$$

The principle of arbitrariness holds that an universal rule cannot determine the link between E and NE, and (1.29) constitutes a very special case. Sentence [1.9] entails that each object in the world has a proper significance due to its physical nature and the mind can but recognize this significance. A natural piece of information conveys information *per se* notably the Nature determines how a signifier and a signified are coincident.

Equality (1.29) could be catalogued as a *tautology* in point of logic; it may be placed close to this identity

$$A \equiv A \qquad (1.31)$$

And may be sensed as a needless repetition of the same element when one takes the formal viewpoint. The development of abstract arguments yields that (1.29) is a negligible expression. Conversely the practical perspective we are following leads to non-trivial conclusions, which we shall expand next.

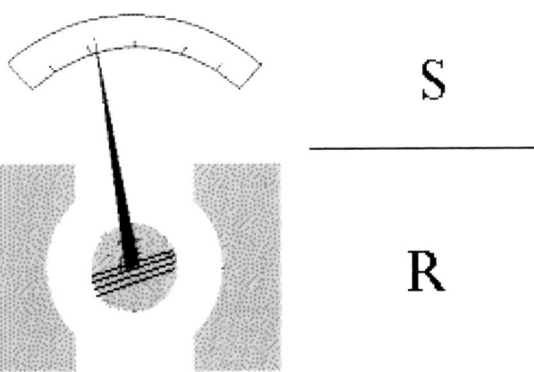

Figure 1.16. Components of an ammeter.

B. Information Independent from the Mind

The generic object E passes from the potential information-state to the real information-state as long as R operates. The probe R lies normally in the generic state R_X and assumes the observation state R_Y when R detects E. Hence one can generalize this concept in the following way:

A physical element that changes state while interacting with an object is an observer.
[1.10]

I bring a straightforward case on how the present account is put into effect.

The ammeter includes the sensor R (Figure 1.16) which basically consists of two magnets and a mobile coil. R detects the electric current E, namely the component R registers the difference between E and the ground value E^*, which is the comparison term. The energy E moves the sensor itself; a physical law determines the appropriate significance which is independent from human awareness. Thanks to this autonomy the ammeter can serve people and communicates the readout to an operator by means of the needle S.

The principle of sharpness leads us to conclude that whatever physical entity that reacts to a solicitation is a potential observer, hence material entities exchange information due to bare mutual interactions. A lifeless object is capable of working as an observer. For instance the Sun warms up the Earth. This simple event, interpreted from the present perspective, yields that the Sun is a signifier and the Earth that changes its state under the Sun's rays acts as R. As second example suppose the body A bumps against the body B that changes position, hence B senses the sign A and plays the role of R. In technical literature one finds that some mechanical sensors work with a principle like that.

Statements [1.9] and [1.10] constitute the theoretical cornerstones for the autonomous acquisition of information achieved by machines. These results establish that a device is capable of conveying information without human intervention and justify systems that handle information completely independent from Man. Robots, automatic systems, and self-controlled devices make cases in cutting-edge technology.

We find examples in the biological realm too. Intricate regulation mechanisms ensure the survival to cells. Biological feedback and feed-forward loops take control of cell organs accordingly to the genetic code. They intervene from the birth of the cell and throughout the life-cycle of the cell beyond any human awareness. These remarks match with the thought of those who take self-reference as an essential property of life (Rosen 1991), (Luhmann et al 1995).

The present conclusions even get close to Stonier's view on information. He draws attention to the atoms and the molecules that make up the mass and movement of the universe and are the most significant information elements. Tom Stonier develops his ideas in (1994) and concludes:

"The first and most important fact is to understand that information is a basic property of the universe, like energy, and like energy it has a reality of its own."

Stonier concentrates on natural information, and insists on the objectivity and autonomy of information assumed as diversity of matter and/or of energy. The present account agrees with Stonier theory and shows how natural items convey information due to relentless mutual interactions. Statements [1.8], [1.9] and [1.10] yield that a system – biological and artificial – is capable of handling information uninfluenced by intellectual opinions.

Measurement occupies a special place in sciences since measurement is the standard mode to acquire information from the physical reality, the signifier E is sharp as much as possible and NE is not affected by personal feelings. Actually the measurement process is obtained through mechanical procedures and provides concrete numbers through a standard unit, e.g. volts, feet, meters. Humanists often see measures as the most vapid and lifeless pieces of information. This is true beyond any doubt, but this defect is compensated by the *precision* and the *objectiveness* of information: two cornerstones for exact sciences (Roche 1998).

7. COMPLETE CATALOGUE

The conclusions expanded in the present chapter lead me toward the complete catalogue of signifiers. The practical perspective which the present book is developing suggests the classification of signifiers according to their origin. The whole set includes *spontaneous, natural signifiers*, like your chair, a street and a tree, and *artificial items*, like this page and the electric signals that a device generates for the special purpose of informing.

This practical criterion for grouping is not new in technical-scientific areas. The classes *natural/artificial* may be found in other disciplines for example chemists keep apart mineral halite from sodium chloride prepared in laboratory. Halite and sodium chloride have identical chemical components and identical molecule: NaCl; but lie apart because of their origins, natural and artificial.

Broken down by the signifier provenance, signs fall into the following groups:

Natural information - The signifier and the signified coincide:
$$E \equiv NE$$
Artificial information - The signifier and the signified do not coincide:
$$E \neq NE$$
[1.11]

This catalogue summarizes the materialistic view on information in the most succinct terms. Finally this description has a further merit: it is divorced from any particular language and covers all the objects and events that exist in Nature that are potential signs.

8. CONCLUDING REMARKS

The present book is an independent attempt to dissect the information technologies on the basis of physical properties and semantic concepts as well.

I deem that both the sides of information can guide us to analyze the machines which are changing people's life-style. Eminent thinkers argue about modern technologies that could determine the shape and direction of our lives, absolutely or to a large degree. I pick out the fundamental contributions by Langdon Winner (1980) and the classical paper by Thomas Misa (1992) from current vast literature on this subject. I believe that the accurate scrutiny of the semantic and the concrete properties of signs could provide a solid support to these philosophers.

Shannon (1949) holds: "Semantic aspects of communication are irrelevant to the engineering problem". A large circle of writers, coming especially from the engineering and technical areas, shares this statement in a radical manner and does not pay much attention or even rejects Semantics. They claim that meanings are affected by personal interferences and are not perceived as a reliable field of research. This present-day position may be concisely described by the following sentence:

"Subjective factors interfere with Semantics, thus a researcher should place Semantics aside".

The premise of this popular way of reasoning: "Subjective factors interfere with Semantics" is true beyond any doubt. Not only the meanings of signs depend on the human soul, but the assignment of significance is an absolutely free action. The preamble of the foregoing implicative sentence proves to be right but the conclusion: "Thus a researcher should place Semantics aside" does not seem obvious to me, and some objections may be made. Normally scientists do not retreat from a field of interest when subjective elements influence this field. I exemplify my mind using the following three cases.

About 1931 Bruno De Finetti and Frank P. Ramsey discovered the subjective value of probability in the mathematical calculus (Gillies 2000). They found out how the probability $p(A)$ of the event A has no relation with the physical reality instead $p(A)$ expresses the degree of belief of an individual upon the occurrence of A. This theoretical issue which apparently seems to be corrosive did not destroy the calculus of probability instead it has triggered fertile studies which have strengthened the statistical field. Presently statisticians, doctors, managers and other decision makers adopt the *Bayesian methods* in every-day activities. The *subjective school* does not constitute a 'group of terrorists' in the scientific territory but is a well appreciated group of theorists which is currently proceeding to improve and to disseminate the Bayesian methods.

Mechanics is the science that establishes the equations for the movements of bodies and the forces that cause interactions. Although the speed does not turn out to be an absolute quantity. The magnitude of the velocity of a body depends on the observer in the sense that two observers can assign far differing values of velocity to a body in a determined situation. This subjectivism undermined confidence on the fundamentals of Mechanics and constituted a heavy theoretical conundrum, but did not convince scholars to give up the question. Conversely theorists attacked the relativism of movement, Galileo and others found the way to circumvent the problem (Brown 2006) and fixed the characteristics and the role of the so called *referential system.*

A medical intervention has no predetermined effects, and the benefits coming from a cure depend on each cured subject. Two patients treated with the same protocol exhibit behaviors that sometime diverge in a drastic manner as one dies and the other survives. The subjective tolerance of drugs and of all the medical remedies did not lead experts to drop the study of medicine. The subjectivism of outcomes does not discourage doctors from taking care of ill persons, and researchers in medicine investigate ever new forms of sickness. Perhaps the most challenging medical treatment emerges in the psychological realm and in particular in psychoanalysis: What is more personal and unrepeatable than the human soul?

Man's psyche – intimate and profound to the extent that the same individual is amply unaware of it – constitutes the greatest challenge of subjectivism, yet Sigmund Freud discovered the *language of dreams* which offers an objective key to decipher the soul of a person down to his unconscious (Freud et al. 2009). An amazing solution indeed!

The aforementioned scientific challenges do not constitute intellectual curiosities or tiny tesserae belonging to the scientific mosaic. The three topics played and still play a noteworthy role in the progress of sciences. The above mentioned areas of research are extremely important and are felt even by laymen in a way:

Who has never doubted whether the probability of winning at the lottery is a pipe dream?

Who did not wonder if his friends were moving or otherwise his train was departing from the subway station?

Who was never afraid of not being cured of a disease?

Scientists cannot destroy the subjectivism of natural phenomena, nonetheless they do not surrender and work hard to enhance the knowledge of phenomena and to delimit the effects of arbitrariness. Researchers accept the challenges of subjectivism and struggle to take the intended sector under control.

I do not see reasons to dodge parallel efforts in information science, and this book represents an attempt to show how Semantics can be discussed on the basis of objective properties and can sustain the study of technology.

BIBLIOGRAPHY

Aristotle (2004) - *On Interpretation* - Kessinger Publishing.
Bateson G. (2000) - *Steps to an Ecology of Mind* - University of Chicago Press.
Berns J.B., van Marle J. (2002) - *Present-Day Dialectology: Problems and Findings* - Walter de Gruyter.
Blazey-Ayoub P.J., Conomos J.W., Doris J.I. (1996) - *Concise Evidence Law* - Federation Press.
Bohm D., Hiley B.J. (1993) - *The Undivided Universe: An Ontological Interpretation of Quantum Theory* - Routledge.
Brier S. (2008) - *Cybersemiotics* - University of Toronto Press.
Brookes B.C. (1980) - The Foundations of Information Science, Part I - Philosophical Aspects - *Journal of Information Science*, 2 (3-4), 125-133.
Brown H.P. (2006) - *Physical Relativity: Space-Time Structure from a Dynamical Perspective* - Oxford University Press.
Bullock J., Boyle J., Wang M.B. (2001) - *Physiology* - Lippincott Williams and Wilkins.

Burgin M. (2009) - *Theory of Information: Fundamentality, Diversity and Unification* - World Scientific Publishing Co.

Carnap R., Bar-Hillel Y. (1953) - An Outline of a Theory of Semantic Information - in Bar-Hillel, *Language and Information: Selected Essays on Their Theory and Application*, pp 221-274, (1964) Addison Wesley.

Chaitin G.J. (1977) - Algorithmic Information Theory - *IBM Journal of Research and Development,* 4(21), pp. 350-359.

Chernavsky D.S. (1990) - *Synergetics and Information* - Znaniye, Moscow (in Russian).

Chomsky N. (1980) - *Rules and Representations* - Columbia Univ. Press.

Csiszár I. (1967) - Information Type Measures of Differences of Probability Distribution and Indirect Observations - *Studia Math. Hungarica*, 2, 299-318.

Cunha G.D.M, Cunha D.G. (1967) - *Conservation of Library Materials: A Manual and Bibliography on the Care, Repair and Restoration of Library Materials* - Scarecrow Press.

Davidson D. (1984) - *Inquiries into Truth and Interpretation* - Oxford University Press

De Kerckhove D. (1997) - *Connected Intelligence, the Arrival of the Web* - Somerville House.

De Saussure F. (1983) - *Course in General Linguistics* - Duckworth, London.

Denning P.J., Comer D.E., Gries D., Mulder M.C., Tucker A., Turner A.J., Young P.R. (1989) - Computing as a Discipline - *Communications of the ACM,* 32(1), pp. 9-23.

Dretske F.I. (2000) - *Perception, Knowledge and Belief* - Cambridge University Press.

Dryer M.S. (2005) - *Word Order, The World Atlas of Language Structures* - Oxford University Press.

Eco U. (1979) - *A Theory of Semiotics* - Indiana University Press, Bloomington.

Everett H. (1957) - Relative State Formulation of Quantum Mechanics - *Reviews of Modern Physics,* 29(3), pp. 454-462.

Fernandez-Dols J.M., Oatley K., Manstead A., Russell J.A. (eds) (1997) - *The Psychology of Facial Expression* - Cambridge University Press.

Fisher R.A. (1950) - *Contributions to Mathematical Statistics* - Wiley.

Floridi L. (1999) - *Philosophy and Computing: An Introduction* - Routledge.

Frege G. (1892) - Uber Sinn und Bedeutung - *Zeitschrift für Philosophie und philosophische Kritik,* 100, pp. 25-50. Traslated as "On Sense and Meaning".

Freud S., Eder M.D. (2009) - *On Dreams* - Cosimo Classics.

Garfinkel H., Rawls A. (2008) - *Toward a sociological theory of information* - Paradigm Publishers.

Gillies D. (2000) - *Philosophical Theories of Probability* - Routledge

Goguen J. (1997) - Towards a Social, Ethical Theory of Information - in *Social Science, Technical Systems and Cooperative Work: Beyond the Great Divide*, G. Bowker et al (eds), Erlbaum, pp. 27-56.

Gordon A. D. (1999) - *Classification* - Chapman and Hall/CRC.

Gray D., Toghill P. (2001) - *Introduction to the Symptoms and Signs of Clinical Medicine* - Hodder Arnold.

Grice H. P. (1957) - Meaning - *The Philosophical Review* 64, pp. 377-388.

Griffin D. (1985) - *Animal Thinking* - Harvard University Press.

Gumperz J.J., Levinson S.C. (eds) (1996) - *Rethinking Linguistic Relativity* - Cambridge University Press.

Hailman J.P. (2008) - *Coding and Redundancy: Man-Made and Animal-Evolved Signals* - Harvard University Press.
Hamilton A., Madison J., Jay J. (2007) - *The Federalist Papers* - Filiqurian Publishing.
Harkevich A. (1960) - On the Value of Information - *Problems of Cybernetics*, 4, pp. 2-10.
Hartley R.V.L. (1928) - Transmission of Information - *Bell Syst. Tech. J.*, 7, pp. 535–563.
Hartshorne C., Weiss P., Burks A.W. (eds) (1931-1966) - *Collected Papers of Charles Sanders Peirce* - 8 vols., Harvard University Press.
Hendee W.R., Wells P.N.T. (1997) - *The Perception of Visual Information* - Springer.
Hirst R.J. (1992) - *Problems of Perception* - Prometheus.
Hooft G. (1999) - Quantum Gravity as a Dissipative Deterministic System - *Class. Quant. Grav.* 16, pp. 3263-3279.
Hübner K., Dixon P.R., Dixon H.M. (1983) - *Critique of Scientific Reason* - University of Chicago Press.
Jablonka E. (2002) - Information: Its Interpretation, Its Inheritance and Its Sharing - *Philosophy of Science,* 69, pp. 578-605.
Klir G. (1991) - *Facets of System Science* - Oxford Pergamon Press.
Kolmogorov A.N. (1965) - Three Approaches to the Definition of the Quantity of Information - *Problems of Information Transmission*, 1, pp. 3-11.
Kotarbinski T. (1968) - Reism: Issues and Prospects - *Logique and Analyse,* 11, pp. 441-458.
Landauer R. (1961) - Irreversibility and Heat Generation in the Computing Process - *IBM J. Res. Dev.*, 5, pp. 183-191.
Landy M.S., Maloney L.T., Pavel M. (1995) - *Exploratory Vision: The Active Eye* - Springer.
Lehmann W.P. (1992) - *Historical Linguistics: An Introduction* - Routledge.
Leff H.S., Rex A.F. (1990) - *Maxwell's Demon: Entropy, Information, Computing* - Princeton University Press.
Levitin L.B. (1992) - Physical Information Theory Part I - *Proc. Workshop on Physics and Computation*, pp. 210-214.
Lewis D. (1969) - *Convention*: a Philosophical Study - Harward University Press.
Loewenstein W.R. (1999) - *The Touchstone of Life: Molecular Information, Cell Communication, and the Foundations of Life* - Oxford University Press.
Longhurst R.S. (1974) - *Geometrical and Physical Optics* - Longman
Losee R.M. (1997) - A Discipline Independent Definition of Information - *J. of the American Society for Information Science*, 48(3), pp. 254-269.
Lucadou von W. (1987) - The Model of Pragmatic Information - *Proc. the 30th Parapsychological Association Convention,* pp. 236-254.
Luhmann N. (1990) - *Essays on Self-reference* - Columbia University Press.
Luhmann N., Bednarz J. (1995) - *Social Systems* - Stanford University Press.
MacInteyer E.R. (2004) - *Stepping Stones to Neurology* - B. Jain Publishers.
McLuhan M. (1965) - *Understanding Media: the Extensions of Man* - McGraw-Hill.
Marschak J. (1971) - Economics of Information Systems - *J. Amer. Statist. Assoc.*, 66, pp. 192-219.
Maturana H. R., Varela F. (1980) - *Autopoiesis and Cognition: the Realization of the Living* - Reidel Publishing Company.
Mazur M. (1974) - Kachestvennaja Teorija Informazii. [Qualitative theory of information] - Mir Publ. (in Russian).

Miller I., Miller M. (1994) - *Statistical Methods for Quality: with Applications to Engineering and Management* - Prentice-Hall.

Miller J.G. (1978) - *Living Systems* - McGraw-Hill.

Misa T. (1992) - How Machines Make History, and How Historians (and Others) Help Them to Do So - *Science, Technology & Human Values*, 17(1), pp. 3-12.

Mityugov V.V. (1976) - *Physical Foundations of Information Theory* (in Russian) - Sovietskoe Radio, Moscow.

Morris C.W. (1964) - *Signification and Significance: A Study of the Relations of Signs and Values* - MIT Press.

Morrison E., Milliken F.J. (2003) - Speaking up, Remaining Silent: the Dynamics of Voice and Silence in Organizations - *Journal of Management Studies*, 40 (6).

Nauta D. Jr. (1970) - *The Meaning of Information* - Mouton.

Ogden C.K., Richards I.A. (1989) - *The Meaning of Meaning: A Study of the Influence of Language upon Thought and of the Science of Symbolism* - Harcourt.

O'Leary-Hawthorne J. (1955) - The Bundle Theory of Substance and the Identity of Indiscernibles - *Analysis*, 55.

Passmore J.A. (1985) - *Recent Philosophers* - Open Court Pub. Co., p. 24.

Partridge L.D. (2003) - *Nervous System Actions and Interactions* - Springer.

Petersen A. (1968) - *Quantum Physics and the Philosophical Tradition* - MIT Press

Pettigrew K.E., McKechine L. (2001) - The Use of the Theory in Information Science Research - *JASIST*, 52(1).

Plato (2004) - *Cratylus* - Kessinger Publishing.

Pratt V. (1987) - *The Evolution of Artificial Intelligence* - Blackwell,

Rastier F. (1990) - La Triade Sémiotique, le Trivium et la Sémantique Linguistique - *Nouveaux Actes Sémiotiques*, 9.

Ritchie D. (1986) - Shannon and Weaver: Unraveling the Paradox of Information - *Communication Research*, 13(2), pp. 278-298.

Robinson H. (2001) - *Perception* - Routldege.

Roche J.J. (1998) - *The Mathematics of Measurement: A Critical History* - Springer.

Rosen R. (1991) - *Life Itself* - Columbia University Press.

Sayre K.M. (1976) - *Cybernetics and the Philosophy of Mind* - Routledge & Kegan.

Schrader A. M. (1986) - The Domain of Information Science: Problems in Conceptualization and in Consensus-building - *Information Services & Us*, 6.

Seckel A. (2002) - *More Optical Illusions* - Carlton Books.

Shannon C., Weaver W. (1949) - *The Mathematical Theory of Communication* - University Illinois Press.

Smirnov A. (1999) - *Processing of Multidimensional Signals* - Springer.

Somjen G.G. (1983) - *Neurophysiology: The Essentials* - Williams & Wilkins.

Stonier T. (1994) - *Information and the Internal Structure of the Universe: An Exploration into Information Physics* - Springer-Verlag.

Tarski A. (1983) - *Logic, Semantics, Metamathematics* - Corcoran J. (ed), Hackett.

Tohm, R. (1975) - *Structural Stability and Morphogenesis* - Benjamin.

Vlaardingerbroek M.T., den Boer J.A. (2003) - *Magnetic Resonance Imaging: Theory and Practice* - Springer.

Wardhaugh R. (2002) - *An Introduction to Sociolinguistics* - Blackwell Publishing.

Weizsäcker von E. (1974) - Erstmaligkeit und Bestatigung als Komponenten der Pragmatischen Information - in Weizsäcker von E. (ed) *Offene Systeme I*, Ernst Klett Verlag, pp. 82-113.

Whaley L.J. (1996) - *Introduction to Typology: the Unity and Diversity of Language* - Sage Publications.

Wiener N. (1961) - *Cybernetics: Or the Control and Communication in the Animal and the Machine* - 2nd edition, MIT Press and Wiley.

Wilson E.B. (1952) - *An Introduction to Scientific Research* - McGraw-Hill.

Winner L. (1980) - Do Artifacts Have Politics? - *Daedalus*, 109(1).

Wolfgang C. (1994) - *Frege's Theory of Sense and Reference: Its Origin and Scope* - Cambridge University Press.

Chapter 2

TWO COURSES OF ACTION

Authors from various fields of expertise recognize that the logic of the machine S depends on the product w carried out by that machine; hence digital and analog systems should be discussed starting from the concept of signifier. I began the present book declaring this special intent and now this declaration has turned into a sort of challenge. The accurate discussion of the semantic triad has just ended and I have to show how the stated plan should be put into practice.

1. NATURAL AND ARTIFICIAL

The complete catalogue [1.11] includes natural signifiers and artificial signifiers, and engineers make use of spontaneous pieces of information or otherwise can prepare artificial signs through mechanical processes in the professional practice. As a matter of fact information items fall into two principal classes and these classes suggest the following conclusion to me:

Engineers either exploit a natural piece of information just in hand or otherwise inaugurate special processes to build up artificial information. [2.1]

I like to explain my inferential reasoning using a parallel with the pharmaceutical domain.

Nature provides medicaments by means of a variety of plants, herbs, lucernes and mineral substances. These medicines have been in use since centuries but fall short of curing complicated ailments and pharmaceutical firms create medicines through industrial processes. We find two lines of products in pharmacology nowadays: on one hand there are drugs derived from natural sources, on the other hand drugs are built up after methodic inquiries. An individual can make use of a medicine of the first category or otherwise of the second category to cure some diseases. If you have a sore throat you are able to cure yourself using *propolis*, a natural antibiotic prepared by bees, or a normal antibiotic.

Herbal remedies took origin from empirical and also occasional discoveries; instead modern pharmacology is grounded upon rational and systematic studies. In parallel I find it reasonable to deduce that two far differing approaches embody the information and communication technology. I infer that engineers are capable of taking advantage of spontaneous information or otherwise creating artificial signs through dedicated procedures. The first *paradigm* (or *method* or *mode*) should employ natural or nature-like pieces of information; the second paradigm should devise signs independently from Nature. Whether the parallel with herbalism and pharmacology is right, the first paradigm should exhibit a somewhat empirical profile instead the second paradigm should be methodic and grounded upon principles. If my reasoning is true, the latter is strongly theory-based and the former is poorly theory-based.

Modern glossaries define '*analogue*' as something having "*the property of being similar to something else, or bearing an analogy to something*". According to my previous deductive reasoning, I mean to say that a technician applies the *analog paradigm* when he/she communicates using a spontaneous signifier or a form resembling an object present in the reality. Otherwise an expert uses the *digital paradigm* which does not imitate occasional information but adheres to standards

Do these conclusions come true in the world?

Is my inferential reasoning correct?

The identity of the digital and analog methods is considered an acute conundrum, emphasized in (Allison et al 2005). I shall spend the next pages to scrutinize how, when and why analog and digital machines operate in the real world. In particular we shall verify whether the previous remarks match with the computer technologies.

2. ANALOG IS CLOSE TO NATURE

An African tribal chief puts a huge leaf over his hut to mark his social status. Inhabitants of Oceania use shells to count. Many people identify the North by means of the Polar star. Dictionaries tell that a person applies the analog paradigm when he/she makes use of a generic object taken from the world to signify something. Thus the above mentioned agents who use leaves, shells and stars to signify something, may be deemed as analog experts from the viewpoint suggested by the dictionaries.

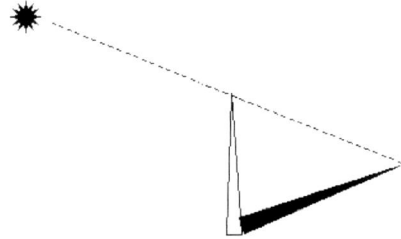

Figure 2.1. A sundial.

I go on along this way and conclude that engineers should have a conduct not so different from the African tribal chief and the Oceania inhabitants.

Experience shows how analog engineers employ natural signifiers and my inference is correct. As an example I quote the Sun which rises in the morning, it reaches its peak and at sunset notifies the day is dying. The Sun is a natural source of information and ancient inventors created the *sundial*: an analog device which exploits the Sun's light, a resource ready for use. All the substances – solid, liquid and gas – expand under the heat, and reduce their volume when cooled. Analog creators invented the *thermometer* that exploits those natural signifiers. The liquid that expands inside the thermometer bulb is a resource just available in Nature and is capable of marking the temperature

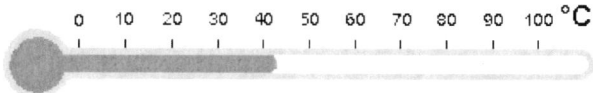

Figure 2.2. An analog thermometer.

Analog designers use signifiers extant in the world or otherwise copy signifiers from the world. Analog devices import or replicate natural information. Take the film of a movie that includes *shots* and the *sound strip*.

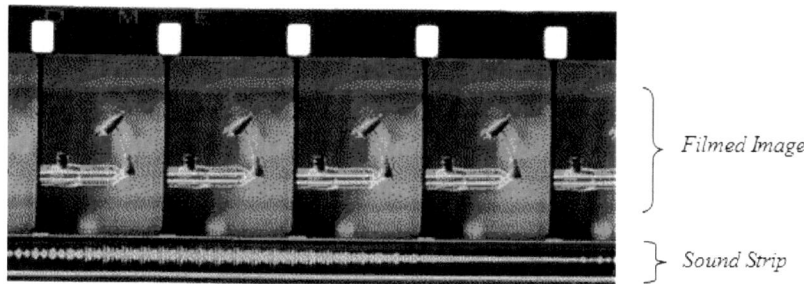

Figure 2.3. A film strip.

A frame exhibits an event which occurred in the world. The sound strip created by a photoelectric cell duplicates the sounds in a simple way. When the sound strip is dark, the original scene is silent; when the white trace is ample, there are many sound sources. In conclusion both the sequence of frames and the sound strip provide true copies of the physical reality, and are analog signifiers.

By contrast digital technicians build up signifiers unrelated to the objects of the world. They learn to use sets of electric pulses, of magnetic energy levels, of flashes of light and dark, and so forth. There is no intrinsic link between each digital signifier and the entity it represents. One cannot find a plausible connection between E and NE to the extent that people have to learn the meaning of each element. As an example take the voltage values E_1, E_2, E_3 and E_4 that provide the *alphabet* (or *base*) for a digital solution

$$E_1 = 1.3 \text{ V}; \quad E_2 = 4.7 \text{ V}; \quad E_3 = 8.1 \text{ V}; \quad E_4 = 11.5 \text{ V}$$

There is no manifest relation between these signifiers and the entities in the world that they are called to represent and that may be any. The contrast between the analog approach and the digital approach appears remarkable.

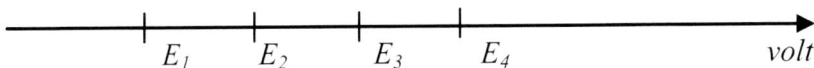

Figure 2.4.

A. Criticism on Naturalism

A circle of commentators agrees that analog information appears somewhat close to Nature. In his essay Antony Wilden (1972) states that the analog is defined by its always having a relation to things. The sign of an analog communication "has a necessary relation to what it represents". Instead discretization produces representations "less real" or "less authentic" than analog forms. Other authors converge toward the same position (Watzlawick et al 1967), (Blachowicz 1998), (Dretske 1981) and the reader could be inclined to sanction the analog/digital paradigms on the basis of the natural/artificial criterion in a definitive way.

But this rigid conclusion raises some doubts.

Digital devices handle discrete signals rather alien to natural forms found in the world. Although this judgment is not absolute: there are digital solutions somewhat close to Nature. Take the sounds that are normally translated into discrete signals. A converter can transmute a continuous wave into a stream of discrete signals (or vice versa) and ensures the realism of the digital sequence. Figure 2.5 exemplifies the parallel between the electric impulses and the intended sound. The *sampling theorem* regulates the conversion between numeric signals and continuous signal, and sanctions the symmetry extant between the analog and the digital representations. As a practical case, digital signals generated at 96 kHz with the resolution of 24 bits make a high-definition format which represents sounds much more accurately than a hi-fi vinyl record.

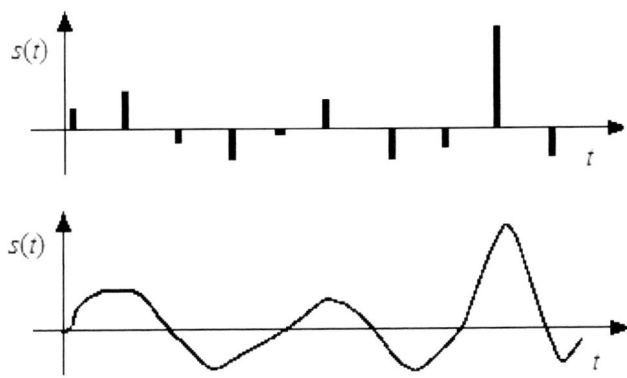

Figure 2.5. Converted digital and analog signals.

As a second case, consider the *classical camera* that creates the chemical image of a house over the film plate. The analog process ends with the faithful photo $\mathcal{A}$ printed on a sensitive paper.

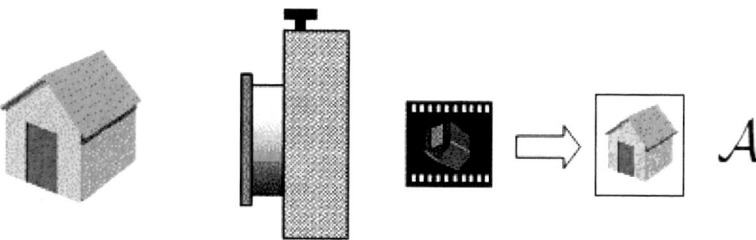

Figure 2.6. Analog camera.

The *digital camera* stores a sequence of bits in a tiny chip and then a computer printer provides the final result on paper. The intermediate outcome does not show any evident connection with the original image, but the final image – consisting of discrete elements – appears identical to the portrayed original. A high-quality digital image – say an image including over 2000 dpi (= dots per inch) on paper – appears absolutely realistic and no one would be able to distinguish between the computer print $\mathcal{B}$ and the traditional print $\mathcal{A}$. Discretization proves to be in keeping with the natural reality in the most perfect way.

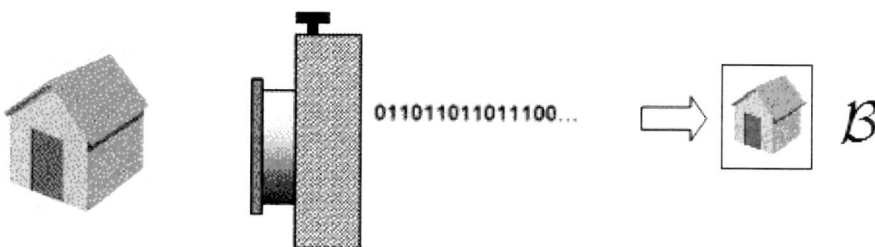

Figure 2.7. Digital camera.

This pair of examples shows how the digital paradigm can create signifiers very similar to the related objects extant in the world. The discrete elements are disposed in such a way as to recreate a realistic image or a natural sound. We find symbols in the digital domain and even icons such as the pictures captured by a digital camera. The popularity of icons and symbols inverts in the analog domain where the majority of signs is iconic.

	Are Icons	Are Symbols
Analog Signals	Normally	Rarely
Digital Signals	Less Frequently	More Frequently

Figure 2.8.

In conclusion analog and digital signs are iconic and symbolic as well. The analog/digital distinction is not coextensive with the distinction between realistic and abstract representations for there are digital elements in pure perception and analog elements in abstract thought. Analog and digital forms are more or less close to Nature and the scientific community agrees that the criterion *natural/artificial* does not provide the definitive answer to understand what is analog and digital respectively.

B. Criticism on Continuous/Discrete

The relation between analog signifiers and Nature has manifest consequences in the sense that physical parameters – e.g. space, time, energy, electric current – are continuous and constitute usual analog signifiers. Conversely distance involves gaps between elements and digital paradigm is systematically grounded on Discrete Mathematics. Analog describes any fluctuating, evolving, or continually changing process, while digital uses pulses that are separated values to represent information. The vast majority of technical writers are inclined to take '*analog information*' as synonymous with a *continuously variable signal* and '*digital information*' as synonymous with a *discrete signal*. The criterion continuous/discrete has many fathers since this idea seems to be self-evident and infiltrated the scientific community in a natural manner.

But some cases bring this criterion into question.

Modern systems handle electric square-waves, and continuous electric waves that – for example – faithfully reproduce a sound. It is obvious how the former signifiers are digital and the latter analog.

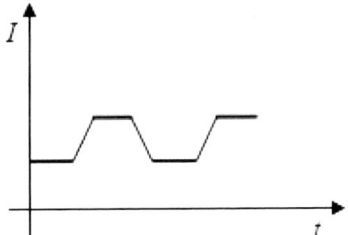 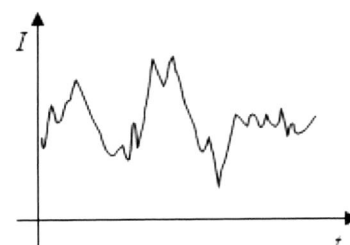

Figure 2.9. Square waves and continuous waves.

However there are waves that cannot be easily catalogued.

Take the Frequency-Shift Keying (FSK), a modulation pattern in which digital information is transmitted through frequency changes of a carrier wave. The signal consists of high-frequency wave-blocks and slow-frequency wave-blocks. All the wave-blocks have the same duration and the final outcome is a continuous wave that creates a bit stream. Thus the electromagnetic wave should be catalogued as continuous signal and discrete signal at the same time.

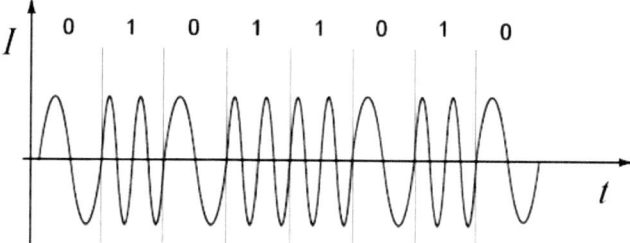

Figure 2.10. Frequency-Shift Keying (FSK).

As a further case, consider the wheel X equipped with the pitch P. When X rotates, P enters between the branches of the cross Y and obliges Y to change position. The shutter converts the continuous rotation X into the jerky movement of the cross that assumes fixed positions. A reduction gear joins Y with a wheel that exhibits ten figures over the border, namely the cross Y is capable of counting the number of revolutions of X. The *mechanical shutter* (X+Y) gets a continuous signal and outputs a discrete signal that is a decimal number. By the way, this device was absolutely common in the past decades: mechanical shutters worked as milometers in cars and measured the oil at petrol stations.

Figure 2.11. A mechanical shutter.

Lastly take the needle which rotates over the scale and is free from jolts. Speedometers, watches, thermometers and many other indicators exhibit mixed continuous/discrete bearings since the needle has a continuous movement and points to discrete values.

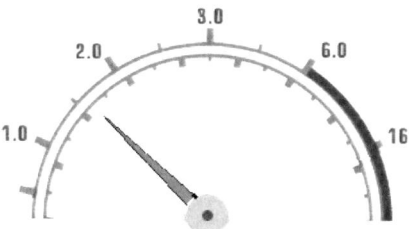

Figure 2.12. A speedometer.

One may wonder: Are the above mentioned solutions to be classified as digital since they deliver numbers? Or otherwise are they analog solutions due to the continuous movements?

Several systems operate in continuous and discrete modes at the same time and show hybrid characters. One could define three classes of products: continuous, discrete and hybrid in order to prepare a brochure for marketing purposes.

But this is not the case.

We are oriented to search for a serious, exhaustive definition of the analog/digital paradigms, and we can but concur with the majority of thinkers who believe that the criterion *natural/artificial* and the criterion *discrete/continuous* do not provide satisfactory answers to the needs. Those criteria illuminate our knowledge upon the digital and the analog domains although they do not clarify the inner substance of things over which we are talking.

I mean to go back to the similarity introduced in the inception of this chapter in the hope that the similarity could suggest an exit strategy. The correspondence with pharmacology should intimate to verify whether the digital paradigm is based on principles and whether the analog paradigm – corresponding to herbal medicine – is less theory-based. We shall try this way and shall attempt to address the various doubts which persist in the scientific community.

3. SHARPNESS FIRST

When we closely examine digital elementary signifiers, we find separation as an evident property. The previous example (Figure 2.4) exhibits the impulses $E_1=1.3$ V; $E_2=4.7$ V; $E_3=8.1$ V and $E_4=11.5$ V which lie 3.4 volts away

$$s = (11.5 - 8.1) = (8.1 - 4.7) = (4.7 - 1.3) = 3.4 \text{ V}$$

In general engineers employ two generic elements E_j and E_k that belong to the continuous metric space ε_m, and take place at a certain distance

$$s = |E_j - E_k| > 0 \qquad (2.1)$$

The distance s highlights how digital engineers look after the distinctness of signifiers and search for high-quality products. The pairs *yes/no, true/false*, and even *all/none* often explain the form of digital signifiers, and emphasize their high quality in fact there is nothing more contrasting than *yes* and *no*, *all* and *none*.

Engineers want that digital signals do not overlap under normal conditions and even under external attacks (Boylestad et al 2005). Rule (2.1) derived from the sharpness principle does not admit exceptions. Attenuation or other disturbances bring E_j and E_k nearer and experts guarantee that signals continue to work under the worst situations. They determine the initial separation s so ample that the digital signifiers remain distinguishable due to a residual distance s_r

$$s \gg s_r > 0 \qquad (2.2)$$

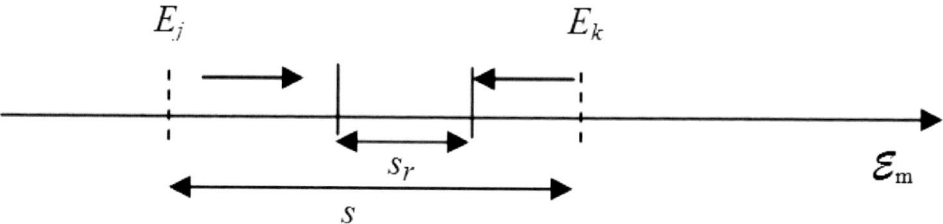

Figure 2.13.

Obviously the larger is s and the higher are the energies spent for storing, manipulating, and transmitting signals; so experts tune up (2.2) with respect to cost-effectiveness of appliances. They balance s and s_r against insulation, power supply and other involved electric parameters.

In conclusion engineers ensure that [1.3] is true within the normal and the critical contexts as well, that is to say eqn. (2.1) and (2.2) calculate the distinction of signs along with the reliability of signs.

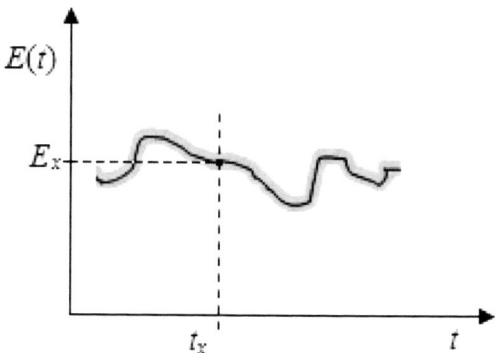

Figure 2.14.

Digital technicians shape elementary signifiers according to the principle of sharpness in this way they give a first testimony to their inclination toward rational behavior. They tend to adopt a systematic style right from the first stage and do not improvise.

Direct comparison between the digital and the analog solutions reveals significant dissimilarities.

Distinctness preoccupies digital designers since the first stage; they create discrete elements because they impose that signals be neat. Instead analog designers import or copy spontaneous pieces of information from the environment, namely they take signifiers from Nature. Experts do not determine the form of signs upon any principle as they take the signifiers at disposal in the context and those signifiers may be more or less confused. The distinctiveness and reliability of signs are secondary features for analog creators.

In Nature usually E belongs to the continuous metric space ε_m and makes a continuous function of the time

$$E = f(t) = E(t) \tag{2.3}$$

An analog signifier is never perfect because $E(t)$ does not derive from a rigorous rule and experts are obliged to apply themselves to reduce the fuzziness of signals. They strive to ensure that at any given moment t_x the subset ΔE_x which contains points common to E_x and to the surrounding subset E^* (Figure 2.15), be negligibly small. Anyway the *absolute error* ΔE_x is never zero

$$\Delta E_x = |E_x \cap E^*| > 0 \tag{2.4}$$

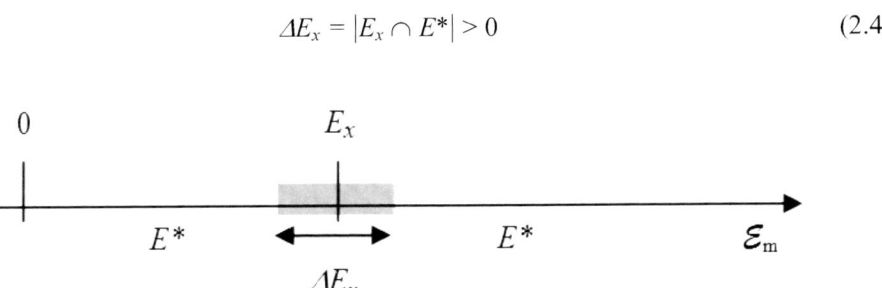

Figure 2.15.

Sometimes practitioners relate the absolute error to the value of the signal in order to see the real impact of fuzziness. For example the analog signal $|E_A|$ is four volts and fluctuates to the extent of more or less 0.1 V, namely $|\Delta E_A|$ is 0.2 V. The ensuing quantity is called as the *relative error* of E_A

$$\partial_{E_A} = \frac{|\Delta E_A|}{|E_A|} = \frac{0.2}{4} = 0.050$$

The signal E_B is clearer than E_A in that the relative error ∂_{EB} is smaller than ∂_{EA}

$$\partial_{E_A} = \frac{|\Delta E_B|}{|E_B|} = \frac{0.4}{12} = 0.033 < 0.050$$

The relative error illustrates the quality of signals in a more accurate manner than the absolute error.

Professional experience shows how E appears more or less blurry. For example, the signals handled by electronic analog devices present defects such as the frequency response shift, the noise floor, and the parasitic effects within semiconductor. The quality of analog information does not prove to be optimal due to (2.4). Analog signifiers do not reach the high standard of digital signifiers even if analog designers attend to the distinctness of $E(t)$.

Analog signals exhibit a certain blurring which takes place under normal conditions and improves in a hazardous environment. Conversely digital signs can resist external interferences and are able to work under the worst conditions.

Expression (2.1) makes evident how discretization is dictated by the criterion which I call 'principle of sharpness' hence digital experts reveal a strong orientation toward methodic behavior from the present perspective. They follow rigorous criteria to build up artificial signifiers since the inception of a digital project. By contrast analog designers tend to improvise and afterward strive to improve the quality of the imported signals. Both groups of experts are concerned with neat signals but exhibit far diverging conducts and obtain products with different degrees of quality. I could conclude that *digital experts act in accordance with rational methodology; whereas analog experts follow pragmatic and eclectic modes.*

However the reader can find this closing sentence somewhat rash and questionable since I have myself defined the principle of sharpness and hold that digital technicians are intelligent because they adhere to my principle. In this case Frenchmen usually quip: "Toujours dans la même boutique (All along in the same shop) !"

Justification of the rational approach followed by digital experts should be proved in a more extensive and complete manner hence I go deep into this argument.

4. AFTER FHE FIRST STAGE

Let us pay attention to how engineers go on after the first step.

A. Minimization

The famous *Ockham razor* may be summed up in the following terms:

"All other things being equal, the simplest solution is the best".

This principle introduced by William of Ockham, a medieval philosopher, is valid everywhere and engineers aim at simplifying artifacts of whatsoever gender. Designers search for straightforward processes to formulate reliable solutions in each sector. They avoid any surplus and any non-essential component to build up efficient products. This rational tendency toward simplification governs all the engineering areas since the larger is the number of parts the higher is the possibility of errors and failures beyond the talent of manufacturers.

Digital experts build up messages by means of elementary signifiers which make an alphabet. Ockham's lesson teaches to reduce the size of that alphabet and technicians aim at being the first in their class. They cut the alphabet back and reduce the set of symbols to two elements. This is the minimum theoretical size in that information relativity principle [1.5] holds that a sole elementary element cannot work

The minimal alphabet includes two elementary signifiers.

[2.2]

Several attacks threaten communications in the physical reality. Noise, perturbations, echoes and a variety of failures are capable of changing the value of signals as we have seen in the previous paragraph. By definition an elementary signal must occupy a fixed place, hence the size of the alphabet increases when a signal shifts. For instance suppose perturbations move the bit E_1 ahead and back. There are four signals in all instead of two in consequence of the disturbances.

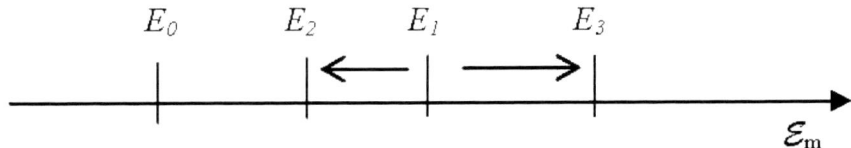

Figure 2.16.

Minimization rule [2.2] goes belly up when the signals shift and it is evident how the binary base must not vary.

Digital experts are concerned about this problem and ensure that the alphabet remains binary notwithstanding the restless attacks from the context. For the purpose they introduce a statement which perfects [2.2] and may be expressed in the following terms

*The minimal alphabet includes **two and only two** elementary signifiers.*
[2.3]

Current literature agrees that digital paradigm is grounded upon the *rule of the excluded middle* [2.3] expressed in formal terms since the classical logic (Anapolitanos et al 1998). This historical precedent induces people to feel the excluded middle rule as a pure abstract tenet. Frequently people mistake practical solutions for ethereal ideas and I immediately examine the engineering ploy that puts [2.3] in a material form.

Digital experts state the separation *s* large enough to maintain the bits clear when interference brings them closer. In addition experts fix the generic point *x* inside the range *s*, and establish that whichever extra impulse at the right of *x* is rounded to E^*. Any extra value at the left of *x* is approximated to E. When noise or other disturbances deform a signal, those effects do not create a new elementary item in that the altered signal is associated to E or to E^*. Anyway a corrupted signifier is a bit and this stratagem guarantees the stability of the binary alphabet.

In the worst situation a bit can invert and anyhow the receiver detects a bit. A new piece of elementary information never comes into existence and the excluded middle rule [2.3] comes true.

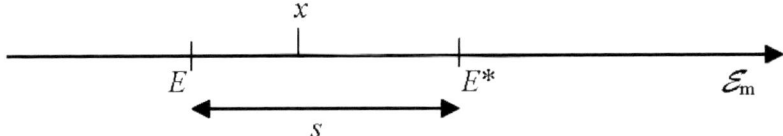

Figure 2.17.

These details bring further evidence on how the digital designers adopt general criteria and are not inspired by suggestions occasionally found in the natural context. The technical advantages are evident: the *robustness* and the *stability of the binary data* resist full-power trails.

From the perspective we are following bits are electric impulses, spots of light and dark, holes in punched cards etc., notably bits are elementary signifiers. They are absolutely physical in the present framework. However bits usually coded with the figures **1** and **0**, are esteemed to be abstract elements in the theoretical studies on Computing. The term '*bit*' contraction of 'binary digit', reinforces the immaterial interpretation of bits as numbers. I shall go back on this interpretation next, for the moment I see how the noteworthy qualities of the digital paradigm such as sharpness, robustness and stability of the binary base do not emerge at all from abstract studies. In addition the ethereal view of binary information cannot explain other facilities of the digital methods which instead we can examine here.

B. A Unified Theoretical Basis

The excluded middle principle ensures the binary basis is stable. A binary device processes bits in any circumstance and consequently digital engineers can work out circuits using a sole mathematical subject: the Boole algebra.

Boole's algebra may be defined as a method of calculus when the variable has only two values (Goodstein, 2007). The Boolean algebra includes a pair of *binary* operations (the adjective '*binary*' means a 'two-inputs' operation) detailed in the following tables:

$$
\begin{array}{ll}
0 \text{ AND } 0 = 0 & \quad 0 \text{ OR } 0 = 0 \\
0 \text{ AND } 1 = 1 & \quad 0 \text{ OR } 1 = 0 \\
1 \text{ AND } 0 = 1 & \quad 1 \text{ OR } 0 = 0 \\
1 \text{ AND } 1 = 1 & \quad 1 \text{ OR } 1 = 1
\end{array}
$$

(2.5)

And a *unary* operation ('*unary*' means a 'one-input' operation):

$$
\begin{array}{l}
\text{NOT } 0 = 1 \\
\text{NOT } 1 = 0
\end{array}
$$

(2.6)

Five properties define the Boolean algebra: *associativity, commutativity, absorption, distributivity,* and *complements* that yield all the statements necessary to calculate a circuit. By way of illustration I quote the famous De Morgan laws devised by Aristotle and discussed by medieval thinkers too

$$
\begin{array}{l}
\text{NOT}(\mathbf{a} \text{ OR } \mathbf{b}) = (\text{NOT } \mathbf{a}) \text{ AND } (\text{NOT } \mathbf{b}) \\
\text{NOT}(\mathbf{a} \text{ AND } \mathbf{b}) = (\text{NOT } \mathbf{a}) \text{ OR } (\text{NOT } \mathbf{b})
\end{array}
$$

(2.7)

I deliberately remind historical quotations in that philosophical and logical topics are worthy of comment.

1. Terminology and Chaos

Classical algebra applies to a wide group of fields: Economics, Physics, Chemistry etc. To exemplify, people execute the arithmetic sum and add up dollars or miles, tons or cars or other quantities. In a similar way the *Boolean algebra* turns out to be a powerful mathematical tool available in different fields and has different applications (Brown, 2003). Hardware and software specialists use the Boole algebra; in addition experts in the set theory and in the bivalent logic adopt the Boolean calculus. Two significant areas in Computer Science – the *hardware* and the *software* – and two abstract disciplines – the *set theory* and the *bivalent logic* – that is to say the *classical logic* – resort to the binary algebra.

Each group of experts is concerned with different quantities used in the four domains and adopts its own terminology.

Electronic engineers call *gates* the operations (2.5) and (2.6) which scramble the bits passing through. Technicians often write plus (+) for OR and a product sign (·) for AND when they design circuits. NOT is represented by a line drawn above the expression being negated ($\bar{a}$). Actually this notation makes it very easy to write complex expressions:

- **1** Binary signifier E,
- **0** Binary signifier E^*,
- · Gate AND,
- + Gate OR,
- $\overline{}$ Gate NOT.

Experts in set theory specify that **0** denotes the *empty set*, and **1** the *universe set* in the *set theory*. They customize significance for each operation and use the ensuing notation:

- **1** Universe set,
- **0** Empty set,
- ∩ Set intersection as AND,
- ∪ Set union as OR,
- ~ Set complement as NOT.

In *bivalent logic* the symbol **0** denotes the value *false*, and **1** the value *true*. The operations are marked by the following symbols:

- **1** True,
- **0** False,
- ∧ Logical AND,
- ∨ Logical OR,
- ¬ Logical NOT.

The Boolean terminology flexes in the four areas in order to highlight the special significance of the operations and the distinguished results obtained in each territory. There is evident separation amongst the above commented domains and the outcomes pertaining to each domain cannot migrate. Rigid separation is valid even in the arithmetic calculus:

Does an oilman perhaps multiply 'meters' instead of 'gallons'?
Or does a tycoon divide 'volts' in the place of 'dollars'?

Or have you ever added 'miles' instead of 'bottles of beer'?

Certainly not. Each individual adopts the terminology pertaining to his job, however one discovers that computer professionals like to import the idiom from unrelated domains into their own sector (Everest, 2007). Besides the terminology appropriate to the hardware and the software techniques, computer experts often call tables (2.5) and (2.6) 'true tables' and use the adjective 'logical' for the Boole operations even if the gates do not achieve any logic calculation but mix up bits that are signifiers. The hardware operations (2.5), (2.6) are used for the purpose of creating original bit-strings and do not explicate 'logical' relationships exclusive to the logic domain. Circuits swap the bits around. Electronic chips do not execute immaterial actions but physical operations in that signifiers are concrete entities.

I find this behavior extremely bizarre and somewhat absurd. I am incapable of finding a reason for such a linguistic initiative.

2. Progressive Standard Assembly

The Boolean algebra comes out as the basic method to calculate binary solutions and this mathematical sector has a very concrete and valuable impact (Tocci et al 2006). Boole's algebra begins with a precise set of operations that manipulate standard signifiers:

1) Signifiers = the *bits*,
2) Operations = the *gates AND, OR, NOT*.

This theoretical premise entails that physical systems are equipped with standard parts of necessity. Whatsoever message and whatsoever circuit are built up using components **1** and **2** respectively. Digital creators sketch any solution by means of well defined groups of initial elements. In practice they join together the listed parts in various ways and obtain an astonishing variety of products.

Of course the fabrication process follows a progressive pathway: the tiniest parts are joined in the first step; the outcomes of previous steps are connected later.

The progressive standard assembly is the fundamental protocol in the digital domain.

[2.4]

The progressive standard assembly is the regulation allowed by the Boole algebra that casts further light into the rational profile of the digital paradigm. I shall concisely discuss the major stages necessary to assemble complex messages and intricate circuits. Technical manuals illustrate details which we do not have space here to explore further.

Stages			Actors
5th	**Hypermedia**	*Rich in Contents* *Imagination*	*Users*
4th	**Texts, Pictures, Sounds etc.**	⇅	*Users/ Software experts*
3rd	**Common Words, Frames etc.**		*Users/ Software experts*
2nd	**Binary Words**		*Hardware experts*
1st	**Bits**	*Poor in Contents* *Calculus*	*Hardware experts*

Figure 2.18. Progressive standard construction of digital information.

3. Assembly of Signifiers

The first stage in preparing a piece of news consists in the design of elementary signifiers – the *bits* – in the intended technology e.g. electrical, optical, mechanical. Then a *binary word* stands for a character, or a figure, a symbol, a sound, a color etc. Thirdly authors prepare a common *word*, a decimal *number* or other compounds by joining binary words. At the fourth stage authors prepare a *text*, a *document*, a *picture*, a *piece of music* etc. by joining together the previous components. Lastly authors assemble various forms previously prepared and obtain a *hypermedia*. A web-page that offers texts, pieces of music, maps, diagrams, films and interactive tools makes a fine example of multimedia communication.

Electronic engineers work around the first two stages; they construct bits and binary words using the formulas just seen and even other measures. Mathematicians have defined a conspicuous number of binary codes in favor of practitioners.

The items at 3rd level are established through rational criteria or otherwise may be created by means of imagination. The items at 4th and 5th levels lie under the domain of creative, artistic or psychological inclination. People set up complex messages according to communicative feeling and it is evident how the outcomes of the upper stages are rich in contents and figment.

Bits are reliable and work in a manner similar to the regular bricks that guarantee a house to be solid. Technicians take care of the initial phases likewise brickworks produce standard bricks. By contrast the interior of a house is designed under the influence of human tastes so levels 4th and 5th rely on peoples' feeling and emotion. On a hand technicians are responsible for the lower rigid assembly steps; on the other hand drawers, creative, users, secretaries, employees etc. contrive the upper pieces of information. The intelligent organization of work is evident.

4. Assembly of Circuits

Whatsoever message consists of bits, hence a binary circuit gets a string of bits and carries on a new sequence of bits. Circuits basically make combinatory tasks and execute very intricate actions.

Boole's algebra defines the most straightforward operations for scrambling bits. The gates AND, OR bring forth four actions, the gate NOT does two actions. They never step out of the lines listed in (2.5) and (2.6) even in case of errors since the excluded middle rule prevents non-bit signals from being generated. Gates have a defined conduct and it is easy for a designer to connect the outputs of one gate to the inputs of another gate. Engineers create whatsoever digital circuit from the AND, OR and NOT like a sort of building blocks. They bring together the gates following regular assembly.

At the second step we find the *complex gates* NAND, NOR, and XOR where the basic gates are wired in series or parallel. For ease NAND is obtained by joining AND and NOT. At steps 3 and 4 we find *combinatorial circuit*s using all the previous gates, and *sequential circuits* that are to be synchronized such as *memories. Digital operations* – at the fifth step – include the components created in advance.

Integration processes, optimization techniques, special calculations and other measures run through the assembly procedure but we omit the analysis of those topics.

Stages		*Actors*
5th	**Operations** (e.g. Addition, Division)	*Hardware experts*
4th	**Sequential Circuits** (e.g. Counter, Register)	"
3rd	**Combinatorial Circuits** (e.g. Coder)	"
2nd	**Complex Gates** (e.g. Nand, Nor)	"
1st	**Gates** (And, Or, Not)	"

Figure 2.19. Progressive standard construction of digital circuits.

Electronic engineers draw a broad variety of equipment following a unique rule from the first stage up to the fifth stage. They design the logic of mobile phones, digital TV, satellite navigators, computers and so forth through the progressive standard assembly of parts. The rigid, exact methods above commented reinforces our view on digital paradigm as a rational mode, strongly grounded on theory.

Ample literature dissects the advantages gained from digital resources. For example digitalized pictures are easily transmitted, stored, corrected, protected, copied and so forth. In reality these benefits can be interpreted as the byproduct of generalized methods. Standard components cross many different areas of application and users enjoy multiple advantages.

5. ENCODING

The digital paradigm shows an elegant style from the formal viewpoint but the reader may perhaps wonder whether the digital mode is powerful enough to comply with the requirements. In particular one may question if the foregoing methods are capable of carrying on all the pieces of information necessary for human communication.

Encoding is the technique that covers three steps out of five in Figure 2.18 and I aim at going deep into this argument.

A. The Exponential Law

Encoding consists in building compound signifiers – usually called *words* or *codewords* – by means of *elements* – also named *modules* – of a prearranged set and later assigning a precise meaning to each word. For the sake of simplicity I shall usually refer to written words, and the modules shall be intended as letters, digits, characters, punctuation marks etc.

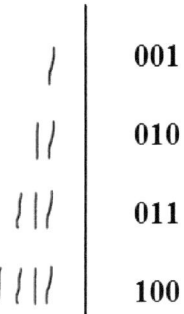

Figure 2.20. Analog and digital numbering.

Coders – namely the persons who prepare a code and assign meanings to each codeword – scramble the elements of the assigned alphabet and ensure differentiated products in accordance to the principle of sharpness. Combinatorics – a branch of pure Mathematics concerning the study of discrete elements – certifies that each codeword differs from any of the remnants. To exemplify, **00, 01, 10** and **11** are obtained by swapping the bits **1** and **0**, and verify the principle of sharpness through six inequalities

$$00 \neq 01; \quad 00 \neq 10; \quad 00 \neq 11; \quad 01 \neq 10; \quad 01 \neq 11; \quad 10 \neq 11$$

Coders do not portray or imitate the objects of the reality as analog creators do. Scrambling is a mechanical and cool operation far different from the creative activities of analog inventors. An iconic reproduction of numbers exhibits – for example – a stroke or another stylized image for each unit to be represented. The author adds a new stroke to the previous ones when the objects rise in number as he alludes to the physical reality by direct way. Instead a coder arranges elements which conform to the principle of sharpness in a systematic manner.

Combinatorial analysis provides the grand total N of the codewords attainable by a coder when the words have the fixed length L and the alphabet has a symbols

$$N = a^L \qquad L \geq 1; a \geq 2 \quad (2.8)$$

To exemplify, the total amount of codewords from **00** to **99** is squared ten

$$N = 10^2 = 100$$

Equation (2.8) is an exponential function of the kind

$$y(x) = a^x \qquad a \geq 2 \quad (2.9)$$

Where x is the variable that potentially ranks from zero to infinity.

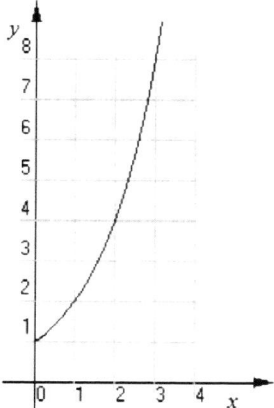

Figure 2.21. Exponential curve ($a = 2$).

The most noticeable property is that (2.9) grows faster than any polynomial function. This feature goes beyond common imagination. I mean to introduce this astonishing mathematical property through a pair of cases which should be useful for readers even if unfamiliar with Mathematics.

Nuclear fission consists of a chain reaction that exponentially expands (Giancoli 1984). The reaction starts with one neutron injected by an external device – this is a first generation neutron – and a uranium-235 atom absorbs this initial neutron and splits into two new atoms releasing an amount of energy and 2 or 3 more neutrons depending on the way in which the uranium nucleus splits. Those 2/3 neutrons are second generation neutrons. Those second generation neutrons prompt the fission of 2/3 uranium atoms and produce third generation neutrons. Nuclear fission chain reaction produces neutrons 2/3 times greater at any generation. Each nuclear reaction generation will produce 2/3 times as many neutrons as went into it. The exponential function depicts how the number of neutrons U bursts on:

$$U(t) = e^{\frac{\alpha}{\tau}t}$$

Where α is a constant; τ is the average lifetime of each neutron before it either escapes from the core or is absorbed by a nucleus and e is the Neper constant approximately equal to 2.718. The energy released by a single atom is extremely modest but the fast progression depicted by the exponential law causes the bursting power of the nuclear bomb well-known by mankind after the Hiroshima and Nagasaki bombings.

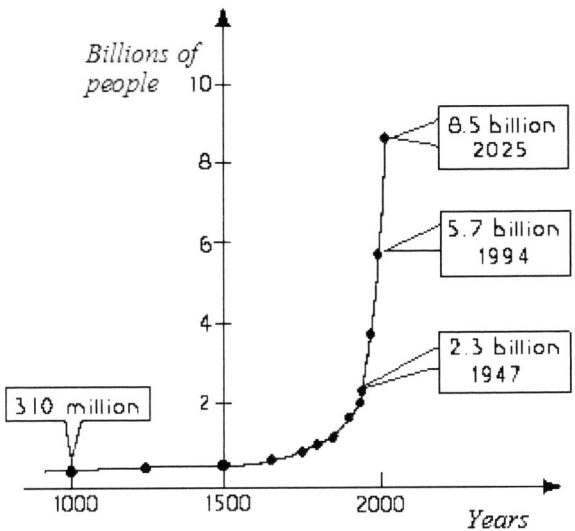

Figure 2.22. Growth of world population (Source UN Fund 1994).

A man and a woman procreate and generate n_1 babies; these in turn give birth to n_2 little ones and so on with geometrical progression over time. The number of people after a certain time t is obtained by the exponential equation:

$$N(t) = N_0 e^{rt}$$

Where N_0 is the starting population at $t = 0$ and r is a constant depending on the values n_1, n_2, n_3, n_4... In the past millennia systematic infant mortality, plagues and exterminations smoothed this theoretical calculation. In the modern era – say from 1500 AD onward – authentic data sustain the exponential growth of population which constitutes an enormous social problem due to its irresistible rising. The expansion of the human race resists the massive losses of lives occurring in various parts of the globe. Earthquakes, wars, famines, tribal carnages, tsunamis, terrorist attacks and other lethal occurrences do not flatten the population growth curve. Even the First and Second World Wars – two horrendous butcheries which provoked millions of deaths – did not slacken off the bursting rise of the masses which bring evidences of the extraordinary force of the exponential law.

Sometimes one finds difficult to perceive the astonishing growth of the exponential function because the initial progress of the function fools people. I like to comment on the deceptive beginning of the exponential function using a nice story.

A legend says that a young man invented the game of chess and brought his invention to his king. The king was enthusiastic of the chess game and offered the inventor any reward he wanted. "All I want is for you to cover this chessboard with corn as follows: one grain for the first square; two grain for the second; four grain for the third square... and so on for all squares". The request amazed the king who suspected the request was much too modest and the young man added: "Your majesty, you have to double that grain of wheat until the chessboard is full". The king ordered baskets of grain to be brought in and the counting began. For the first row of the chessboard (eight squares), the payment was 1, and 2, and then 4, and then 8, and then 16, and then 32, and then 64, and then 128 grains of corn. Far less than a bushel and the king was smiling. For the next row, the payment was 256, and then 512 and at the end of the row 32,768, almost a bushel. For the third row, the final square totaled 8,388,608 grains. The king was flabbergasted, and the operations stopped since the king could not provide enough grains to give the inventor a chessboard's worth of grains. Why?

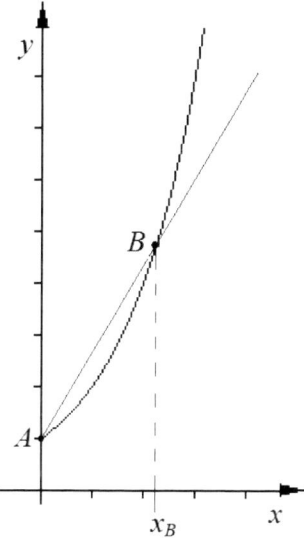

Figure 2.23. Initial profile of the exponential curve.

The chessboard problem involves adding up 64 exponential terms that make the ensuing geometric progression

$$2^0, 2^1, 2^2, 2^3, \dots, 2^{63}$$

The grand total of grains is a number of twenty digits, exactly 18, 446, 744, 073, 709, 551, 615 grains. There are not enough grains in the whole world to give the young man the sum. H.J.R. Murray (1985) in *"The History of Chess"* estimates that the required quantity of grain is such as to cover England to a depth of 12 meters: an incredible amount respect to the modest quantity covering the first two rows of the chessboard.

One may believe that the exponential growth starts suddenly, and the steep slope begins immediately. Instead this idea is somewhat misleading and one falls into a trap. I take the following straight line as a good comparison term for (2.9)

$$y = mx + 1 \qquad\qquad m > a \geq 2 \qquad (2.10)$$

Suppose $m=(a+1)$ for the sake of simplicity (Figure 2.23), the line climbs immediately behind the point A; instead the incline of the curve $y=a^x$ is lower in the initial range and carries on high values solely beyond the point B where the exponential function surpasses the straight line (2.10).

The exponential curve produces modest outcomes in the initial range but shortly later climbs in an irresistible manner. It may be said that $y=a^x$ has a *cool start*. The size of the 'cool start' period – say the interval (0, x_B) – depends on the base. The smaller is a and the more the cool period turns out to be deceptive. The minimum base of (2.9) yields a so ample cool period as to fool the king of the previous story.

The 'cool start' results in a special effect on coding, notably a small alphabet requires long codewords to represent a large number of objects. For instance binary words which are 10 bits in length codify a little over 1,000 objects; but only 3 decimal figures are enough to symbolize 1,000 objects. A natural language handles a number of topics that go far beyond 1,000 and people should exchange monster-binary-words if they adopt the binary alphabet. It is evident how humans labor to handle words containing dozens of symbols and prefer short words. As an example I mean to cite several English *grammatical words* that have one or two letters such as *I, we, in, at, if, of*, etc. The '*Short Word Rule*' deals with those grammatical words and with the *content words* which sound similar to short grammatical words and have a few redundant characters in the written version such as *in/inn; of/off; be/bee* (Carney, 1997).

Digital appliances manipulate voluminous words without efforts, whilst people like better to use large alphabets that generate words far smaller than binary words. The throughput of a modern written alphabet that brings forth a lot of short words is evident. For example the numbers of words compiled with the Latin alphabet are the following ones

$$26^1, 26^2, 26^3, 26^4, 26^5, 26^6 \ldots$$

The first term spells out there are 26 monograms in all; next there are 676 bigrams which are words made up of two letters; 17,576 trigrams; 456,976 words of four letters, 11,881,376 words of five letters; 308,915,776 words of six letters. It is enough to stop here, and to see how words with six letters in length are capable of signifying billions of objects, events and ideas.

The human preference for large alphabets is apparent. There are 26 letters in the Latin alphabet, 28 basic letters in the Arabic alphabet, 29 in the Cyrillic alphabet, and the Hebrew alphabet consists of 22 letters. The "*Guinness Book of World Records* (1995 edition)" lists the Khmer or Cambodian alphabet as the largest alphabet in the world which consists of 33 consonants, 23 vowels and 12 independent vowels. The Khmer language is the official language of Cambodia and approximately 12 million people use it in Cambodia, Vietnam, Laos, Thailand, and China. Thai language with 44 consonants, 15 vowel symbols and 4 tone marks is the second largest alphabet in the world. On the other hand we learn that the Rotokas alphabet, used by some 4,000 people in Bougainville, an island to the east of New Guinea, contains only 12 letters and is considered to be the smallest written alphabet.

In short the smallest alphabet has a dozen letters and the largest about sixty letters, rough speaking the alphabets familiar with humans are about ten times greater than the binary alphabet.

Six-letter words written with the Latin alphabet are enough to see how three hundred thousand million words is an incomparable quantity with respect to about 3,000-10,000 words sufficient for a layman to make himself understood. The enormous surplus of words generated by each human alphabet clarifies why a sole written alphabet can serve dozens of languages with modest overlapping. The Latin letters are used by nine languages out of the 30 most spoken languages such as English, Spanish, Portuguese, French, Indonesian and German (in order of popularity). The grand total of the Latin-alphabet users reaches about 1,713 million people.

Further comments on alphabets follow in Chapter 10.

B. A Monster Number

The function $y=a^x$ ensures the massive production of signs which go beyond the needs of any community. A population adopting whatsoever alphabet does not bring into play all the words available in that alphabet. The used words make a small fraction of the writable words which constitute an enormous set. The exponential law surpasses the writing needs of people at an unimaginable level.

"The Library of Babel", a lovely allegory written by Jorge Luis Borges (1994) seems to me very efficacious in spelling the force of digital encoding. This story deals with the surrealistic library containing every possible combination of a book which is 410 pages in length; each page containing 40 lines; each line 80 letters. "In the vast Library there are no two identical books" and there are treasures beyond measure. Borges writes:

> On the shelves somewhere are "the minutely detailed history of the future, the archangels' autobiographies, (…) the Gnostic gospel of Basilides, the commentary on that gospel, the commentary on the commentary on that gospel, the true story of your death, the translation of every book in all languages, the interpolations of every book in all books, the treatise the Bede could have written (but did not) on the mythology of the Saxon people, the lost books of Tacitus".

How is it possible to make a search inside that library?

> The faithful catalog of the library is supplemented with "thousands and thousands of false catalogs, the proof of the falsity of those false catalogs, a proof of the falsity of the true catalog".

Borges' suggestive tale holds a great amount of meanings. The title referring to the biblical tower of Babylon intends to highlight the confusion generated by a wealth of information. In addition it may be said that the imaginary book collection foreshadows the impressive amount of data gathered in the World Wide Web. The author also intimates a parallel between the Universe and the Library of Babel that "exists ab aeterno" and whose books are entirely placed in hexagonal bookshelves in order to occupy all the available space in the Universe

"The universe (which others call the Library) is composed of an indefinite and perhaps infinite number of hexagonal galleries, with vast air shafts between, surrounded by very low railings. From any of the hexagons one can see, interminably, the upper and lower floors. The distribution of the galleries is invariable. Twenty shelves, five long shelves per side, cover all the sides except two; their height, which is the distance from floor to ceiling, scarcely exceeds that of a normal bookcase. One of the free sides leads to a narrow hallway which opens onto another gallery, identical to the first and to all the rest. (…) In the hallway there is a mirror which faithfully duplicates all appearances. Men usually infer from this mirror that the Library is not infinite (if it were, why this illusory duplication?)"

The dimension of the Babel library cannot be fully described in words. Even a great writer such as Luis Borges has no suitable terms to fulfill his duty. Solely Mathematics can describe the fantastic honeycomb structure of the Babel universe. A book with the dimensions mentioned above contains 1,312,000 characters

$$410 \cdot 40 \cdot 80 = 1,312,000$$

Borges adds that the orthographical symbols are twenty-five in number. Using the exponential function we obtain the number of books in the Library of Babel

$$25^{1312000}$$

One can put this quantity down on paper in an easy way but this quantity is literally unimaginable. I use an astronomical parallel in the attempt to explain this number.

The most remote objects we observe in the interstellar space are *quasars* that lie at billions light-years of distance. All that we see in the Universe is included in a sphere of nearly 26 billion light-years in diameter. W. L. Bloch in his recent book (2008) claims that if each book of the Library were the size of a proton – a nuclear particle – our universe would still not be big enough to hold anywhere near all the books. Neither two nor tree universes are enough. We should have billions and billions of Universes to host the Babel Library when each book is so tiny as an invisible particle!

Borges' tale starts with a normal book with 410 pages and leads to a monster quantity.

The Borges nice metaphor offers an aid to grasp the growth property of the exponential law and in turn the power of the digital paradigm which is capable of preparing endless pieces of news.

C. Measures of Distance

Encoding conforms to the inequality $E \neq E^*$ since a generic codeword belonging to a code differs from any other word of the same code. Technicians should like to measure how much two any words differ, but this measurement is unachievable at large.

One finds a nice exception with the binary alphabet.

The dissimilarity of the binary words E_j and E_k is given by the number of positions at which the corresponding symbols are different. For instance, all the corresponding bits mismatch between E_j=**0101** and E_k=**1010**. They are absolutely different as the distance between E_j and E_k reaches the maximum that equals the length of each word

$$d_{jk} = L_{jk} = 4$$

Given a code, experts calculate the distances between two any pair, and the minimum value of these distances – named *Hamming distance* – specifies the overall quality of that code (Russell 1989). Technicians appreciate the reliability of a code through insecure media using d_H. The higher is d_H, the more that code is reliable. For example $d_H = 1$ in the ensuing code {**00,01,10,11**}. When the first bit inverts, the codewords **00** and **10** become identical and are no longer distinct. The following code {**0000,0011,1100,1111**} is more reliable in the face of risks than the previous code, in fact $d_H = 2$. At least two bits should invert to make a codeword equivocal.

D. Assignment of Significance

A written codeword does not resemble anything in the world and coders assign the significance to words without preliminary restrictions. Coders enjoy of the principle of arbitrariness with full degree of freedom because of the independence of codewords from the intended items.

DE	*Deutchland*
FR	*France*
IT	*Italia*
ES	*España*
PE	*Peru*
AR	*Argentina*

Figure 2.24. Semantic table

In the computer sector coders adopt an algorithm or otherwise the *semantic table*, a two-entry table that mirrors the scheme $E \rightarrow NE$ in a direct way. Coders are rarely guided by imagination, they pursue scientific objectives for example they handle meanings in order to speed up the circuit operations, to reduce the store size etc.

Coders apply some intelligent expedients to enhance the quality of a code. For example gaps amongst the words make the *discrete code*. New codewords will be inserted in the discrete code which can include random updates. Natural languages inspire *mnemonic* codewords which are easy to remember. As an example the *country code* consists of two letters copied from the country name which makes each word something effortless to recall to mind.

Coders adopt variable-length coding to reduce the size of storage and the time of transmission. For example, instead of occupying 20 bits (= 4•5) using the following fixed-length words

0000 0001 0010 0011 0100

The following variable-length solution occupies 9 bits (= 1+1+2+2+3) that implies 55% of memory reduction and transmission time

0 1 10 11 100

Coders assign the meanings to words accordingly to the *occurrences* (or *frequencies*) of the words and this trick reduces further more the elapsed shifting time due to transmission and the amount of store occupied by variable-length codewords.

In practice a coder orders the codewords according to their lengths in the semantic table and places the subject contents to be represented according to the frequencies of use which follow the inverse order. That is to say a coder assigns the shortest word to the most frequently used message; and couples the most cumbersome codewords to rare subject matters. S. E. Morse applied this criterion when he wrote his famous code. One dot symbolizes the letter **E**, the most frequently employed in English; the letter **Q** far less used consists of two dots and a dash. Communication systems adopted the Morse code over one century – longer than any other electronic encoding system – and made minor changes due to Morse's efficient design.

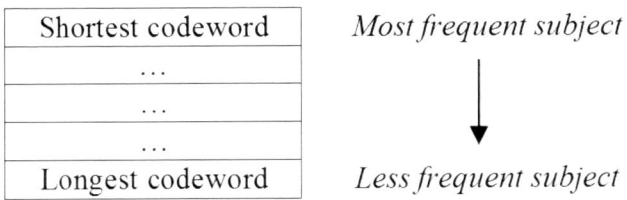

Figure 2.25. Ordered semantic table

6. CONCLUDING REMARKS

The present chapter makes an effort to ascertain the profile of the digital paradigm which proves to be grounded upon principles that can be formally expressed. In particular we have seen how the digital way begins with:

- ✓ The sharpness principle that ensures neat elementary signifiers.
- ✓ The excluded middle principle fixes the binary alphabet.
- ✓ The binary alphabet implies that the Boolean calculus stands as unique and uniform mathematical basis.
- ✓ Boole's algebra enables engineers to implement solutions using standard components and adopting standard assembly rules.
- ✓ The exponential law ensures immense amount of signifiers when one adopt encoding as an assembly method; and the principle of arbitrariness enables accurate, flexible assignment of meanings.

The digital paradigm emerges as a theory-based paradigm from the previous comments. Digital machines lie under the umbrella of a consistent theory whose concepts and equations we have examined step by step.

BIBLIOGRAPHY

Anapolitanos D., Baltas A., Tsinorema S., Athenon P. (eds) (1998) - *Philosophy and the Many Faces of Science* - Rowman & Littlefield.

Allison A., Currall J.E.P., Moss M., Stuart S. (2005) - Digital identity matters - *J. of the American Society for Information Science and Technology*, 56 (4), pp. 364-372.

Blachowicz J. (1998) - *Of Two Minds: the Nature of Inquiry* - Suny Press.

Bloch W. L. (2008) - *The Unimaginable Mathematics of Borges' "Library of Babel"* - OUP USA.

Borges J.L. (1994) - *Ficciones* - Grove Press.

Boylestad R.L., Nashelsky L. (2005) - *Electronic Devices and Circuit Theory* - Prentice Hall.

Brown F.M. (2003) - *Boolean Reasoning: The Logic of Boolean Equations* - Dover Publications.

Carney E. (1997) - *English Spelling* - Routledge.

Dretske F. (1981) - *Knowledge and the flow of information* - MIT Press.

Everest B.M. (2007) - *Philosophy and Fun of Algebra* - Chapman Press.

Giancoli D.G. (1984) - *General Physics* - Prentice Hall.

Goodstein R. L. (2007) - *Boolean Algebra* - Dover Publications.

Murray H.J. (1985) - *History of Chess* - Benjamin Press.

Russell D. (1989) - *The Principles of Computer Networking* - Cambridge University Press

Tocci R., Widmer N., Moss G. (2006) - *Digital Systems: Principles and Applications* - Prentice Hall.

Watzlawick P., Beavin J. H., Jackson D. D. (1967) - Some Tentative Axioms of Communication - In *Pragmatics of Human Communication: A Study of Interactional Patterns, Pathologies, and Paradoxes*, W.W. Norton & Company, pp. 48-71.

Wilden A. (1972) - Analog and Digital Communication: On Negation, Signification and the Emergence of Discrete Elements - *Semiotica*, 6(1), pp. 50-82.

Chapter 3

THE EXTRAVAGANT REALM

The tenets lying at the basis of the digital paradigm and the procedures followed by practitioners seem to sustain the similarity between the digital sector and pharmacology intended as the systematic study of drugs.

I have gone into the digital mode and attempted to develop inferential reasoning with the aid of some evidences. Though the argument turns out to be somewhat weak, I have placed little attention on the analog machines which constitutes a nontrivial section of ICT. The presumed parallel with herbalism entails that analog experts should determine the logic of machines thanks to chance discoveries, and should not follow a unique pathway. Designers should exploit a variety of ideas to arrive to the blueprint of systems and signifiers.

I shall use this chapter to verify if this similitude comes true in the world.

1. ECLECTIC PROFILE

Technical literature tends toward a common view (Lipták 2005) (Weik 2000) and places modern analog equipment in the ensuing classes:

1. Instruments for observation and measurement,
2. Equipment for calculus,
3. Process control appliances,
4. Communication media,
5. Converters.

Those devices are based upon several mechanical laws, physical rules, chemical reactions, and special effects. It appears rather demanding to examine those products and to append explanatory notes. The reader would probably get bored and in addition my account should be considered incomplete since a very ample assortment of techniques gives birth to analog machines and analog information.

A. Historical Digression

The historical approach provides a better key for surveying the analog domain and presents stimulating explanation of facts (Fox 1998).

1. Early beginnings

The seeds for the analog mode were planted very early when individuals suffered the impossibility of detecting vital information through direct perception or otherwise perception turned out to be unreliable. In primitive societies people wanted to know for example the weight of a commodity exchanged in a commercial transaction, the hours of the day and the dimensions of a rural field. Men felt the need for suitable instruments of measure and the analog paradigm was inaugurated under the pressure of very practical demands (Derry 1993). Archeologist findings – rude *balances*, *poles* and *strings* – agree with the present analysis and with ancient reports. The Greek historian Herodotus (2007), who lived in the fifth century B.C., relates:

> The pharaoh Sesostris "distributed the land to all the Egyptians, giving an equal square portion to each man, and from this he made his revenue... and if the river should take away any man's portion... the king used to send men to examine it and to find out by measurement how much less the piece of land had become, in order that for the future the man might pay less".

The measurements here referred may placed around 1400 B.C. and were made with the use of *ropes* in which knots had been tied at pre-determined intervals.

People began to measure time, spaces and weights using primitive instruments. The acquisition of information through analog appliances had remarkable impact on those primeval economies. In addition rough measuring tools assisted the government of those communities and individuals in everyday life. For ease the *abacus* supported the earliest population censuses.

The analog paradigm proceeded to sustain human civilization for millennia. The best evidences may be found in the Mediterranean area. Architects built up extraordinary edifices – say the Egyptian pyramids, the Parthenon, the Coliseum – using analog tools such as *levels* and *dip-sticks*. Calculation tools were employed in shops, markets, and customs long before the adoption of the written modern numeral system (Kren 1985). Instruments of measure offered essential aids to craftsmen, to sailors up to armies.

2. After the Middle Ages

The earliest analog devices were invented to obtain essential information in line with people's naïf lifestyle. When living became more prosperous and complicated, experts perfected the instruments in use and implemented novel tools to gain sophisticated information. After the year one thousand and especially from the Renaissance onward the analog method progressed at growing speed. Technicians employed original mechanisms to measure day-hours. For ease they introduced water clocks comprising complex gearing, sometimes those clocks were connected to fanciful automata. Al-Jazari, an Arab engineer, made a monumental clock – at present reconstructed at Dubai – that moved gates, musical equipment and human-like machines.

Significant advances in clock construction occurred in Europe during the 14th century when clock makers introduced new sources of power to keep the clock going and used repetitive oscillatory processes – e.g. the swing of a pendulum – to control the clock movement. Complex mechanical devices were intended for marking the time and even for modeling the solar system. Large *astronomical clock* dials exhibited the sun, the moon phases, the planets and even a star map.

The progress of precision mechanics taught clever artisans to build up refined *compasses* and *calipers* (Bruton 2004). For ease Galileo Galilei invented a compass performing a variety of geometric and arithmetic operations. One may remind astronomical instruments such as the *torquetum* to calculate the calendar date, the position of the Sun and the stars. The *astrolabe* and the *sextant* were introduced for navigation. The *planimeter*, the *nomograph*, and the *slide rule*, which may have a linear shape, a circular or cylinder shape, were used as mathematical implements. A group of analog tools was invented to assist drawers such as *pantographs, polygraphs, beam compasses,* and *splines*.

Printing techniques will be commented with particular attention in Chapter 10.

Figure 3.1. Astronomical clock at Prague (1410).

Significant use of lenses did not occur until the 12th century. This analog component made slow progress in Europe and boomed from the 14th century when first optical instruments – say *refracting telescopes, reflecting telescopes*, and *microscopes* – were strongly appreciated by sailors, militaries, and astronomers.

3. From the Industrial Revolution onward

From the eighteenth century onward a broad variety of sophisticated units were progressively introduced to supervise industrial processes and artisan production alike. Feedback and feed-forward loops ensured massive output rates and standard quality (Mutambara 1999). Analog components governed civil and military appliances as well. The analog technology that had sustained primitive economies became greater in the modern era when it penetrated numerous areas.

Obviously each analog appliance has its special history (Bennett 1979, 1993), and I restrict myself to three significant cases.

In the sixteenth century Cornelius Drebbel, a Dutch alchemist, developed a mini-oven in which automatically regulating the temperature to the desired value was possible. He found the first *thermostat* that was massively employed decades later.

The invention of the working steam-engine is usually credited to Thomas Savery, an English military engineer. He contrived the *'fire-engine'* as he called the first prototype, in 1698. The rotation speed of steam engines varied significantly; controlling the motors was so difficult that for decades this defect rendered steam motors scarcely useful. James Watt introduced the *centrifugal governor,* and put the steam engine under control in 1776. The fork with 'flying balls' commands the inlet valve of the steam engine in order that the steam flow decreases when the rotation speed is too high. The regulated motor provided the necessary source of energy to manufacturing and propelled the industrial era in Britain and later in the world. Authors agree that Watt's solution ushered in the industrial revolution.

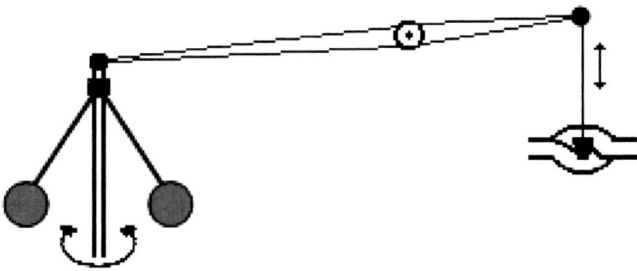

Figure 3.2. The centrifugal sensor and the valve control.

Currently an entire advanced sector such as the aerial and spatial navigation depends on an analog device: the *gyroscope*. Usually gyroscopes take the form of a disc shaped object that spins on its axis at high speed. This disc resists changes of direction and thanks to this property is capable of indicating the right direction with precision; in fact the gyroscope rotor maintains its spin axis direction regardless of the orientation of the outer frame. Each modern flying device – missiles, satellites, space vehicles, projectiles, civil and military aircrafts – can follow its planned course thanks to the assistance of a gyroscope that proves to be irreplaceable in several circumstances.

First working gyrocompass was developed to steady ships; Elmer A. Sperry built up the first automatic pilot for aircraft using gyroscopes in 1909. At present companies offer a broad variety of gyroscopic models: from instruments for small airplanes up to complex *inertial guidance systems.*

The 19th century is very special; it emerges as the 'gold era' of communication media. Astonishing analog solutions broke through the following order:

- *Photography* (1820),
- *Telegraphy* (1830),
- *Telephony* (1870),
- *Cinema* (1895),

> *Radio* (1898),
> *Television* (1930).

At successive stages those media promoted radical changes for the life of individuals and for the human society. Analog devices which monopolized the sector provoked outstanding changes in people's behavior which for the first time in history had at their disposal enormous amounts of data, images, music and other vivid information resources.

The term '*computer*' usually denotes a system capable of executing an entire computing process without human intervention. The catalogue of ancient computers prevalently based on mechanical technology turns out to be uncertain and controversial. During the Second World War experts designed the first *electric/electronic analog computers* for military scopes. One of the first was Whirlwind a flight simulator to train bomber crews built at the MIT (Massachusetts Institute of Technology).

Figure 3.3. Whirlwind: an analog electronic computer (1943).

A number of analog computer models were developed up to the seventies in the West countries and in the East alike for various purposes. Those models compared with similar digital computers proved to be promising due to the higher performances of electronic analog circuits. However a series of managerial (see Chapter 8, Paragraph 4, Section C) and technical problems (see Chapter 2, Paragraph 3) discouraged the continuation of experiments in the analog domain.

After millennia, the beneficial support of the analog paradigm to human progress gave the impression to cease all at once. In the second half of the twentieth century we attended the astonishing spreading of digital machines which invaded the market and replaced analog devices. The analog appliances which boosted the advance of humankind seemed to be definitively destined to vanish despite their outstanding support to civilization. As dinosaurs and other species of animals suddenly became extinct million years ago, so the analog devices appear to be convicted to definitive death.

This impression however is questionable. It will be very interesting to examine closely the nature of analog components and the role of analog equipment in modern economies. And I shall spend some pages on this topic.

B. Heterogeneous Components

The previous historical excursus should be enough to show the reader how analog designers do not adopt standard components when they intend to acquire information, but designers take advantage from assorted suggestions emerging from the environment. The ensuing popular cases should make the multifaceted analog appliances even more evident:

- A *sundial* shows the umbra shadow cast by the Sun's light;
- A *photo camera* works with the principle of the obscure chamber;
- A *long-case clock* runs thanks to the regular movement of a pendulum;
- A *sextant* gauges the height of the stars varying with the latitude;
- A *spirit-level* makes evident the different relative densities of a liquid and the air;
- The *litmus paper* is an indicator of acidity made by a mixture of different dyes extracted from lichens;
- Early *microphones* took advantage from the properties of the coil under the solicitation of the voice;
- An *optical telegraph* uses flags or other visual elements;
- *Electrical telegraphs* works with electromagnets and manual switches;
- A *phonograph record* detects mechanical vibrations from a rotating disc made of polyvinyl chloride.

Normally an analog appliance utilizes an original effect, which has nothing to do with the remaining machines. Scientists adopt odd principles even to design only one instrument:

- *Thermometers* exploit the thermoelectric effect or the capability of a liquid to expand such as mercury.
- A *mechanical calculator* employs complicated gears and leverages, or a simple mobile line (e.g. the slide rule).

Some analog solutions comprise similar components but obtain far different outcomes. For instance, *microscopes, telescopes* and *cameras* are equipped with converging lenses that result in three optical effects and the three instruments offer distinct services.

Whereas all digital systems use gates, analog experts copy a mechanism that works in a device already in use or otherwise employ occasional criteria. The analog paradigm brings in expedients and tricks from many domains. Sometimes an analog solution appeared after a special research work such as the *phonograph* by Thomas Edison. Other appliances were discovered through occasional events or were imported through fortuitous occurrences. As a case, the modern *magnetic compass* seems to be copied from previous Chinese equipment.

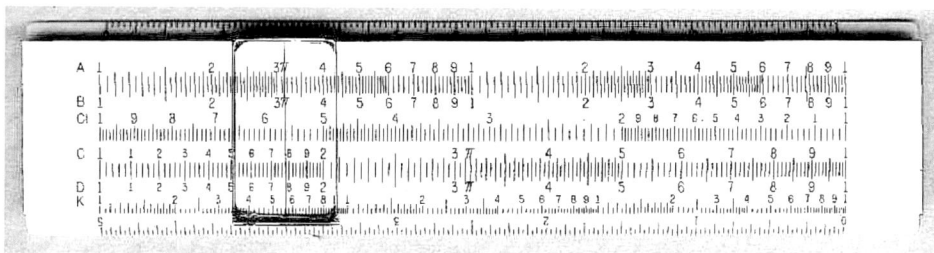

Figure 3.4. A linear slide rule.

The eclectic style of the analog becomes self-evident when the reader disassembles an ancient mechanical calculator, and sees a tangle of wheels and levers. Bizarre mechanical arrangements include curious gears, leverage and works (Pucher 1974). Multiplications, divisions and summations are achieved by works that appear extravagant to us. The creative style shared by analog designers should emerge from the ensuing three examples.

The *worm* thread is engaged tangentially with a *worm-wheel* so that one turn of the worm moves the worm-wheel one tooth. This mechanism achieves the division of the rotation x, notably the unit in Figure 3.5 divides x by y that equals the number of teeth on the worm-wheel. The revolutions z of the wheel constitute the outcome of the division

$$z = x / y \qquad (3.1)$$

For example the worm revolves 400 times and the worm-wheel has 50 teeth, thus the wheel turns eight times and z equals to 8.

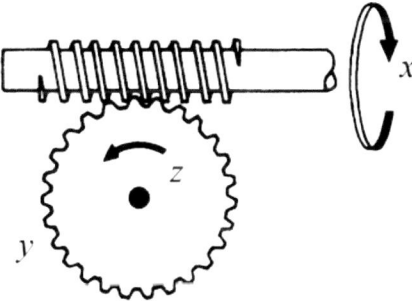

Figure 3.5. Worm and worm-wheel.

A mechanical *lattice* is used to multiply the input length x by a constant that depends on the distance y. Because the distance y is three times greater than t, the unit in figure multiplies x for 3:

$$z = y \bullet x = 3 \bullet x \qquad (3.2)$$

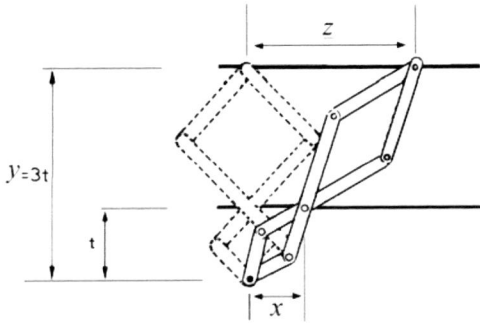

Figure 3.6. Mechanical lattice.

The subtraction of x from y is obtained by means of the *geared differential*. This apparatus consists of four bevel gears, two of which rotate about a fixed axis but on separate in-line shafts. The lateral gears are used to introduce the variables x and y. The other pair of bevel gears is carried on a cross-head mounted on a shaft having the axis z, the same axis of rotation as the input x. The shaft for x is hollow and accommodates the output shaft z whose rotation speed is the output of the difference. All four bevels have the same number of teeth. The inputs of the subtraction are the rotation speeds x and y of the shafts. The directions of x and y may be any namely they can represent positive or otherwise negative values. It turns out that z may be positive or negative according to the direction of its rotation:

$$z = x - y \qquad (3.3)$$

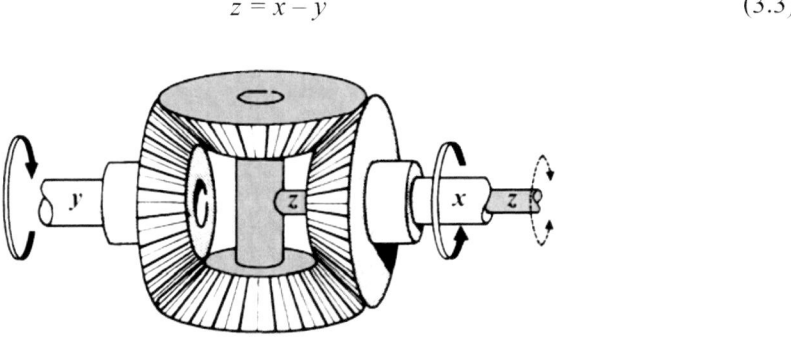

Figure 3.7. Geared differential.

For instance suppose x and y follow the arrows in Figure 3.7 and have the same speed

$$x = y = v$$

The shaft z does not rotate and the result of the subtraction is zero

$$v - v = 0$$

The reader can grasp the fantasy of analog designers when I append the common usages of those works:
- The *geared differential* is a component belonging to a car that transmits the movement to the posterior wheels.

o The *lattice* is used to transmit electric current from the aerial-line to the railway power car.
o The *worm wheel* is frequently employed to reduce the speed of an electric engine.
o The *mechanical shutter* illustrated in Chapter 2 (Figure 2.11) is a component of mechanical film projectors.

Counterexamples in electric technology exhibit components that have nothing to do with the mechanical components (Williams 1995). For ease multiplication and sum of electric values are obtained using electric coils placed at the extremes of a balance. Two coils (similar to the telephone induction coil) are solicited by the current *x* and *y*, and are mounted at the left end of the balance. The coils are connected in two different ways to multiply and to add as shown in the Figure 3.8. The results are detected by means of an identical induction coil at the right end of the balances.

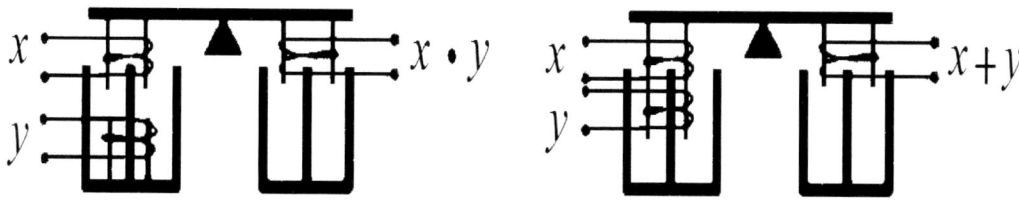

Figure 3.8. Electric coil units.

More recent analog electronic computers employ transistors, diodes and other electric elements that make a *component circuit*. Components constitute the macroscopic hardware parts of a computing machine. A significant component is the *operational amplifier* (op-amp) credited to a number of inventors such as G.A. Philbrick, C.A. Lovell and J. Loebe (Korn et al 1956). An operational amplifier is a high-gain electronic voltage amplifier with two inputs and a single output (Figure 3.9). An op-amp produces an output voltage that is typically many times larger than the voltage difference between its input terminals. An operational amplifier has high direct-current stability and high immunity to oscillation, generally achieved by using a large amount of negative feedback. Operation amplifiers are used to arrange a broad variety of hardware functions, e.g. op-amp can work as an *inverter, voltage comparator, differential amplifier, precision rectifier, voltage and current regulator,* and *waveform generator*. Besides amplifiers, electronic calculators employ other components such as *precision resistors* and *capacitors, multipliers, potentiometers,* and *fixed-function generators*.

An analog computation is executed by a collection of electronic components that are interconnected in such manner as to produce the predefined set of time-variant voltages. Technicians set up the analog computer and join the circuit components in accordance to the intended scheme.

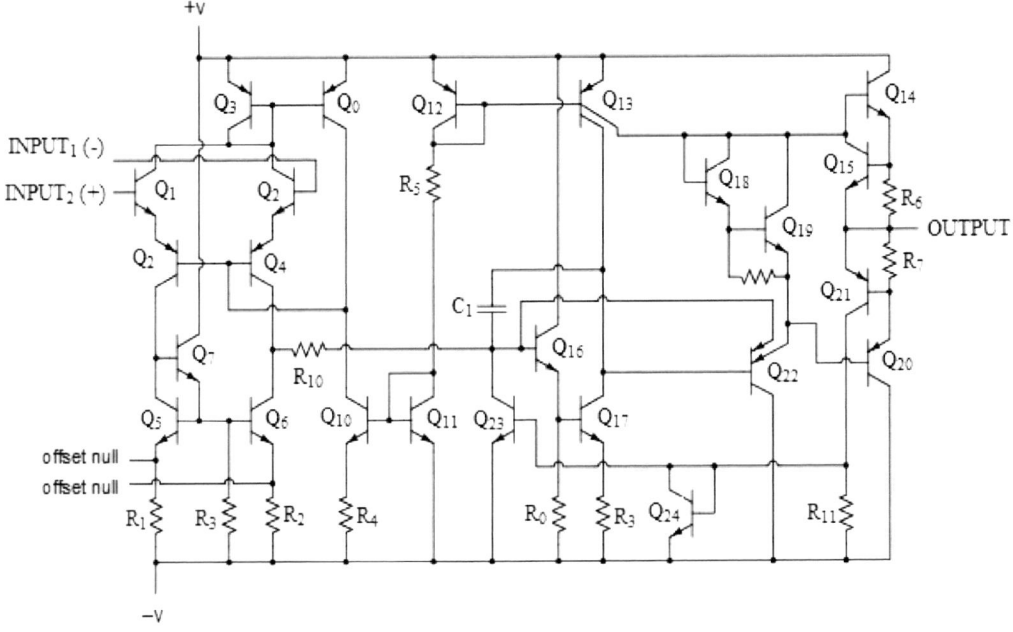

Figure 3.9. Operational amplifier electronic scheme (Fairchild Corp.).

For instance the *full-wave rectifier* (Figure 3.10) is obtained by two amplifiers, four resistors and two transistors

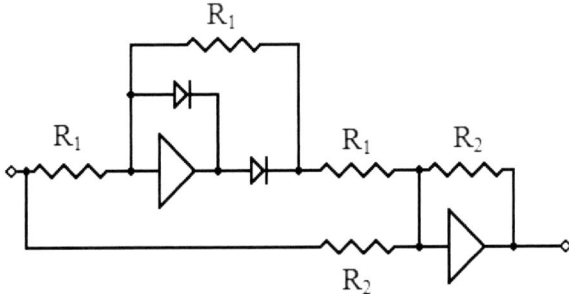

Figure 3.10. Scheme of a full-wave rectifier.

An analog calculation normally proceeds along a continuum constituted by several component circuits that are joined using commutators, push buttons, switches, wires and other physical tools. The front of PACE 231R (Figure 3.11) exhibits the panels and the knobs necessary to set up this analog system.

Figure 3.11. PACE 231R (Electronic Associates Inc. - 1961).

Connectors can make an intricate compound and can be made to vary in numerous dimensions (Truitt et al 1960). In fact analog electronic systems are especially suited for the solution to complex non-linear equations, for the reproduction of multi-dimensional processes, for parallel and continuous simulation (Strong et al 1962). Such simulations may be conducted in real time or at greatly accelerated rates, allowing experimentation by performing many runs with different variables.

This bird's eye view on the analog domain aims at showing the astonishing variety of solutions. This scenario should consolidate the conviction that analog designers do not adopt standard components and do not follow a systematic pathway as digital experts do. They exploit a broad variety of laws coming from Mechanics, Optics, Electro-physics, Magnetism, Chemistry, etc.

2. VARIOUS MATHEMATICAL THEORIES

Perhaps the reader considers my account, based on practical cases, rather unsatisfactory, so I append a short comment on the mathematical tools that mirror the prismatic nature of the analog paradigm.

The large number of mathematical corpora employed in the analog domain appears impressive. One finds the *dynamical systems theory,* the *signal processing theory,* the *communication theory,* the *control theory*, the *stochastic system theory,* and many others. Those theories do not deal with the roots of the analog paradigms, they do not cast light upon unified principles that do not exists but barely provide instruments of calculation for engineers.

I mean to focus on the dynamical systems theory where systems are subdivided into *continuous time* and *discrete time* systems. And I concisely shall make mention of the mathematics for the first sub-group: the *linear continuous time systems*.

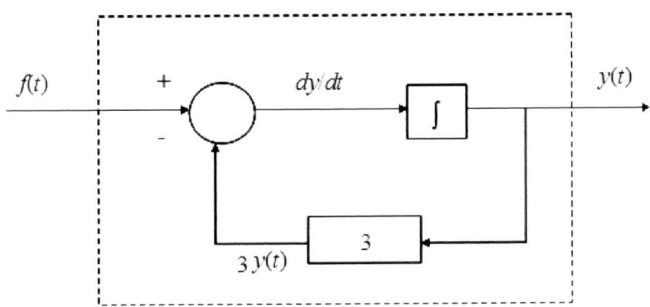

Figure 3.12.

A. Linear Continuous Systems

A system is *linear* when it depends linearly from the state parameters and from the input variables (Reid 1983).

When a system qualifies as a linear system, it is possible to introduce the following method. Suppose a complex stimulus x_1 enters into a linear system and we measure the responses y_1. Next, we present a second stimulus x_2 and obtain y_2. If the complex stimulus ($x_1 + x_2$) solicits the system, then the forecast response will be just the sum of its responses to each of the two stimuli presented separately ($y_1 + y_2$).

Linearity simplifies the analysis of systems significantly, and hence there is a large body of mathematical techniques and results, referred to as *linear system theory*.

Engineer in the analog sector are concerned with the calculation of behavior and equilibrium of systems whose variables x, y, z ... change with time (Sarachik 1997). These variables include system inputs – e.g. external causes of change or excitation – and system outputs – e.g. measurable outcomes or effects of the behavior, response, or dynamics of the system – as well as variables describing internal states of the system.

In order to perform this analysis and to make a correct design, relationships between the system variables are described by a set of formulas known as the *model* of the analog system. That is to say the dynamics of a linear continuous system are represented by analytical time-dependent functions.

1. First Order System

The simplest model relates the input variable x to the output y through a temporal function

$$y = f(x,t) \qquad (3.4)$$

For example a component is moved over the space x and this equation $y = k\, dx/dt$ gives the speed of that component. An important class of systems is calculated using differential equations of this kind

$$a_1 \frac{dy}{dt} + a_0 y = f(t) \qquad (3.5)$$

Where $f(t)$ is the *forcing function*, roughly speaking it describes the system solicitation; $y(t)$ depicts the reaction of the system to the input; a_1 and a_0 are constant. As an example, the block diagram in Figure 3.12 depicts this mathematical model

$$\frac{dy}{dt} + 3y = f(t) \qquad (3.6)$$

A significant class of machines is *stationary* or *time-invariant*, namely the system parameters do not depend on time such as equation (3.5). In practice time invariance means that whether we apply an input to the system now or t seconds from now, the output will be identical, except for a time delay of the t seconds. The standard form of the homogeneous first-order equation, obtained setting $f(t) = 0$ in (3.5) and $a_0 = 1$, is the same for all the system variables and generates the response of the system which has this form

$$y(t) = k \cdot e^{-\frac{t}{\tau}} \qquad (3.7)$$

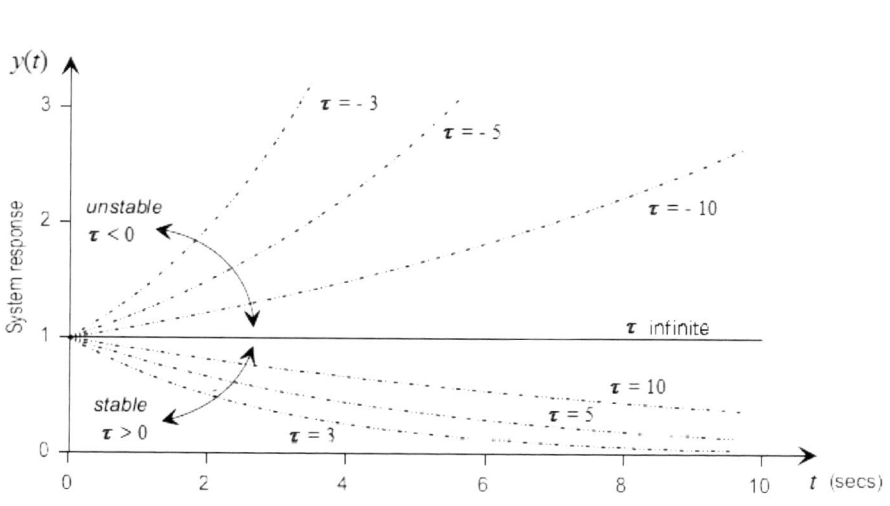

Figure 3.13.

The constant τ is the *system-time constant* – previously written as a_1 – responsible for the time scale of system responses. If $\tau > 0$ the response of any system variable is an exponential decay from the initial value toward zero and the system is *stable*. If $\tau < 0$ the response grows exponentially for any finite value of the system variables and the system is *unstable*. The family of curves displayed in Figure 3.13 exhibits the responses of stable systems ($\tau > 0$) and unstable systems ($\tau < 0$).

The *unit step function* $f(t) = u(t)$ is commonly used to characterize a system subjected to sudden changes in its input at time $t=0$

$$u(t) = \begin{cases} 0 & t < 0 \\ 1 & t \geq 0 \end{cases} \qquad (3.8)$$

The characteristic *unit step response* is obtained using the method of undetermined coefficients

$$y_s(t) = k\left(1 - e^{-\frac{t}{\tau}}\right) \qquad (3.9)$$

The unit step response $y_s(t)$ asymptotically approaches the steady-state value as shown in Figure 3.14 that exhibits normalized values

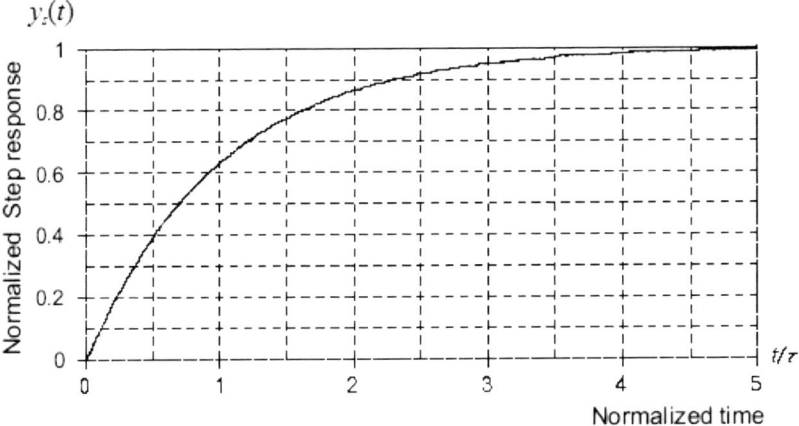

Figure 3.14.

The *impulse function* $f(t) = i(t)$ is defined as the limit of a pulse of duration Δt when Δt approaches zero and calculates the response of a system to an impulsive input. The characteristic response to the impulse is the following one

$$y_i(t) = \frac{1}{\tau} e^{-\frac{t}{\tau}} \qquad t \geq 0 \qquad (3.10)$$

This illustrates an exponential decay.

2. Laplace Transform

Analog designers resort to other mathematical tools.

They describe the behavior of a system using the so-called *transfer function* that is frequently expressed through *Laplace transform*. In fact the Laplace transform converts linear differential equations into algebraic expressions which are easier to manipulate. The transfer function is the ratio of the output Laplace transform to the input Laplace transform assuming zero initial conditions

$$H(s) = \frac{L\{y(t)\}}{L\{x(t)\}} = \frac{Y(s)}{X(s)} \qquad (3.11)$$

The Laplace transform converts functions with a real dependent variable – such as time – into functions with a complex dependent variable (such as frequency represented by s). E.g. the transform L of input signal $x(t)$ is

$$L\{x(t)\} = X(s) \qquad (3.12)$$

Important characteristics of dynamic systems can be determined from the transfer function.

3. Second Order System

The first-order system is described by a first order differential equation such as (3.5). The second-order system is described by a second-order differential equation

$$a_2 \frac{d^2 y}{dt^2} + a_1 \frac{dy}{dt} + a_0 y = f(t) \qquad (3.13)$$

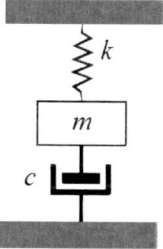

Figure 3.15.

To exemplify a second-order system let us take the *spring-mass-damper* system (Dorf et al 2008). The mass m is moved by the force of gravity and is sustained by a spring; at the bottom a damper provides viscous friction or damping (Figure 3.15). The damper consists of a piston and an oil-filled cylinder. Any relative motion between the piston rod and the cylinder is resisted by the oil because the oil must flow around the piston (or through orifices provided in the piston) from one side of the piston to the other. The damper does not store any kinetic or potential energy, but essentially absorbs energy. The response of the system is the function $y(t)$ obtained from the following mathematical expression

$$m \frac{d^2 y}{dt^2} + c \frac{dy}{dt} + ky = 0 \qquad (3.14)$$

Where *m* is the mass of the body, *k* is the constant of the spring, *c* denotes the viscous-friction coefficient.

3. Nonlinear Systems

Sometimes dynamical evolution problems involve *nonlinear systems* that are very hard to solve explicitly, thus experts attempt to decompose or to approximate a complex machine to linear subsystems that can be treated more easily. For example it is possible to study a nonlinear system behavior in a limited range of values of inputs and outputs around an operating point with the help of linear approximations. The time constant τ offers a fine support, in fact one can generalize the time constant and τ_G allows approximating the second-order system to a first-order system when the input signal evolves with time t much greater than τ_G (Codenotti et al 1991).

Even if this survey covers only one section of one mathematical theory – the dynamical system theory – we have found three classes of systems: first-order linear systems, second-order linear systems and non-linear systems. We have seen different functions such as the impulse functions and the unit step functions; and various methods of calculus such as the Laplace transforms. This brief review should aid reader's intuition and should just give an idea of the heterogeneous mathematical weapons employed by engineers. I mean to underline how the equations necessary for an analog expert do not derive from unified and consistent principles and this eclecticism highlights furthermore the differences with the digital mode. Assorted theoretical studies give support to the analog paradigm which has been associated to the variety of resources available in the world.

The comparison between analog and digital is not over, and we proceed across two further relevant engineering topics in the next sections.

3. METICULOUS DESIGNERS

A computing machine must produce a predefined answer from the input and no exception is allowed. This demanding quality is necessary for digital and analog appliances alike, and one can but assume the following *principle of precision*:

A system put into operation repeatedly without adjustments, must achieve the same correct result given the same input conditions and operating in the same environment. [3.1]

Firstly the principle of sharpness [1.3] entails that a signifier must not be confused with anything else. Secondly appliances must comply with [3.1] since an error can cause disasters in the working environment. Precision is the taxing principle for systems – no matter whether they are analog or digital – due to theoretical and pragmatic reasons.

Facts sustain [3.1] in that both the paradigms comprise a significant group of procedures, methods and tools of design to ensure the precision of machines. Once again we shall remark the far different styles of the digital and the analog modes.

A. Accurate States

Each digital circuit handles a finite set of binary codewords, hence the hardware of a digital machine passes through a predefined set of *states*. A digital process may be subdivided into finite states because whatever operation manipulates discrete elements.

A corrupted bit does not generate a new signal thus a state never handles vague values and never has undetermined conduct. A state is responsible for carrying out a predetermined function, or pointing to the correct action. A state has transitions to other states, which are caused by events or actions within that state. A state of the digital system cannot have multiple roles. No two states have the same reaction to a specific event and the set of states is unique. These qualities allow digital designers to program the actions of a machine with absolute precision.

Engineers usually develop the *finite state machine* (FSM), the mathematical model that describes the exact behavior of a digital system (Kam et al 1997). FSM encompasses a finite number of states, transitions between those states, and actions. Using a simplified formalism FSM is a sextuple

$$FSM = (I, O, S, s_0, \delta, \omega) \qquad (3.15)$$

Where:
- I is the *input set* of binary symbols,
- O is the *output set* of binary symbols,
- S is the *set of states*,
- s_0 is the *initial state*,
- δ is the *state-transition function* that regulates the transition to the subsequent state,
- ω is the *output function* that relates the binary output to the input, namely ω connects an element of O to an element of I in a way.

Also a wrong string of bits can trigger a state in the physical reality thus it is not adequate for the author of FSM to plot only regular situations. A finite state machine is drawn on the paper to manage even inconsistent events otherwise the implemented machine will be at a deadlock or will produce wrong results. Hardware designers forecast breakdowns using the FSM model so that the constructed machine complies with the requirements for precision.

Elegant subsidiary models give support to designers. For ease the *state transition table* (STT) places under control the principal transitions occurring in FSM. STT in Figure 3.16 allocates the states A, B and C driven by events *1*, *2* and *3*. The first condition causes the system to fall from whatsoever state into A; the last condition keeps the system in the initial state; the second condition drives the system in the states recorded in the second row.

Initial State →	A	B	C
Condition 1	A	A	A
Condition 2	B	C	A
Condition 3	A	B	C

Figure 3.16. State transition table.

All the possibilities, even rare and accidental ones, are held by the system blueprint. Formal models – e.g. FSM and STT – and automatic tools assist designers who are driven by general rules and criteria.

B. Improvements

Analog designers take inspiration from the surrounding nature; they make up a draft and in the second stage improve the precision of their solution.

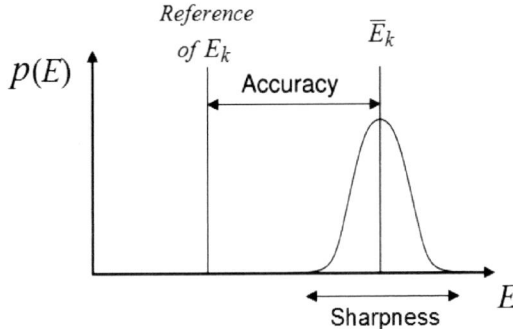

Figure 3.17. Sharpness and accuracy of an analog signal.

1. Signals

The analog experts copy or import pieces of information from the world. The dispersion of the various values should narrow and experts are forced to improve the precision of signals. Sharpness can be characterized in terms of *error factor* and *standard deviation*, that anyway are never null (see Chapters 1 and 2).

In the second place an analog signal cannot shift apart from the true value. The *accuracy* is defined as the difference between the mean $\overline{E}_k$ and the reference value E_k (Figure 3.17); this difference has to be minimal.

The calculations and the techniques accomplished to ensure the precision and the accuracy of analog signals constitute a wide topic which cannot be summed up here.

2. Devices

Analog designers discover a mechanism or take a device within their grasp to produce information. But designers cannot use it in the original form because of the principle of precision [3.1], so designers transform the original mechanism into an accurate appliance. They streamline an arrangement through refined improvements to suit it to the information domain.

Identifying and correcting for bias is necessary for the calibration of a system. Inventors devise several techniques to construct an analog machine with very low degrees of approximation, but the rules are extremely diversified in this area. Specialists cannot follow uniform methods – as digital experts do – to ensure precise systems because systems have differing provenances.

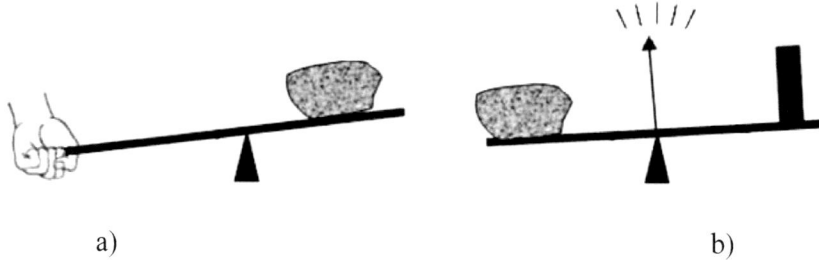

Figure 3.18. A lever to take up and a lever to weight out.

Engineers resort to a wide assortment of expedients and mathematical formulas that go beyond the scopes of the present book. I confine myself to discuss macroscopic measures undertaken in the field. Let us see two cases which should aid reader's intuition.

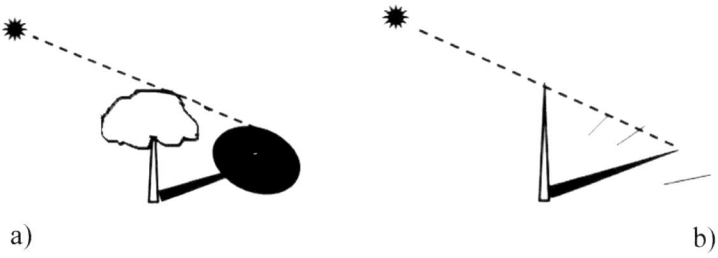

Figure 3.19. A tree and a sundial.

A lever offsets a force against a weight. The lever must be robust to lift a gross weight. Precision is inessential for a lever in a normal context; instead the analog equipment is required to be exact. Thus ancient engineers perfected the lever movement and its position was sensed by a needle to register the minimal deviation: the lever became a balance.

A tree shields the Sun's rays and the crown's shadow moves around all day long: a good idea for signaling the day-hours. The ancient started to measure time by the position of the Sun. However the crown of a tree turns out to be irregular and experts made a sharp stick, called *gnomon*. They added lines all around so that the sundial indicated each hour of the day with precision.

This couple of cases should cast light on how analog authors consider principle [3.1] as an obligation which one cannot bypass. The commitment of technicians toward precision is evident in literature to the extent that commentators classify analog mechanical appliances into the sector named *Precision Mechanics*.

4. PARADIGMS AND TECHNOLOGIES

The nouns '*paradigm*' and '*technology*' have two distinct meanings even if they are related in a way. The term '*paradigm*' is synonymous with "*method, mode or methodology*", and denotes rather "*abstract guidelines and general rules*". The term '*technology*' stands for "*practical activities, specific objects and materials, optimized rules for production*". Hence a paradigm enables the use of different techniques. An engineer adopts a paradigm and in principle he can follow the technology A or B.

A. Flexibility of Digital Paradigm

The digital mode saw the light before the Second World War and became a well-established methodology in the sixties. The models of *finite state machine* devised by George H. Mealy (1955) and Edward F. Moore (1956), and the *maps* by Maurice Karnaugh (1953) constituted the solid cornerstones for engineers. In those years the electronic technology took off and was systematically associated to digital equipment. Electronics opened the doors to massive production of appliances and has been successfully in the foreground since more than half a century. To the best of my knowledge I have never seen a book presenting the digital paradigm as a general method apart from electronic technology. The clause "*digital technology*" has over 3,500,000 occurrences in the Web (January 2009) and provides further evidence on how people relate the *digital mode* to the *electronic technology* in a systematic manner. The reader perhaps doubts that the term '*paradigm*' is a mistake of mine or that I have voluntary overstated the digital sector using the pompous expression '*digital paradigm*' instead of '*digital technology*'.

We can but go deep into the matter more thoroughly because of the high popularity of the expression '*digital technology*'. I should examine how the digital paradigm is a method independent from technologies, how one can implement a digital solution using different objects and resources but follows a unique logic.

The present account pinpoints two groups of universal components:

1) Signifiers = the *bits*,
2) Operations = the *gates AND, OR, NOT*.

I mean to verify how those parts can materialize using whatsoever physical support; in particular we should see how researchers have explored the use of disparate resources which gained more or less success in the market. Let us analyze points **1** and **2**.

1) Modern digital devices manipulate bits very different from the physical viewpoint, I quote randomly:
   - *Electric impulses* (square waves) along the wires,
   - *Electromagnetic waves* (modulated waves) along the wires,
   - *Light* and *dark* in optical fibers,
   - *Holes* and *solid spots* in a punched card,
   - *Pits* and *plane-surface* in an optical disk,
   - *Magnetic spots* and *neutral spots* in a hard-disk,
   - *Pixels* in the display screen.

2) Let us take the gate AND as an example of circuit:

$$
\begin{array}{cccc}
I_1 & & I_2 & O \\
0 & \text{AND} & 0 & = 0 \\
0 & \text{AND} & 1 & = 1 \\
1 & \text{AND} & 0 & = 1 \\
1 & \text{AND} & 1 & = 1 \\
\end{array}
$$

(3.16)

The implementations of AND based on various technologies verify the flexibility of the digital mode.

- One can use transistors – e.g. TTL, RTL, or CMOS transistors – to implement the gate AND in *electronic technology*.

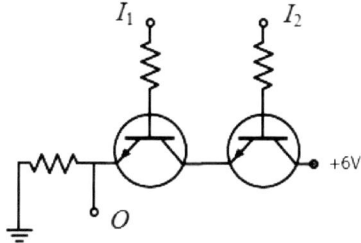

Figure 3.20. – Electronic AND.

The type of transistors determines the *logic family*, namely a circuit pertains to *TTL logic*, or to *RTL logic*, to *DTL logic* or to *CMOS logic* etc. The family of transistors fixes the high and the low electric values of the bits, and all the other physical parameters of a circuit. The example in Figure 3.20 pertains to TTL logic and is equipped with two transistors. Bits, which enter in I_1 and I_2, and exit in O, are obviously square waves.

- Two relays make the gate AND in *electromagnetic technology*. The electric currents in input keep the relays open or closed (the relay on the left is closed and the relay on the right is open in Figure). The electric current at bottom carries on the output bits. The current does not pass through O unless both the relays are closed.

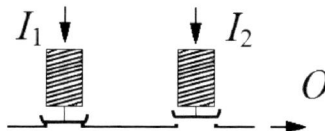

Figure 3.21. Electromagnetic AND.

➤ Two valves make the AND in *pneumatic technology* (Krivts et al 2006). The input flow of gas can pass through as long as both the valves are open. The states open/close of the valves I_1 and I_2 make the input bits; the gas flow makes the output bits in O. The first valve is open and the second closed in the next figure, hence the output bit is zero.

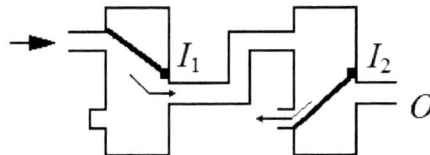

Figure 3.22. Pneumatic AND.

➤ The previous gate works with gas at high pressure. When the gas pressure is shortly higher than atmospheric pressure, the air has laminar movement and the gate AND works in *fluidic technology* (Foster 1970). This unit consists of two ports that convey the laminar air into the gate. Three pipes convey the output. If the laminar flows in input are balanced – namely both the input bits I_1 and I_2 are ones – then the output bit is one in O. In all the other cases the vents **a** and **b** convey the air flow outside and the flow is null in O, namely the output bit is zero.

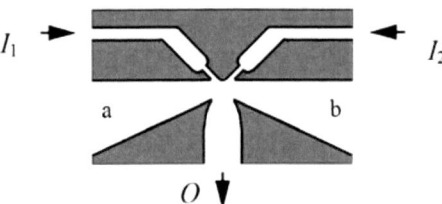

Figure 3.23. Fluidic AND.

The above-quoted cases mean to show in a tangible manner how a digital designer can employ the technology A or B; anyhow he develops a unique scheme to build up the intended system. The digital paradigm is independent from past and present-day technologies.

Other innovative technologies appear on the horizon and in broad strokes I comment on the chances promised by Biology and Quantum Physics.

B. Biological Computation

The discovery of the genetic code, achieved in 1953, inspired the biological approach to ITC a few decades later (Margham et al 1983).

All the instructions in a genetic code are 'written' solely with four chemical components: *adenine, thymine, guanine,* and *cytosine*. The letters A, T, G, and C symbolize the four chemical components and one may say that A, T, G, and C make the genetic alphabet. The information units, called *codons*, are triplets namely the four chemical components spell out 3-letter 'words' which are 64 in all in accordance to the exponential law

$$N = 4^3 = 64$$

The various codons generate a personal genetic code for each individual, in other words the genetic code fixes eye color, stature and all the features which make an individual unique. All the biological functions are directly related to the sequence of codons. If a scientist changes the genetic code, he/she modifies the entire biological processes in a cell.

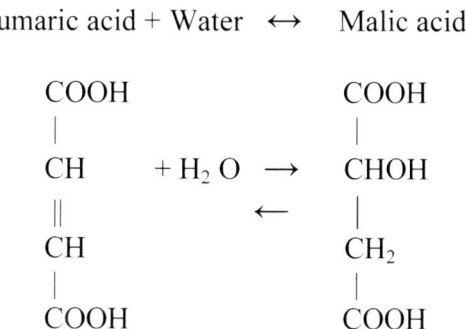

Figure 3.24.

The fundamental property is that cell operations are highly selective and exclusive. Biological actions are characterized by a rigid selection of agents and exclusion of alternative agents. That is to say the molecule A reacts with B and is inert with all the other molecules included in the cell. Even if the molecule X is very similar to B, A does not work with X. A well-known example is given by Fumarase, an enzyme that catalyzes the hydration of Fumarate (or Fumaric acid) to L-malate (or Malic acid) inside the Krebs Cycle.

There are two forms of Malic acid: called L-malic acid and D-malic acid which have identical components and symmetrical structures. L-malic acid is symmetrical to D-malic acid, alike the right hand appears identical to the left hand and one can confuse a hand with the other hand in a mirror. L-malic acid and D-malic acid are called *optical isomers* due to this symmetry. The enzyme Fumarase hydrates exclusively L-malic acid and does not operate with D-malic acid notwithstanding their evident similarity. The reaction in Figure 3.24 runs if and only if malic acid is the L-isomer. This means the enzyme Fumarase discriminates L-malate from D-malate and isomers are signifiers

$$\text{L-malate NOT}=_{\text{Fumarase}} \text{D-malate} \qquad (3.17)$$

Biological reactions show qualities consistent with the principle of sharpness [1.3] and the principle of precision [3.1].

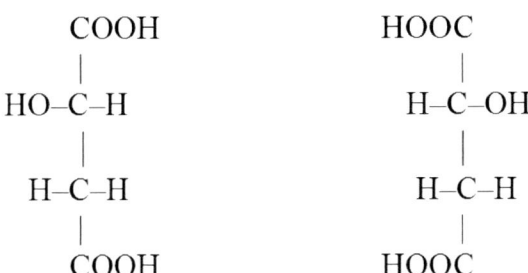

Figure 3.25. L-malic acid (left hand) and D-malic acid (right hand).

Biological computation took off when biologists noted the articulated set of exact operations achieved through DNA in a cell. Distinct reactions make up systematic threads to follow in the labyrinthine paths inside the cell and elucidate how a DNA sequence results in precise work rules for the whole biological system. The molecules A, T, G, and C, and codons show how biological computation may be developed in digital form; the selectiveness of biological reactions guarantees the precision of a system. Hence in the nineties biologists began to work around the idea of using DNA to store and to process information.

Currently a biological device can only perform rudimental functions, and has no practical applications. Biological Computing is still in its infancy and new outcomes are in the offing. In terms of speed and size DNA computers surpass conventional computers and are able to carry on massively parallel processes whereas silicon circuits basically achieve sequential operations. While silicon chips cannot be scaled down much further, the DNA molecule found in the nucleus of all cells can hold more information in a cubic centimeter than a trillion music CDs. A spoonful of cells contains an amount comparable to trillions of biological computers whose energy-efficiency is more than a million times that of a PC.

C. Quantum Computation

Intriguing experiments have been developed to apply the digital paradigm with quantum physics (Le Bellac 2006).

A binary implementation could start with the use of particles with two spin states: *up* and *down*. Each quantum state makes a *quantum bit* – a term contracted as '*qubits*' – which is intrinsically dissimilar from a classical bit. Actually a normal device assumes either the value **0** or **1**, it cannot have both the binary states at the same time. Conversely a quantum particle can simultaneously embody both the qubits **0** and **1**. This quantum law, called *superposition*, means that a particle enters a superposition of states, in which it behaves as if it were in both states simultaneously. Each utilized qubit can take a superposition of both **0** and **1**.

Quantum storage is capable of containing more information than normal storage thanks to superposition. Whereas a 2-bit register in an ordinary computer can store only one of four binary configurations at any given time, a 2-qubit register in a quantum computer can store all four numbers simultaneously

00 + 01 + 10 + 11

The storage capacity increases according to the exponential law in quantum computers

$$M = 2^n \qquad (3.18)$$

Where n is the number of qubits in the memory and M is the grand total of stored words.

Another property of quantum particles, named *entanglement*, shows an astonishing view in the future of Computing. Particles that have interacted at some point retain a type of connection and can be entangled with each other in pairs. For ease knowing the spin state of one entangled particle allows one to know that the spin of its mate is in the opposite direction. Quantum entanglement enables qubits that are separated by incredible distances to interact with each other instantaneously and the interactions are not limited to the speed of light. No matter how great the distance between the correlated particles, they will remain entangled as long as they are isolated.

Superposition and entanglement are real phenomena the mechanisms of which are not yet fully explained. The lack of exhaustive quantum theory and the original properties of quantum particles make Quantum Computing a great challenge for theoretical and experimental scientists.

More than a dozen different ways of creating qubits have been developed to date. Software programmers write algorithms for quantum computers but a general purpose quantum computer has not yet been built. Such a machine stimulates much research efforts and probably will absorb the best minds for decades. Researchers are optimistic even if a practical device is years away.

D. Rigid and Flexible Relations

The foregoing somewhat concise survey should be sufficient for us to conclude how the digital paradigm is flexible and works in various technologies: electrical, mechanical, pneumatic, biological, quantum etc. Technologies do not subvert the logic of a digital machine established on the paper. Even if each technology carries on dissimilar implementations, the organization of the designed machine, based on the gates, is independent from each adopted technology. Digitalization has always involved and will involve a variety of technical domains that lie under the control of a unified and consistent theory.

The versatility of the digital paradigm stimulates a dynamic view on the market. Very likely modern electronic devices will be surpassed by novel techniques in the future whilst the universal components – bits and gates – will continue to ensure the correct logic for each machine.

The same cannot be said about the analog domain.

The analog way is fractioned into several special technologies, one cannot separate the principles from the techniques, the logical solution from the physical components. The analog mode resorts to different resources based on unlike criteria. A digital circuit is independent from the technology namely the digital system X may be implemented in the technology A, B or C and in principle one may bring forth three versions X_A, X_B or X_C of the same machine according to customer inclinations, market fashions, costs, performances etc. Instead each analog solution depends on its technology through an indissoluble bond. The analog machine Y_A is built up in technology A and there is no easy way to migrate from A, to B or C since the technology A shapes the equipment Y_A to a complete degree. Each analog appliance is bound up with a discipline: Mechanics, Electronics, or Chemistry etc. This relationship is so strong that it determines the catalogues in literature; commentators commonly assign an appliance to a special field. For ease telescopes, cameras and microscopes fall into the group of *optical instruments*; voltmeters and ammeters take their place among *electrical equipment* and so forth.

5. Concluding Remarks

The present chapter has chiefly discussed:
- The heterogeneous components adopted by analog designers.
- The logic of the various machines which one cannot compare.
- The broad assortment of mathematical methods in use.
- The rigid connections between the structure of an analog system and the implemented technology.
- The eclectic approaches used to improve the precision of analog equipment.

The systematic methods followed by digital designers clash with the improvisation typical of analog authors tend to reinforce the vision of the digital paradigm as an engineering approach strongly based on theory and systematic criteria of work.

A. Annotations on Current Literature

The multifaceted nature of the analog machines has frustrated any complete survey so far. Each commentator tends to describe a single class of analog appliances for example *analog integrated circuits, analog filters,* and *analog to digital converters*. The exhaustive inventory of the analog solutions has not yet been written and also historians prefer to follow a single class of appliances when they recount the technical progress in the time scale. In literature it is easy to find titles such as *"History of calculators"*, *"History of regulators"*, *"History of printing"*, *"History of clocks and watches"* and other nice titles that disclose intriguing episodes of mankind's advance.

Analog methodology is so fractioned into several areas as not to seem a distinguished sector. Somebody claims:

> "'Analog systems' is an easy way to pile up dissimilar technical solutions that do not follow any common idea".

This paradoxical statement sounds right in a way and contributes to highlighting the lack of uniform principles and the impossibility to detach the logic of a machine from the intended technology.

B. Reasons for a Defeat

Current literature places the paradigms analog/digital close to the binomials natural/artificial and continuous/discrete. This parallelism is right in a way but rather insufficient to decipher completely the analog and digital methods of work. It may be said that the tenets natural/artificial and continuous/discrete cast light on the surface of the paradigms; they depict the appearance. The substance of the argument proves to be far more tricky and serious.

We have seen how people instinctively import signs whose meanings are rather immediate, and the pragmatic conduct of an analog designer may be compared to the herbalist who goes about the prairie and picks up medical herbs which he has not sown and cultivated. The first stages of the analog way are guided by imagination and seem absolutely attractive.

Problems crop up later.

Signs are low quality and experts try hard to make them sharp to a suitable degree. Analog machines are obliged to work with precision but each solution follows its own way and has to be tuned up using a special rule. The lack of universal components entails that each analog device has a proper logic; and often designers come up with expedients to prepare this logic. The occasional solutions make the construction of a device tricky and venturesome. One cannot change technology at ease in the sense that a new technology is intended to intimate a complete new organization for the analog machine. The parts and the whole equipment are to be re-designed if the technology changes. The rigid link between the blueprint of an analog machine and its physical implementation does not imply that faster technology results in more efficient equipment, and one cannot make optimistic forecasts for the future.

In my view, these evident defects corroborate how analog equipment has lost ground in the ICT market. Analog systems sharply declined after centuries of success and presently very few systems are installed. Digital appliances progressively have taken the place of analog devices in use. *Digital cameras, digital radio, digital TV, digital channels, digital phones* have thrown out the parallel analog media. *Digital thermometers, digital balances* and other instruments have surpassed the corresponding tools. This book offers cues to those who aim at analyzing the reasons that lay at the base of the 'defeat' of the analog paradigm as the dominant method in ICT which occurred from the sixties onward. It is an attempt to demonstrate how the digital mode exhibits rational, systematic features alien to the analog mode.

Digital designers do not commence with an easy idea; they make the elementary signals conform to the *sharpness principle* that also ensures the reliability of signals. Digital experts make the binary base stable through the *excluded middle principle*. The *principle of arbitrariness* facilitates the assignment of significance to signifiers. These solid premises lead to the *Boolean algebra* which guarantees uniform assembly procedures to obtain whichever piece of information and whichever circuit. *Bits* are enough to build up any gender of message and solely three components are sufficient to achieve whatsoever circuit: the *gates AND, OR* and *NOT*. Solutions and technology are really independent, and researchers are able to improve the services of a digital appliance adopting the best cost-effective material support. This flexibility stimulates optimistic forecasts, and the discovery of novel technologies will empower the digital systems even more in the future.

The variety of spontaneous information extant in the world inspires the analog authors' fantasy whereas digital experts enjoy the advantages offered by a corpus of rules and by flexible implementation. It may be said that the first group of experts adopts a behavior guided by practical experience and not theory; conversely the second group guided by theory is capable of exploiting the most productive resources.

We shall see how the analog paradigm is not drawing to a close despite its dramatic failure. The next pages will show how the analog mode is called upon to carry out conspicuous duties that only the analog mode can achieve.

C. Objections

The reader may object that electronic engineers calculate the Boolean circuits but, for example, are unaware of the sharpness principle. They are rather unfamiliar with the terms *signifier* and *signified* and with other topics introduced in the previous pages.

I put forward the following answer.

Some concepts discussed heretofore are rather obvious, for example the notions of signifier and signified are consistent with the common sense. It appears as a somewhat spontaneous fact that a piece of information has a physical basis and stands for something. Layman's experience shows how signs must be sharp and distinguishable. The principle of arbitrariness merely claims that people can assign meanings without restrictions. Hence the lack of official statements may be considered as unessential in the working environment. Experts are capable of grasping fundamental rules through intuition; they can adopt rational principles on the digital sector even if unstudied. This way of action is not new in the history of sciences. Primitive men invented the wheel while they were absolutely unaware of the principles of Mechanics. Mankind proceeded by trial and error for millennia. Practitioners built up astonishing devices, buildings, military equipment and excogitated other outstanding solutions through perspicacious minds; they had no formal statements in hand which were formulated far later.

The reader may even object that the principles presented in this book sound somewhat linear.

This is absolutely true. Dictionaries tell that a 'principle is a basic truth', and usually a straightforward issues expresses a principle. For instance the second law of Mechanics holds the proportionality of acceleration and mass to force:

$$f = m \bullet a$$

An essential cornerstone of Mechanics is no more than a multiplication. Also Chemistry, Optics, Electronics and other disciplines include principles expressed through rather simple statements.

A basic law usually exhibits a simple form, and does not require much effort to be understood by a reader by constrast it was long the way to arrive at this law. The scientific method is based on gathering observable, empirical and measurable evidence, and the formulation of a conclusion must match with tests and practical verification. Principles require weary labor to be defined as an author has to dissect a lot of documents and facts, and has to ponder all of them. A gold-digger sifts out gold from tons of sand, and in a similar manner a theorist filters large amount of experimental evidence to obtain a principle that covers a wide area of interest. It is not accidental that the present book grounds discussion on a large number of down-to-earth cases, examples and counterexamples.

I find very illuminating the following sentence by Donald E. Knuth (1991):

"My experience also strongly confirmed my previous opinion that the best theory is inspired by practice and the best practice is inspired by theory"

BIBLIOGRAPHY

Bennett S. (1979) - *A history of Control Engineering 1800-1930* - Peter Peregrinus Ltd.
Bennett S. (1993) - *A history of Control Engineering 1930-1955* - Peter Peregrinus Ltd.
Bonocore J. (2001) - *Commanding Communications: Navigating Emerging Trends in Telecommunications* - John Wiley and Sons.
Bruton E. (2004) - *The History of Clocks & Watches* - Book Sales Incorporated.
Codenotti B., Leoncini M. (1991) - *Parallel Complexity of Linear System Solution* - World Scientific.
Dorf R.C., Bishop R.H. (2008) - *Modern Control Systems* - Pearson Prentice Hall.
Derry T.K., Williams T.I. (1993) - *A Short History of Technology: From the Earliest Times to A.D. 1900* - Courier Dover Publications.
Foster K., Parker G.A. (1970) - *Fluidics: Components and Circuits* - Wiley-Interscience.
Fox R. (1998) - *Technological Change: Methods and Themes in the History of Technology* - Routledge.
Kam T., Villa T., Brayton R.K., Sangiovanni-Vincentelli A.L. (1997) - *Synthesis of Finite State Machines: Functional Optimization* - Springer.
Karnaugh M. (1953) - The Map Method for Synthesis of Combinational Logic Circuits - *Trans. of the American Institute of Electrical Engineers*, part I, 72(9), pp. 593-599.
Korn G.A., Korn T.M. (1956) - *Electronic Analog and Hybrid Computers* - McGraw-Hill.
Knuth D.E. (1991) - Theory and Practice - *Theoretical Computer Science*, 90, pp. 1-15.
Kren C. (1985) - *Medieval Science and Technology: A Selected, Annotated Bibliography* - Garland Publisher.
Krivts I.L., Krejnin G.V. (2006) - *Pneumatic Actuating Systems for Automatic Equipment: Structure and Design* - CRC Press.
Le Bellac M. (2006) - *A Short Introduction to Quantum Information and Quantum Computation* - Cambridge University Press.
Lipták B.G. (2005) - *Instrument Engineerings' Handbook* - CRC Press.
Herodotus (2007) - *The Landmark Herodotus: The Histories* - R.B.Strassler, R. Thomas, A.L. Purvis (eds), Pantheon.
Margham J.P., Hale W.G. (1983) - *Basic Biology: An Introduction to Biological Computing* - Collins Educational.
Mealy G.H. (1955) - A Method for Synthesizing Sequential Circuits - *Bell System Tech. J.*, vol 34, pp. 1045-1079.

Moore E.F. (1956) - Gedanken-experiments on Sequential Machines - *Automata Studies, Annals of Mathematical Studies*, 34, Princeton University Press, pp. 129-153.

Mutambara A. (1999) - *Design and Analysis of Control Systems* - CRC Press.

Pucher G.H. (1974) - *Introduction to Control Techniques* - Pitman Publishing.

Reid J.G. (1983) - *Linear System Fundamentals: Continuous and Discrete, Classic and Modern* - McGraw-Hill.

Sarachik P.E. (1997) - *Principles of Linear Systems* - Cambridge University Press.

Strong J.D., Hannauer G. (1962) - A Practical Approach to Analog Computers - *Instruments and Control Systems*, 35(8).

Truitt T.D., Rogers A.E. (1960) - *Basics of Analog Computers* - John F. Rider Publisher Inc.

Weik M. (2000) - *Computer Science and Communications Dictionary* - Springer.

Williams J. (1995) - *The Art and Science of Analog Circuit Design* - Newnes.

Part 2

Chapter 4

SYSTEM ARCHITECTURE

The likeness between the digital paradigm and pharmacology, and the similarity between the analog paradigm and herbalism sound rather reasonable after the first pages. Although I restricted the field of discussion to static topics, I did not examine what digital experts do when they design a device, when they build up an infrastructure or optimize a secure medium.

Electronic engineers create a broad assortment of solutions and one wonders if they are guided by rational criteria also inside factories and laboratories. The reader could query whether the principles seen in the previous chapters go on inspiring digital creators. The resemblance of digital experts with chemists should be validated in the professional practice, when customers demand and pay an appliance or a service.

The next pages aim at exploring the working environment and will plunge into the ensuing significant areas:

- *The architecture of digital systems* – Chapter 4,
- *Computer networks* – Chapter 5,
- *Storage* – Chapter 6,
- *Protection/security measures* – Chapter 7,
- *Software programming* – Chapter 9, 10.

I shall follow this way: I shall present an inference in abstract, namely I shall describe a work criterion consistent with the logic of the digital mode discussed in the previous pages. In the second stage we shall check whether the criterion of work deduced on paper has been adopted in the professional practice.

Cellular phones, digital control stations, electronic instruments, embedded computers, robots and other equipment make a broad assortment that exhibits various degrees of specialization. The reader could not have good knowledge of each machine thus the Chapters from 4 to 10 preferably refer to general-purpose (GP) computers for the sake of simplicity. The restriction is not severe: GP machines are the most popular digital systems.

1. FROM INFORMATION TO UNITS

Computing machines are required to manipulate a broad variety of information: numbers, as well as texts, pictures, graphics, music, symbols, and sounds. Those systems achieve mathematical operations and graphical elaboration, they assemble, store and correlate messages and execute endless algorithms. Because of such an ample assortment of services, I am inclined to conclude that the architecture of a digital system exploits the properties of information in a systematic manner. I assumed that the internal of the machine S relies on the qualities of the product w that S brings forth, thus the following features should determine the operations of a computing machine according to the criterion discussed in the inception:

(1) *A signifier has a physical basis,*
(2) *A signifier stands for something.*

A computer should transform E and NE respectively; a computing machine should fully exploit properties (1) and (2) in order to manipulate information without restrictions. I proceed by deductive reasoning and conclude that a system should achieve two families of processes determined by (1) and (2), and this pair of functions should have the following profiles:

[1] The first process should consist in changing the concrete form of input data, namely this operation transmutes the signifiers and keeps the meanings of input and output unaffected.
[2] The second process should output novel semantic contents respect to the input. This function elaborates the subject matter of the input messages and delivers original pieces of news through an automatic process while the physical appearance of signifiers steadies.

Let us check if these conclusions are true in the world.

A. Converters

People can use exclusively information perceivable by the senses; they cannot work with electric impulses and need messages presented in a clear and striking manner by means of video screens, printers etc. Electronic devices detect physical parameters such as temperature, hours, and pressure that are to be displayed in readable forms. Facts show how electronic appliances handle a variety of information required by users and environmental entities, and special devices cross certain types of boundaries from continuous to discrete, from a physical form to another physical form and so forth. Each digital system is equipped with components specialized to convert the physical body of signs.

Technical literature places the conversion devices into the hereunder principal classes:

1) *Sensors* transmute a physical signal into another physical signal for example an optical signal into electrical.

2) *Actuators* are used to transform a signal into a motion. They are typical components of robots.
3) *Analog-to-digital converters* (ADC) change the form of an electric signal from digital to analog (and vice versa);
4) *Modulators* change square waves into continuous waves and vice versa;
5) *Transcoders* change codewords from a coding system to another coding for example from ASCII code to EBCIDIC code;

Conversion equipment comes in many dissimilar types because of the phenomena they measure, how they work, what they are made of, their function, their cost and their accuracy; it turns out that two devices belonging to the same class can have far differing shapes, volumes and prices. We find a converter as small as a tiny chip and a converter as huge as a unit equipped with sophisticated electronic circuits. Printers, display screens, loudspeakers, microphones, keyboards, and faxes are popular conversion units that exhibit different appearances and dimensions (Doyle 1999).

By definition analog machines handle natural information, and solely an analog element can transmute the physical body of signs. Conversion operations are under charge of analog components. The most significant converters belong to classes 1 and 2 and have been inventoried in the inception of the previous chapter as analog equipment. A device 1 or 2 can include digital circuits, but those circuits work for the analog part that transmutes the signifiers in input and is the core of the device. A key in the keyboard offers the most straightforward example of an analog transducer. When you press the key **A** on the keyboard, you enter a piece of information which is mechanical. The key is a switch that receives a mechanical signal and emits a sequence of electric impulses, namely it converts the material nature of **A** from mechanical to electrical.

LED (Light Emitter Diode) is another popular analog component that transmutes electric signifiers into light.

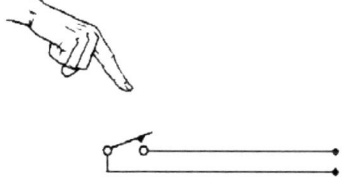

Figure 4.1. Analog conversion mechanical-electrical.

A variety of analog transducers have been invented for printers that change electric impulses into ink letters on the sheet; for display screens that convert electric bits into bright points; for loudspeakers that transmute electric waves into sounds; for disk-drivers that switches magnetic bits into electric impulses. CCD, LED, magnets, electric motors and others parts provide examples of analog components employed for conversion purposes and elucidate how statement [1] comes true in the world. Facts prove that the process defined in [1] seems to be correct.

B. Data-Processing

Let us conduct an accurate examination into what data-processing really consists.

1. Numerical Data-Processing

We commence to scrutinize numerical data-processing which probably is the most familiar form of data-processing. Take the following subtraction where each number has specific significance: the input signifies the cost of a product, and the payment by cash

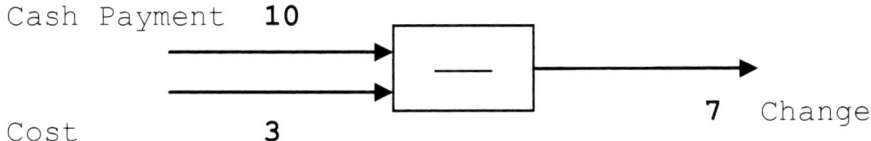

Figure 4.2. Numeric processing of data.

The output of this subtraction stands for the change that the cashier has to give to the client. Note how the outcome symbolizes something new with respect to **10** and **3** in input and for this reason **7** is useful to the cashier. The result of data-processing conveys information quite different from the input numbers, namely the electrical device creates novel pieces of news.

As a further example, suppose a satellite flies around the Earth. The speed of the satellite is obtained by the time derivative of the space function $s(t)$ and the acceleration is given by the second derivative of $s(t)$

$$v(t) = \frac{ds(t)}{dt} \qquad a(t) = \frac{d^2 s(t)}{dt^2}$$

The control station achieves the derivatives, and minute by minute exhibits the results on the control panel. Numerical data-processing proves to be precious because in advance of computation the parameters v and a are unknown pieces of news for the flight controllers.

Numerical data-processing brings to light fresh information and reasonably matches with definition [2].

2. Verbal Data-Processing

Probably the reader has read a sentence of this kind: "Data-processing consists of automatic mathematical calculations". This definition has something true but unfits with the variety of operations executed by modern systems. Besides numerical data-processing more forms of data-processing are widely in use.

All the day long modern computers manipulate linguistic information. Suppose you press the key-word CELLULAR in a search engine, and in a few seconds you obtain several news and offerings from the Web.

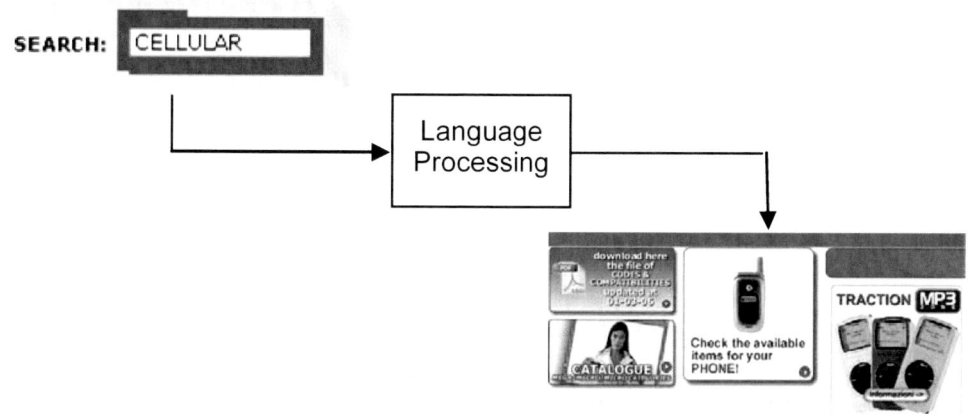

Figure 4.3. Linguistic processing of data.

You can purchase mobile phones at low cost, namely the system has provided messages whose contents absolutely differ from the input key-word.

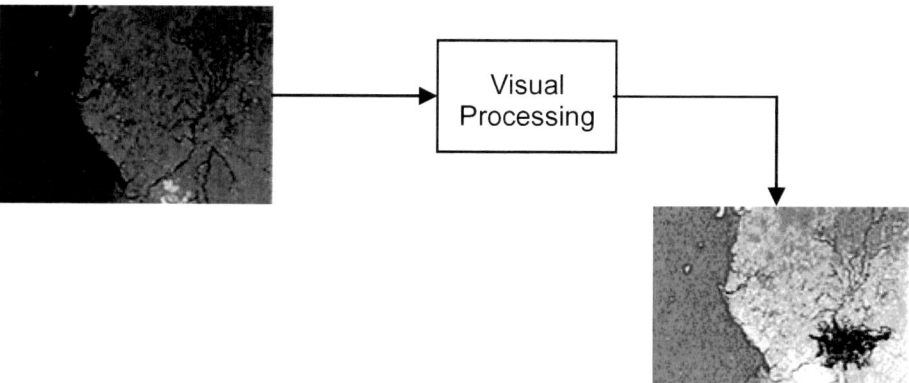

Figure 4.4. Visual processing of data.

3. Visual Data-Processing

Suppose that a satellite takes a snap and a special coloring program highlights the area rich in mineral resources using false colors. The announcement of bonanza is the final message ignored in advance of visual data-processing.

4. Operational Data-Processing

The outputs of data-processing just seen are symbols, images etc. The output may even be an operational signal that guides a device. For example the subtraction in Figure 4.2 can control a mechanical cashier that gives the change to a customer through automatic equipment.

5. Static and Dynamical Responses

Data-processing provides single data items or otherwise provides dynamic results and portrays a real event, or a state of affairs. When the system displays realistic images and allows the operator to use realistic devices, then we have a *simulation*. For example a flight-simulator immerses the operator in a virtual world and the operator has the impression of flying anywhere in the world by means of a joystick.

Figure 4.5. Flight simulator.

Simulation is used in many contexts, including Physics, Chemistry and Biology as well as engineering and even Economics and Social Science, for the purpose of gaining information about phenomena which occurred or will occur.

Practical evidences show how data-processing transforms the input subject matters and prepares novel pieces of news; it delivers original messages; it makes unexpected representations of the reality and conforms to definition [2].

In current literature authors talk about "transformation of content" and mean to describe the translation of a text into a more useful format or into a more meaningful structure. This operation occurs especially in the Web where different platforms and systems communicate (Stojanovic 2009) but this special *transformation of contents* has nothing to do with the present argument.

6. Impact of Data-Processing in the World

It may be said that most economic processes are information-based in the modern world. Managers and leaders make influential decisions with success as long as they have trusty elements in hand, but the manual acquisition of information normally requires exhausting efforts and remarkable investments. The possibility of obtaining pieces of news via speed machines turns out to be an extraordinary opportunity. The mechanical production of pieces of news has a vital value and a great effect in the civilized world and in emerging economies.

The proposed concept of data-processing, which is grounded on Semantics, offers an aid to explain why computers support people everywhere, how computers assist individuals and communities and have dominant success.

Conversely one is inclined to underestimate the relevance of systems to modern economies when he/she assumes that digital systems treat ethereal values. Computers have a considerable influence on our lives and strongly affect the course of events and human relations because the strings of bits represent dollars, euros, gallons, products etc. If by absurd computing machines ran with abstract data, they would have a negligible impact on real life. Very few people would be concerned with data that has a generic reference to the physical reality. The extraordinary contribution of data-processing evaporates and the importance of computer systems vanishes in the mind of those who have some sort of ethereal view on Computing.

The abstract approach to Computing prevails in the scientific community which overlooks the semantic aspects of data and many believe that data-processing coincides with calculus. This idea was not completely wrong in the pioneering age: most software programs were mathematical programs.

Things no longer go in the same way. Nowadays a lot of programs handle sounds, texts, letters, and pictures which have nothing to do with numbers. Surveys conducted on the use of programming languages hold that mathematical computations make a minority group with respect to the other forms of data-processing. Mathematics-oriented languages such as Fortran and APL hover around 5-10% of programmers' work-time in mainframe environment. Fortran ranks the last place of popularity for PC programmers (Norton et al 2002). Other recent statistical results mean that currently numerical data-processing is not a large portion of computer applications. Innovative data treatments – linguistic, visual, multimedia etc. – are overwhelming and the percentage of mathematical programs is decreasing day by day.

The present interpretation of data-processing is based on the accurate analysis of meanings and consists with practical experience. The abstract culture on Computing hints the idea that the systems handle exclusively *abstract numbers* – see Chapter 1, Paragraph 5, Section D, Subsection 4 – and therefore prevents the reader from grasping definition [2]. I am not sure that one can realize in what processing of data consists in the reality as long as he/she deforms the significance of numbers.

7. Creative

Data-processing – the most astonishing activity of computers – brings into existence original pieces of news through mechanical rules. It is not exaggerated to claim that data-processing simulates human thought, in fact thinking is the improvisation of something which has never existed before. A creative reasoning is the process which people use when they come up with a new idea. And the processes illustrated from Subsection 1 to Subsection 5 in this paragraph exhibit something like creative thinking.

Since the seminal article by Turing who introduced the *'test for consciousness'*, scholars argue about the possibility of reasoning for computers and conduct endless debates on whether a machine can discover something new (Koch et al 2008).

The controversy centers upon two elements: the computing machines and the human mind. The former appears rather complex and the latter really constitutes an authentic knotty conundrum. The two obscure terms of the problems – the computer and the brain – expect to be clarified, and the present logical framework offers a small contribution toward that goal.

The proposed definition of data-processing casts light on the *creativity/ inventiveness* of humans and machines. From the present view, data-processing proves to be a *creative* process as long as the computing machine generates original pieces of news. Though data-processing does not constitute an *inventive* process in that digital systems apply the procedures assigned by programmers who govern the manipulation of symbols through the software instructions. A processor does not concoct an answer because it cannot operate on the basis of an original idea as man does. Intuition does not trigger an appliance that instead rigidly executes the scheduled operations even in the most advanced applications in Artificial Intelligence.

8. How Data-Processing Comes to be True

Perhaps the creativeness of data-processing puzzles the reader who wonders how data-processing works in reality. The doubt may be expressed in the following terms:

How can a computer system convey novel information if that machine is unconscious, if circuits are unaware of data meanings?

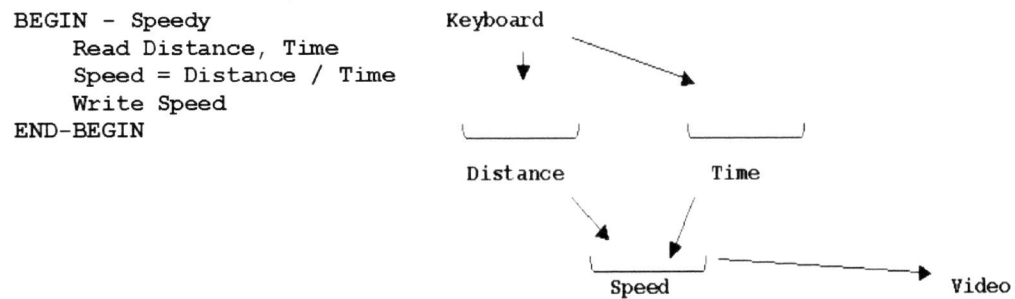

Figure 4.6. The complete program **Speedy.**

Usually authors tackle this argument through philosophical glasses. Thinkers debate the autonomy and the consciousness of machines; instead I like better to dissect the material elements of digital systems that carry on data processing.

Data-processing brings forth novel messages thanks to *complex sets of operations* coordinated through cells of memory called *data-fields* (and also *areas, elements, spaces* etc.). Computer operations handle strings of bits in various manners: they move bits, they store bits, they multiply etc. A data-field is a portion of space which keeps a piece of information for a short while and to which the software programmer can assign a label (Kraft 1979) (Scott 2008). In substance, a specialist designs and implements data-processing applications by means of correlated instructions and data-fields. Thanks to this couple of tools a specialist commands a machine to bring forth novel contents through an automatic process.

A very short software program should elucidate how things go. Suppose a computer operator enters the distance covered by a car and the time spent by this car. The program **Speedy** displays the velocity of the intended car. Figure 4.5 exhibits the list of the software instructions on the left side, and the data flows through the data-fields on the right side. Let us examine the algorithm step by step.

The computer executes the first instruction; that is to say the computer operator is allowed to insert the numbers respectively into the fields **Distance** and **Time** using the keyboard. The first couple of arrows show how the **Read** instruction runs in the practice. In the second step the division is executed and the result is placed unto the field **Speed** – see the second couple of arrows at the right side. Lastly the content of **Speed** is displayed on the video screen.

It is evident how the software program provides a new item of information – the velocity of the car – thanks to the set of statements and data-fields prepared by the software programmer. Ahead of time the programmer is unaware of the numbers that the computer operator will enter, but this ignorance does not debar the programmer from planning the overall plan of work. He is capable of organizing the items necessary for the machine to obtain the intended results. The correlated arrangements of operations and fields constitute the factual answer to the serious problems that proved to be intractable from the philosophical stance so far.

The algorithm **Speedy** turns out to be a straightforward case, deterministic and static. One could doubt that advanced applications deviate from the aforementioned scheme.

Many problems in Artificial Intelligence such as problems in *reasoning, planning, learning* and *robotics* require an agent to operate with incomplete or uncertain information. *Genetic programming* creates *evolutionary* applications. Advanced software applications are incommensurable more complex than **Speedy**, nonetheless the previous conclusions remain true in the sense that instructions and fields are the irreplaceable elements of any software construction. The methods of work and the algorithms developed in the living environment cannot be compared with the scholastic example related above. AI solutions are intricate in a superlative manner but the substantial elements of data-processing – instructions and fields – are always the same, and these elements enable us to infer further conclusions.

9. What Software Programmers Can and Cannot do

Thinkers explore the limits of the computer tasks. They question what a computer can and cannot do long since.

In formal terms a mathematical problem is said *computable* if it can be solved in principle by a computing device. Common synonyms for '*computable*' are '*solvable*' and '*decidable*' (Cooper 2003). Hilbert believed that all mathematical problems were solvable, but in the 1930's Kurt Gödel, Alan Turing, and Alonzo Church showed that this is not the case. There is an extensive study and classification of which mathematical problems are computable and which are not. Later theorists investigated the *computational complexity classes* that classify computational problems according to their inherent difficulty (Epstein et al 1990). While a number of intricate questions are awaiting a complete answer, one can develop practical issues on the basis of the elements just introduced.

Software designers obtain the project specifications of what a computer system is required to do by customers and investigate whether a set of instructions and fields meets with those requirements. There is no cookbook for software designers: sometimes the algorithm is immediate; other times it is hard to devise the algorithm; lastly a software solution may be simply unachievable in practice. Normally it is not a question of abstract 'decidability' in companies, business and institutions; it is a question of several pragmatic details which turn out to be fuzzy, uncertain and unknowable by professionals. It is a matter of difficulties that expect to be translated into practical terms. One could hold that *a computer can treat all the problems that software experts are capable of analyzing and converting into instructions and data fields.* Instructions along with fields are the 'silver bullets' for software practitioners but there is no simple and infallible rule to implement an effective software application.

2. TWO MODELS FOR A DIGITAL SYSTEM

By definition a digital system manipulates signs which consist of signifiers and signified. Facts make clear that a computer manipulates E and NE using distinct units. A conversion process modifies the forms of information while meanings are kept untouched:

$$E_{IN} \neq E_{OUT}$$
$$NE_{IN} = NE_{OUT}$$

Data-processing carries on novel meanings while signifiers are uniform from the physical viewpoint:

$$E_{IN} = E_{OUT}$$
$$NE_{IN} \neq NE_{OUT}$$

Practical experience shows how definitions [1] and [2] are true in the working environment but the analysis is incomplete and one may wonder:
What is the overall structure of a digital system?
How do functions [1] and [2] work together?

A. Star Model

Converters adapt the pieces of information in aid of the processor that works with physically uniform signals. Therefore a digital system should be equipped with the data-processing unit placed at the center and a number of conversion units placed all around. The *radial model* (or *star model*) should exhibit the correct displacement of parts in a computer system.
Let us see whether digital engineers comply with this inferential reasoning.

Authors coined the term '*central unit*' for the data-processing unit because of its position, while the conversion units were called *peripherals* or *input/output units*: the latter devices lie around the former and prove the radial configuration is correct.
The radial model identifies an external unit even if integrated and rather hidden. For instance the star model pinpoints the hard disk as a distinct input/output unit whereas the central box in a personal computer encapsulates the disk drive and conceals this unit from human sight.
The radial model justifies recent trends in technology.
Devices lately sold as regular stand-alone devices, are becoming peripherals of modern computer systems. This modern visible tendency in the computer sector is currently known as

digital convergence. The USB (Universal Serial Bus), a plug-and-play interface between a computer and add-on devices such as audio players, joysticks, keyboards, telephones, scanners, and digital cameras, reinforces the connectivity of a portable or fixed system. The Internet facilitates digital convergence as hypermedia information can be instantly transferred from the Web into a personal computer (Sullivan et al. 2004).

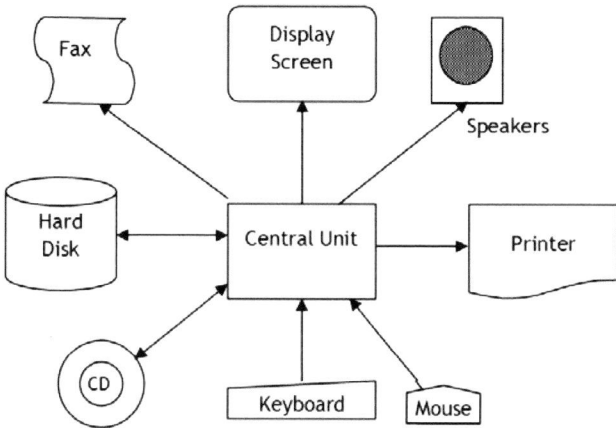

Figure 4.7. Radial Model.

Probably the future world will become a place without books, letters, post cards, billboards, telephones, photographs, movies, televisions, stereo systems, and fax machines. In lieu of the media that we now take for granted there will be the one digital medium that will take full advantage of the star model.

B. Hierarchical Model

The central unit needs homogeneous signals and can run provided the input and output flows are homogeneous. Process [1] adapts the physical forms of data in function of process [2] and it may be said that peripherals are servants of the central unit. Peripherals appear to play a subordinate role with respect to the central unit according to the present reasoning. A principle of operational mastery which may be associated to the arguments treated in (Pattee 1973) should govern the computer system from the current viewpoint and the *hierarchical tree* (Salthe 2001) should complete the description of the computer architecture.

Let us see the internal of systems and check whether the previous inference is correct.

Common practice shows how it is not sufficient for a conversion unit to be connected; this unit can only run under the central unit grant (Brookshea 2004). There is no other way to put a peripheral device into action; an input/output unit is idle unless the central unit empower this unit. In other words all the peripherals lie under the operational supervision of the central unit.

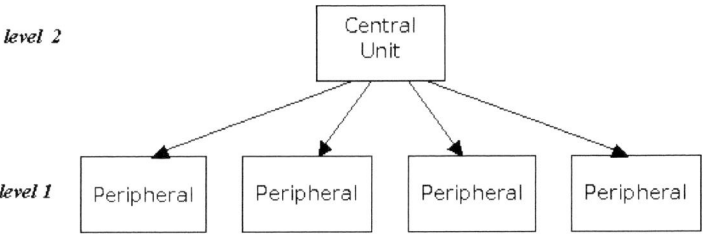

Figure 4.8. Hierarchical Model.

Computer designers strengthen the natural hierarchy of a system and place the *control unit* (CU) into the central unit: a circuit specialized for the operational control of the overall system. Normally CU integrates into a chip named *central processing unit* (CPU) together with other circuits, and the acronyms CU and CPU are frequently used as synonymous (Green 1988).

A computing machine is equipped with hybrid devices, and CPU orchestrates the varied components in order to avoid conflicts amongst the parts and to optimize the overall performances. In this way the CPU reinforces the supervision role played by the central device and one can conclude that the tree model turns out to be even truer.

Several hardware procedures relate minutely how CPU practices its operational supervision. I cannot look closely at those rules, and confine myself to three examples that should clarify the style of the central unit which rules over the other units.

- A peripheral device cannot get or emit data unless the CPU enables this peripheral to work, namely any external operations cannot commence without the central authorization. The periphery does not run autonomously but relies on the center.
- As soon as a peripheral ends a task, the CPU checks the results of the input/output operations that have just come to an end. In other words, all the outcomes are tested and assessed with care by the central device that undertakes the appropriate initiatives to manage the situations.
- When a special event occurs – e.g. a circuit breaks down – all running operations come to a halt at that moment and the Central Processing Unit takes full control of the machine and handles this event. This proves that the CPU leads all the units during ordinary jobs and special occurrences alike.

3. CONCLUDING REMARKS

A logical chain leads us from the properties of signs, to the system units, and in turn to the radial and the hierarchical models which depict the overall digital system. The architecture of systems conform to the logical conclusions developed in this chapter independently whether a system is *stand alone* or *connected* to a net, whether a system is *embedded* in a machine or a big *supercomputer*. One can verify the models above discussed in cellular phones, hi-fi pods, satellite navigators, flight control equipment and so forth.

The deductive reasoning which attempts to justify the machine S starting from the product w seems a good method of proving conclusions in the computer field too, and casts further light on the intelligent methods adopted by digital experts. Designers have contrived productive and profitable manipulations of signs and created the architecture of systems.

A. Annotations on Current Literature

The classical structure of a computing machine equipped with a stored program was presented in the "*First Draft of a Report on the EDVAC*". The overall organization of systems was illustrated in this paper dated 30 June 1945, which includes this synopsis:

> "The three specific parts [that make the central unit n.d.r.] correspond to the associative neurons in human nervous system. It remains to discuss the equivalents of the sensory organs or afferent and the motor or efferent neurons. (…) These are the input and output organs of the device, and we shall now consider them briefly. (…) There remains (…) the necessity of getting the original definitory information from outside into the device, and also of getting the final information, the results, from the device into the outside." (Neumann 1993)

Von Neumann compares input/output devices to the human sensory organs and associates data-processing to the neural nets theorized by McCulloch and Pitts in those years. This analogy with the human nervous system raises vivid suggestions (Boden 2008) but appears rather questionable on the intellectual plane. Neumann aims at explaining an unknown topic – say the peripherals and the data-processing unit – by using a comparison term that is even more enigmatic. Usually scientists follow the opposite direction. Doctors illustrate a complex biological organ using a device, for ease the bones of the arm and the forearm are compared to a mechanical lever; the heart looks like a pump, the blood vessels are similar to pipes. In fact a machine, designed and built by engineers lies normally under the full control of those engineers; by contrast living beings are ready in Nature and scientists have to decipher their complex functions. Biologists and physicians help themselves by means of technical concepts when they make easier to understand biological parts.

Neumann seems to adopt the opposite method which sounds rather strange; he attempts to elucidate the functions of a computing system by means of the parallel with the human brain which is still a challenge for researchers world-wide. It is evident that the '*von Neumann model*' constitutes a cornerstone in Computer Science but deserves discussion. This basic assessment of the computer architecture should be brought into the open and its merits debated.

Figure 4.9. Input-Process-Output Model.

Unfortunately the project did not go on. Theorists give the impression to me to consider the hardware structure of a computer system as a rather trivial argument. They do not proceed to the study of particulars. This passive orientation is not a trifling matter since a number of fallacies and misconceptions, which derive from theorists' negligent behavior, may be found in current literature especially in educational texts.

- ✓ Textbooks and manuals describe the structure of a computer system on the basis of the von Neumann model and illustrate this model using a linear graph with three blocks (Forouzan 2003). The *Input-Process-Output model* (IPO) may include the memory, the CPU and other details: these variants are inessential for the moment. One may remark:

    - The IPO model is linear and simplifies the radial structure to the extent that a reader cannot understand the *digital convergence* and its enormous factual impact.
    - The linear chain implies – in conformity with *Markov's chain theory* – that the central block depends on the input block, instead the contrary is true. The process unit governs all the external operations and an input unit cannot run until the central unit has not enabled the operation in advance.
    - A lot of systems in various sectors of production – e.g. agriculture, mining, hydraulics, etc. – share the IPO scheme in the sense that several automatic systems are served by units that introduce raw materials and bring out manufactured goods respectively. The labels *input*, *process* and *output* sound rather generic in the computer sector until a commentator does not specify in what the peripheral processes and the central processes consist. If theorists do not illustrate the special treatments undergone by information crossing the computer system, the overall purposes of the system appear ephemeral.

- ✓ Scholars do not accurately examine in what data-processing really consists and are inclined to conclude that data-processing and calculation came to mean the same thing; instead digital systems treat various forms of data in the real world and do not restrict their intervention to numbers.
- ✓ The lack of an accurate description of the digital systems entails that technical manuals seem to be written as cookbooks. As a cookbook provides an effective guide for cookers, so modern, up-to-date textbooks are able to assist students who really become wizards in daily tasks. Theoretical principles are unnecessary for those wizards, but prove to be necessary to those who manage or implement an ICT infrastructure. We shall see next how a number of computer disasters are caused by poor education (Dvorak 2004), namely the consequences of the above mentioned problems are not of little significance and value.

The behavior of digital designers appears intelligent and theory-based, but the benefits deriving from the digital paradigm sometimes do not fully benefit the people involved.

BIBLIOGRAPHY

Boden M. (2008) - *Mind as Machine: A History of Cognitive Science* - Oxford University Press.
Brookshea Glenn J. (2004) - *Computer Science: An Overview* - Addison Wesley.
Cooper S.B. (2003) - *Computability Theory* - CRC Press.
Doyle L.F. (1999) - *Computer Peripherals* - Prentice Hall.
Dvorak J.C. (2004) - *The Bottom 10: Worst Software Disasters* - PC World Magazine, 8.
Epstein R.L., Carnielli W.A. (1990) - *Computability: Computable Functions, Logic and the Foundations of Mathematics* - CRC Press.
Forouzan B.A. (2003) - *Foundations of Computer Science, From Data Manipulation to Theory of Computation* - Thomson.
Green D. (1988) - *Digital Electronic Technology* - John Wiley & Sons Inc.
Koch C., Tononi G. (2008) - Can Machines Be Conscious? - *IEEE Spectrum*, 45(6), 55-59.
Kraft G.D., Toy W.N. (1979) - *Mini/microcomputer Hardware Design* - Prentice-Hall.
Neumann von J. (1993) - First Draft of a Report on the EDVAC - *IEEE Annals of the History of Computing*, 15(4), pp. 27-75.
Norton P., Clark S. (2002) - *Peter Norton's New Inside the PC* - Sams Publishing.
O' Sullivan D., Igoe T. (2004) - *Physical Computing* - Muska & Lipman.
Pattee H.H. (1973) - *The Organization of Complex Systems* - in Hierarchy Theory: the Challenge of Complex Systems, Pattee H.H. (ed), Braziller, pp.1-27.
Salthe S. (2001) - *Summary of the Principles of Hierarchy Theory* - MIT Press.
Scott M.L. (2008) - *Programming Language Pragmatics* - Morgan Kaufmann.
Stojanovic D. (2009) - *Context-Aware Mobile and Ubiquitous Computing for Enhanced Usability* - IGI Global Publ.

Chapter 5

NETS AND SPOTS

Information is required to be transported and stored, and these services are so mandatory and so valuable that currently ICT infrastructures cover the entire world. The modern global market could not run without the support of communication networks and capable memories. Electric lines and magnetic stores shoulder the burden of frantic decisions and activities crossing the continents. Present-day infrastructures are sustaining the advance of economies.

According to the purposes of this book I go on to verify the behavior of digital engineers when they construct channels and stores.

1. ANALOG COMPONENTS

The material origin of signs leads us toward a similitude. A sign lies in a certain place and exists over a certain period of time in a manner similar to whatsoever object. It is evident how signifiers are situated in portions of place and span over ranges of time. The comparison between normal objects and signifiers is intended to intimate that preservation and transport of signs are services analogue to the preservation and transport of goods. One can proceed with this reasoning and conclude that the core components of networking and the basic elements of data storing comply with the essential criteria shared in other sectors. The rules of transportation and warehousing should be uniform and the units responsible for modifying the displacement of information and for extending the temporal existence of information should be analogue to units that achieve similar works in various fields, in short: *channels and storage are analog appliances.*

This concept is unusual in current literature and I have to provide the accurate illustration of this idea.

A channel moves an item of information from the place p_1 to the place p_2 and in this way changes the spatial characteristic of that item. A storage unit keeps an item of information over the interval (t_1, t_2), namely it may be said that a store moves a piece of news from the instant t_1 to t_2. Channels and stores transmute physical features of signifiers and it is reasonable to conclude with the following statement:

Channels and storage manipulate the spatial and the temporal characteristics of signifiers. [5.1]

Stores and channels modify the space values and the temporal values of information, therefore these components may be classified as *conversion units* in accordance to the description given in the previous chapters. Solely analog components are capable of transmuting signifiers. We have just seen how the core of peripherals is analog and [5.1] yields that modern *ICT infrastructures are based on analog components*.

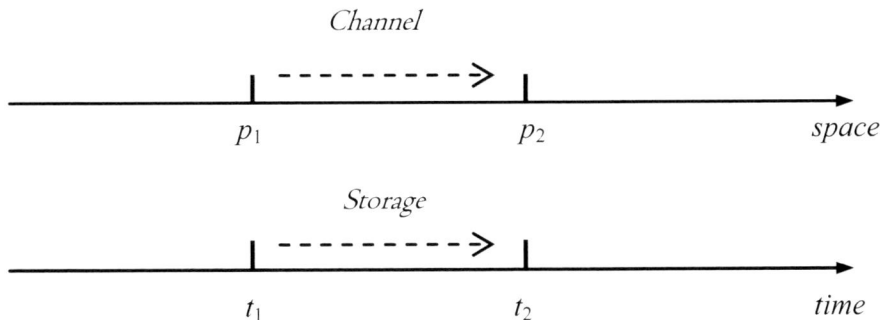

Figure 5.1.

Current literature overlooks the idea that storing and telecommunications are grounded upon analog concepts. I do not mean to say that somebody disputes this interpretation but simply that the whole argument does not seem to merit attention. Because of the lack of references, issue [5.1] inferred in abstract is to be accurately verified in the physical reality. In particular one has to ascertain whether digital engineers who design and build up networks and archives adopt transport and logistic rules; whether they optimize operational parameters; whether they minimize resources etc. in analogy to engineers who design pipelines, railways, and highways.

We shall see the prominent characteristics of networks here and of storage in the next chapter.

2. CHANNELS

Hardware channels widely differ from one another. They make up an assortment, which technical writers do not tend to express in a uniform mode. I am forced to make a complete inventory of channels – even if it is succinct – in order to pursue the objectives of this book.

A. Telephone Cables

In modern countries the telephone lines reach any home. In the US the *Public Switched Telephone Network* (PSTN) was the two-wire phone line system originally designed and used for voice. Today, PSTN incorporates backbones that improve the speed and quality of signals transmitted from private premises. As a consequence, modern telephone cables make the local loop from subscriber's premises to the local central office switches and some trunk circuits.

Copper wires transmit pure electric signals; they can also carry *electromagnetic* (EM) signals over short distances at low frequencies (up to about 1 GHz).

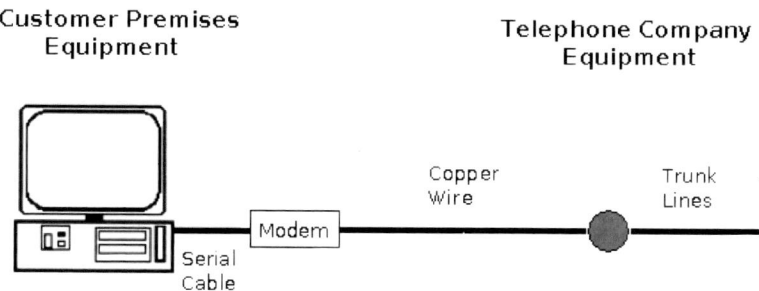

Figure 5.2. Telephone system.

B. Waveguides

High rate transmission consists of EM waves that propagate down the line and propagate even into the space surrounding the wires. Copper lines have evident undesirable defects at high-speed transmission. Waveguides solve these problems by confining the electromagnetic wave to the space inside the guide. A standard microwave guide consists of a strip of space (or dielectric) surrounded by metal, in effect it is like a metal pipe with a rectangular or circular section.

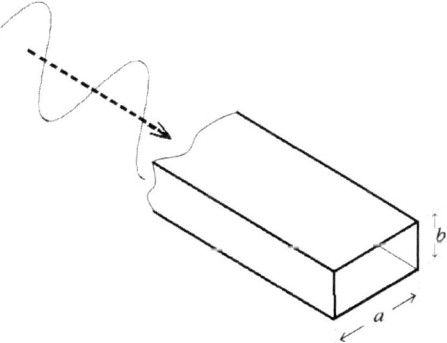

Figure 5.3. Waveguide for microwaves.

Waveguides are long, axially symmetric, hollow conductors with open ends. The sides a and b are in the order of millimeters. A signal flows from place to place inside the pipe, because EM fields which try to radiate away from the metal simply bounce off the opposite wall of the pipe. Hence the electromagnetic power is 'trapped' and forced to flow along the pipe.

Waveguides are high-frequency transmission lines, roughly wave frequency ranges 3 GHz to 30 GHz.

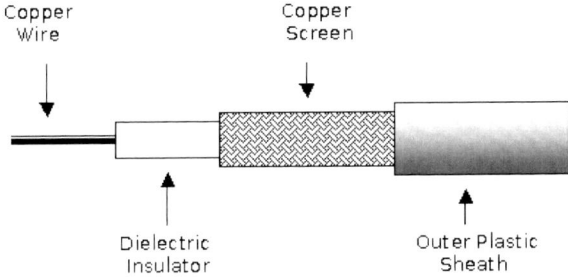

Figure 5.4. Coaxial cable.

C. Coaxial Cables

Coaxial cables are more popular than the aforesaid waveguides. Laymen frequently see those cables connecting aerials to TV appliances.

A coaxial cable consists of a copper wire, surrounded by an insulating spacer, surrounded by a cylindrical conducting screen, and lastly surrounded by a final insulating layer. Coaxial lines confine the electromagnetic wave to the area inside the cable, between the copper wire and the copper screen. The transmission of energy in the cable occurs totally through the dielectric inside the cable between the conductors. Coaxial lines can therefore be bent and twisted without negative effects, and they can be strapped to conductive supports without inducing unwanted currents in them. This cable of a few millimeters in diameter carries a high-frequency or broadband signal (at least 3 GHz).

D. Optical Fibers

Optical fibers make the third class of waveguides besides hollow conductors and coaxial cables. They boomed over the past decades and currently optical fibers are backbones for high-speed, local and long distance communication inside PSTN.

A fiber optic is a wire, generally of glass or plastic, which guides light through its length by using refraction. The light can get through the fiber without escaping because light reflects at the inner surface of the fiber. Light is trapped in a step-index fiber by total internal reflection. An electronic device pumps tiny flashes into fiber optic, at the rate of tens of billions tiny flashes per second. An electronic device receives and transmutes the optical signal at the other extreme of the fiber. At present, the maximum pulse rate that can be handled in telecommunication systems reaches up to about 10 billion bits per second (10 Gb/s). Another virtue of fibers is the fiber minuteness; a fiber optic is as thin as a few μm (10^{-6} m) in diameter.

Figure 5.5. Optical fiber.

E. Space

I complete the inventory and append the unique *natural channel* that is the *open space* to the principal *artificial channels* just quoted.

The open space comes out as the most astonishing and important resource to communicate. Firstly, space has unconfined form, it is boundless in size since it covers the Earth and even reaches stars and galaxies. Secondly space conveys a large assortment of signals: light, radio waves, microwaves, sounds, and infrared waves all around. The third big advantage of space is easy of use, namely a device can connect anywhere without the need for wires. As fourth, wireless communication strikes mobile devices which move around the world and cannot be plugged in, that is why the term '*wireless communication*' often is synonymous with mobile communication. One device can detect the signals everywhere on the understanding that a receiver is correctly tuned to the transmitter. Lastly space is a free resource, it has not to be installed and paid. In conclusion the natural channel, which is the only one of its kind, shows the following outstanding features:

1) Space is boundless,
2) Space gives off a broad variety of signals,
3) Space connects a device without the need for wires,
4) Space reaches a device even when this device is mobile,
5) Space has no cost.

F. Improper Channel

Besides artificial channels – wires and waveguides – and the natural channel – space – operators use *improper channels*, which are lines devoted to a special purpose and in addition transport information.

The electrical power grid constitutes the most popular improper channel as it supplies electricity and also delivers data. Companies and institutions save money using the cables already installed instead of connecting computers with cables which have to be purchased and installed.

The exhaustive inventory of channels shows how space offers extraordinary and unique benefits for transmission and the reader can deduce how users surcharge space and hazard confidential communications. Technicians remedy with linear conduits that link predefined users. Artificial channels are called to make up for the overcrowded space channel.

The foregoing inventory spanning from Section A to F should make the reader aware that channels convey analog signals and digital signals as well; in consequence digital and/or analog protocols govern channels; lines connect digital devices and/or analog devices. A physical channel is able to serve multiple technologies and this serviceability risks to be confusing. Managers and operators who make investments on technology often are unaware of the exact meanings of the terms. Sometimes the bare words in use confuse people.

3. Systems for Transmission

The definition of channels as analog resources entails that experts should tailor an infrastructure in accordance to operational criteria; they should determine the size of flows, the capability of conduits, the speed and priority of operations, and so forth (AA.VV. 1961).

The thorough, minute examination of facilities goes beyond the scopes of the present book. Let us verify whether telecommunications infrastructures are in agreement with some basic criteria on transport and mobility.

In principle a channel can convey signals toward one-way or otherwise can throw forth information in several directions at the same time. In the living world we see how artificial channels connect point-to point and can but adopt the first method. Instead the space can serve multiple points simultaneously.

Let us start with the first type of systems.

A. Single Direction

Several stretches of line make a net are capable of covering a broad territory.

1. Planar Nets

Suppose n nodes are to be linked, in principle there are two extreme arrangements: the *linear graph* and the *complete graph* (Deo 2004).

The linear graph consists of a sequel of nodes and looks to be the most straightforward and consequently the cheapest pattern for transport. As a counter balance the linear graph is the puniest solution because the whole system fails if only one stretch breaks down.

The complete graph whose nodes are fully connected constitutes the most robust system since the system collapses only if all the edges break down. Each node is bound up with all the remaining hence this net emerges as the most intricate and expensive pattern. The complete graph is reliable in return for the investment.

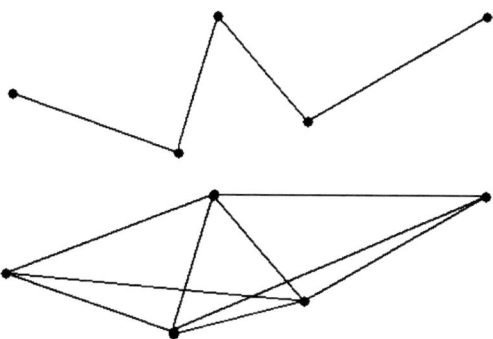

Figure 5.6. A linear graph and a complete graph.

It is evident how these networks have strong points and weaknesses, and engineers balance pros and cons depending on customer requirements, geographical constraints, peaks of traffic and so forth. For instance when the telecommunication system covers a small area – e.g. the nodes are placed within the internal areas of a company or a business – risks are improbable and weak. Experts prefer *local area networks* (LAN) which assume the linear shape and whose architectures are known as Ethernet and Token-ring (Chowdhury 2000).

When the nodes scatter over a large area, the possibilities of disruption are very high, and engineers make a *mesh*, namely they make a trade-off between the complete graph, the traffic requirements and the costs they can meet. Designers establish the *geographic network* (GN) as a mesh in order to counteract frequent transmission flaws.

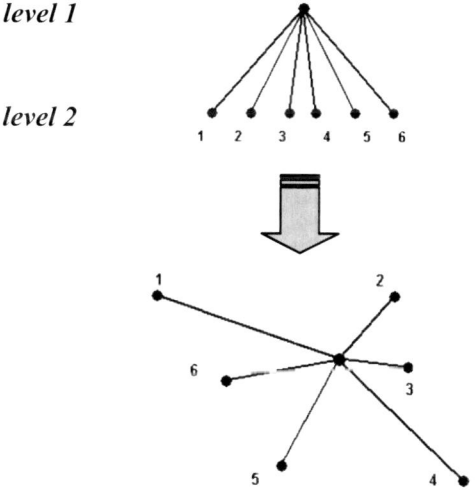

Figure 5.7. The origin of hierarchical net.

2. Hierarchical Nets

Now we append a special hypothesis. Let us suppose that a node monitors the remaining nodes in a net. By way of illustration, take a switching center that manages the telephone-numbers 1, 2, 3, 4, 5 and 6. The switching node supervises the other nodes and the hierarchical tree illustrates the role of the switching node (Salthe 2001). The *tree model* results in the form that the hierarchical net assumes over a physical territory (Figure 5.7). In fact controlled nodes scatter over the ground and the tree becomes a star in order to keep the connections with the centre. The *star net* comes from the hierarchical order erected amongst the nodes.

Engineers build stable radial shaped infrastructures when the hierarchy of the nodes is definitive. Instead, when the hierarchical relationships established among the nodes vary over time, the star cannot be plugged in. The physical net has a form that cannot be specified. The hardware structure is any while special software programs establish star-connections in accordance to the needs of the moment. This variable pattern turns out to be a normal arrangement in the Internet as we shall verify next.

We shall return to the telecommunication control in the next paragraph.

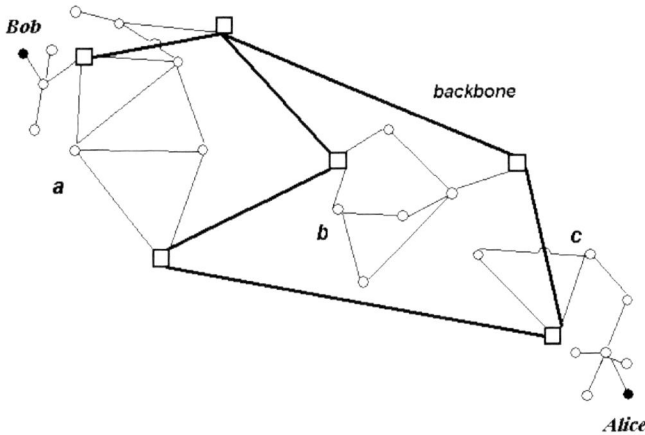

Figure 5.8. Backbones.

3. Backbones

The Internet exploits odd installations existing in the world: wireless and channeled infrastructures, fixed and mobile systems, stars, lines and meshes. The Internet crosses the planet through those resources, which can potentially reach any individual. The overall system of connections though cannot fulfill its duties by means of mere joining subnets already in use. For example, three arrangements cover the neighboring countries **a**, **b** and **c**. Alice emails a message to Bob, and her text should pass through three intricate pathways and should take so much time that the service becomes rather useless.

Engineers remedy this sort of shortcoming by *backbones* that link geographical areas with long-distance interconnections. Backbones make a broad mesh – or *second order mesh* – that overlap small meshes – or *first order meshes* – serving small territories. Backbones ensure swift connections among distant points and confirm that meshes are solutions specialized to cover wide areas (Bonocore 2001).

Engineers on telecommunications optimize the data flows, they reduce the stretches to cover, they balance costs to benefits, they size the cells up in relation to the crowding and the mobility of subscribers to strike and so forth. Solutions do not derive from the principles of the digital paradigm; the hardware of transmission systems is not involved in discretization, in the Boolean algebra and in other topics typical of the digital field.

ICT experts design a transmission system which comply with transportation and operational concepts which are familiar in other sectors: highways, aqueducts, railways, etc. For example ordinary routes make a first order mesh, highways make the second order mesh and work very likely to the arrangement in Figure 5.8. The logic of telecommunication nets proves to be close to the logic of systems equipped with routes, pipes, rails, canals or rivers.

B. Multiple Directions

A broad set of users are daily assisted by the space-channel. In fact a transmitting station serves a territory where are placed fixed and mobile handsets. E.g. portable computers, cell-phones. The portion of territory is proportional to the distances amongst fixed stations and to the mobility of the users to strike. The wider is the movement of the served users, the wider is the served area.

The most significant broadcasting systems split into three major groups.

1. Short-Range Wireless Systems

A short-range wireless system serves users working within an office or a plant. Computers can be up to 100 feet or so apart.

2. Medium-Range Wireless Systems

A medium-range wireless system serves a portion of territory – called *cell* –ranging from one to twenty kilometers (or even more) in diameter.

Cellular technology allows for the hand-off of subscribers from one cell to another as they travel around. This turns out to be the key feature to enable a user to be mobile. A computer constantly tracks mobile subscribers of units within a cell, and when a user reaches the border of a cell, the computer automatically hands-off the call and the call is assigned to a new channel in a different cell.

3. Long-Range Wireless Systems

Long-range systems of telecommunication serve distant receivers. E.g. two fixed operators placed at the West and the East coast. E.g. a ship crossing the ocean. Mobile and fixed units are related by means of *radio-stations* that act as end-points and *relay stations* that capture the messages and resend them forward.

Repeaters usually fly in space like the *geostationary satellites* for communication. Satellites, which work as either active or passive repeaters – a passive repeater runs as a bare reflector of signals – occupy predefined spots in the sky so that the Earth stations easily locate them and direct the dishes. A geostationary satellite can see approximately 40 percent of the earth's surface because it flies at around 36,000 kilometers (some 22,300 miles) above the earth. Three such satellites, spaced at equal intervals, can provide coverage of the entire civilized world in theoretical terms.

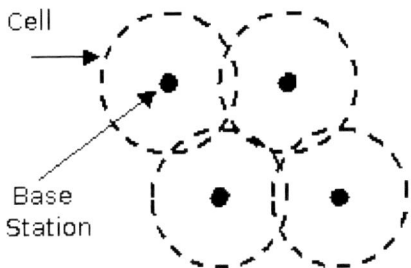

Figure 5.9. Cluster of cells.

4. CONTROL OF COMPUTER NETS

Signifiers are not car drivers who are able to control their own movement. Signals are passive travelers and need to be transmitted, conveyed and checked in advance of each movement and at the end of each transport step alike. The control of transmission is a dominant question in networking and includes a lot of functions.

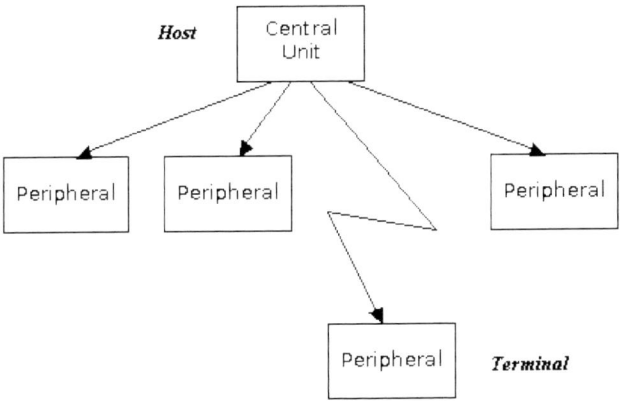

Figure 5.10. The computer architecture and a monocentric net.

The present book cannot be extensively devoted to this topic, and we focus on the *hosts*, the major actors of communication control. Technical literature defines as host the computer that takes the full control of operations in a net; while *routers, gateways* and other systems bring forth a more limited set of control operations.

In principle a network can include either one host or many hosts, thus we have *monocentric* and *polycentric* computer nets. There are two basic models of computer networks, no matter the channels installed.

A. Monocentric Net

A monocentric net is wholly consistent with the architecture of computer systems illustrated in Chapter 4, Paragraph 2, Section B. I mean to exploit the tree model presented in the previous chapter in order to decipher the principal properties of monocentric nets.

1. Rigid Control

When a technical team designs a monocentric net, the team moves one or more peripheral devices several miles away and basically keeps the hierarchy of the computer system illustrated in Figure 4.7. Experts place all the distant appliances under the operational control of the central unit which is the unique host of such a *hierarchical net*. The peripherals placed all around the country take the reasonable name of *terminals* due to their subordinate role (Figure 5.10).

The simplest computer network has the radial form over the territory in accordance to the tree model. Special *protocols* embody the inflexible dominion symbolized by the tree. For ease, a terminal cannot open a session on its own; instead the host polls the terminal-system which is allowed to transmit under precise requisites.

2. Multilevel Functions

When there are several terminals, a number of intermediate systems are required to aid the central supervisor. A *terminal-system* rules over a group of terminals, simultaneously the central host overviews its functions. The terminal-system has the operational overview over a portion of the network, and at the same time it acts as a terminal with respect to the host. In substance, the terminal-system ranks in the middle between the host and the final terminals (Tanenbaum 1981), and a complex hierarchical exceeds over two levels.

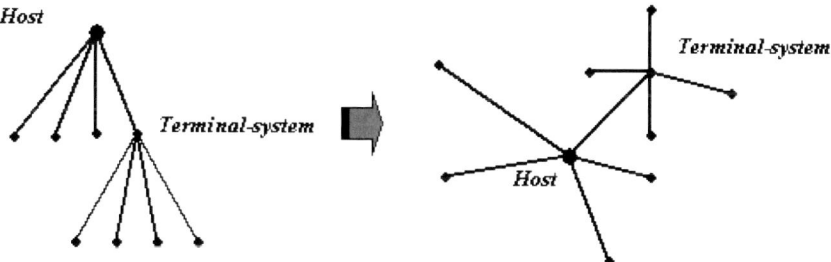

Figure 5.11. Multilevel hierarchical net.

Monocentric nets prove to be very efficient since the host ensures secure communications amongst the nodes: no bit can travel outside the central control. Technical commentators coined the contraction *master/slave* to elucidate the rigid authority erected in the hierarchical networks. Somebody holds the term 'master/slave' may sound offensive and a number of writers prefer the terms '*primary/secondary*'.

B. Polycentric Net

When engineers join several hierarchical nets and even other sorts of nets – e.g. LAN, wireless – the new infrastructure is no longer monocentric. The *polycentric net includes a large number of hosts*, necessarily peer due to the lack of any principle of operational mastery. No host can supervise the other installations and no procedure can give a node an edge over the others. All the nodes rank the same level namely the hierarchical tree vanishes. This is the case of the Internet.

1. Insecure Connections

Host's supervision makes the hierarchical secure from attacks. The mechanical governor forbids violations of the software and the hardware resources which lie under its severe control. A polycentric net conversely is insecure in the sense that experts cannot install a general supervisor. No appliance is capable of monitoring the whole infrastructure. This implies that Internet cannot include any superior checkpoint either today or tomorrow. It hasn't any automatic center of control and will never have one.

The shortness of a mechanical governor does not exclude that countermeasures are available to make communications in the Internet secure. Anti-virus products, anti-spamming and cryptographic programs are examples of defense tools available to consumers and institutions. The so-called *firewall* screens a partial net, somehow a firewall divides the *intranet* that is protected from the rest of the world. The firewall, a compound of hardware components and software programs, constitutes the essential shelter of the Intranet. The *filter* allows authorized traffic to pass in and out the corporate net and make a special class of firewalls. Only selected operators can run through the filter that ensures protection to the private resources. The *proxy*, a second firewall, logs all the transactions and makes the data ready for investigations, for violation documentation, etc (Griswold 1997).

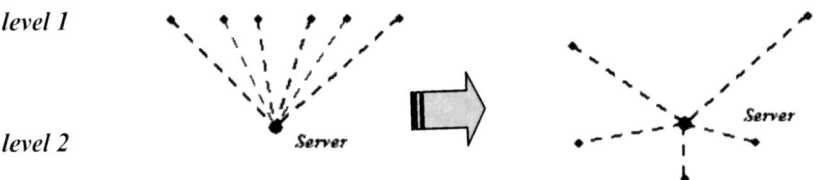

Figure 5.12. Client/server hierarchy.

2. Mutable Control

All the organizations must be controlled and this rigid issue is necessarily true even for the polycentric net.

What rules give an order to operations?
Which sort of hierarchy does the Internet apply to?

An example proves to be useful to illustrate the control available in a polycentric net.
Suppose an operator at the host *A* looks for some data stored in *B* and downloads a file from *B*, namely the host *B* offers its services to *A*. It is evident how the operations of *B* depend

on *A*. They rank two hierarchical levels: *A* lies on top and *B* which is serving at bottom. However this kind of operational hierarchy can change. For example, shortly after *B* demands a service to *A* which satisfies the request. The hierarchical relation inverts: *B* ranks on top and *A* that serves *B* lies at the bottom.

Fig 5.13. Visualization of traffic in a section of the Internet.

The foregoing example brings evidence on how the concept of hierarchy is still valid in the polycentric net, in fact there are precise priorities, and each session needs to be supervised. However the control has a behavior far different from the static authority erected in the monocentric net. Hierarchies vary time and again in a polycentric net. The management of the operations, light and changeable, looks like the relation emerging between the shopkeeper and a customer. The *client/server hierarchy* takes place in the world-net in place of the rigid master/slave hierarchy (Johnson 2001).

The client/server model entails two original issues. First, the eye of the radial structure does not manage the peripheral nodes; on the contrary the central node is servant and supports the periphery. The hierarchical order exhibited in Figure 5.7 overturns. Secondly roles are unstable and invert time and again. The mutable connections are established through software programs. Dashed lines in Figure 5.12 mean the relations between a server and its terminals are subject to change (Shafe 1995). These conclusions find evidences in the Internet. Visualization of the Internet traffic exhibits the star as the basic pattern of the net. Authors use the grayscale to represent the intensity of the traffic in each line (Figure 5.13).

5. CONCLUDING REMARKS

The basic features of computer networking examined in this chapter may be summed up as follows:

- o Channels are hardware conduits, and conform to common rules that regulate transportation and movement of materials. See the division between single direction channels and multiple directions channel. The former are subdivided into linear nets, tree nets and meshes. The latter are subdivided into short, medium and long range broadcasting systems. Traffic requirements and other logistic criteria guide the decision makers who design meshes, backbones, stars etc. We have seen each solution in relation to a precise logistic problem.

o   The control of telecommunications is centered upon the concept of hierarchy which teaches us to recognize two basic organizations: monocentric and polycentric nets; which in turn lead to the *master/slave* and the *client/server* models that illustrate somewhat opposite styles of control. Those metaphors cross various domains and mirror relationships that one can find in Economics, in Ethology, in Sociology etc. This is a further aid to see the channels as analog resources and the control of telecommunications analogue to other forms of control.

Customers feel different needs and present requirements which normally overlap, hence an infrastructure includes a mixture of hardware components: analog and digital; wired and wireless; fixed and mobile; hierarchical and TCP/IP. The multiform nature of an infrastructure redoubles the serviceability of the present account that tends to sum up various concepts and rules.

A. Annotations on Current Literature

The *theory of queues* (Cox et al. 1971), the *theory of graphs* (Diestel 2006) and *Operations Research* (OR) (Gass 1981) have given a solid support to researchers on telecommunications. Various studies in OR matured specialists' minds and led to '*Transportation Science*', the foremost journal in the field of transportation analysis. Unfortunately theorists concerned with the technologies of communication at a distance are not inclined to develop a general terminology; they do not love to harmonize the topics crossing various fields. Albrechtsen (1997) claims:

"A majority of so-called 'information scientists' are not really scholars/scientists but are people working with information technology or with practical problems without any ambition to formulate theoretical principles or seeking empirical justification for their decisions".

As a consequence of this narrow view, one may note in literature how:

- Writers do not present the open space as an extraordinary channel and give account – usually incomplete – of the various bandwidths for EM waves. Moreover the accounts on bandwidths are not uniform. Some non-technical books make channels more comprehensible by describing their relevant properties (Sebeok 1991).
- Authors usually present six graphs to depict networks: bus, star, ring, mesh, tree and hybrid, and a variable number of sub-graphs. But they do not relate each graph to a special problem of transportation and in addition the various accounts remarkably disagree.

- Commentators neglect the concept of operational control of nodes and for this reason they introduce the client/server model and the master/slave as occasional features of transmission protocols. For instance, the client/server mode emerges as a property of TCP/IP protocols in technical handbooks. The master/slave hierarchy is a secondary aspect of VSAM nets. Important features are mixed up with negligible particulars.

Significant principles on networking lie in the background and what is worst readers are not aided to see each solution as an answer to an operational problem. Insufficient studies on telecommunications lead to fuzzy definitions and to some mixtures between the analog and the digital parts that are included in an infrastructure. Readers labor to grasp the rational qualities of the infrastructures devised by digital engineers. The effects of current narrow studies become tangible when operators and managers attempt to compare pros and cons of different architectures. In the telecommunication world, understanding analog versus digital is not as easy as comparing one item to another.

These defects do not prevent authors from writing monumental books that dump tons of notions on systems used in transmitting messages electronically over a distance. Beyond any doubt those huge heaps of notions improve the skills of the readers in a way, but the exhaustive knowledge on networking is being delayed.

BIBLIOGRAPHY

AA.VV. (1961) - *Transportation Design Considerations* - National Academy of Sciences-NRC, Publication 841.

Albrechtsen H., Hjørland B. (1997) - Information Seeking and Knowledge Organisation: the Presentation of a New Book - *Knowledge Organisation*, 24.

Bonocore J. (2001) - *Commanding Communications: Navigating Emerging Trends in Telecommunications* - John Wiley and Sons.

Chowdhury D.D. (2000) - *High Speed LAN Technology Handbook* - Springer.

Cox D.R., Smith W.L. (1971) - *Queues* - CRC Press.

Deo N. (2004) - *Graph Theory with Applications to Engineering and Computer Science* - PHI Learning Pvt. Ltd.

Diestel R. (2006) - *Graph Theory* - Springer.

Gass S.I. (1981) - *Operations Research, Mathematics and Models* - AMS Press.

Griswold S. (1997) - *Corporate Intranet Development* - Premier Press.

Johnson E.J. (2001) - *The Complete Guide to Client/Server Computing* - Prentice Hall.

Sebeok T.A. (1991) - *A Sign is just a Sign* - Indiana University Press.

Salthe S. (2001) - *Summary of the Principles of Hierarchy Theory* - MIT Press.

Shafe L. (1995) - *Client/Server: A Manager's Guide* - Addison-Wesley.

Tanenbaum A.S. (1981) - *Computer Networks* - Prentice Hall PTR.

Chapter 6

STORAGE

Storage is the place where data is held in electromagnetic, printed or optical form for access. Archives are analog components from the perspective that the present book is developing and that is anchored on the idea that information has a body. This assumption entails the parallel between stores of data and stores of commodities. Designers of data organizations should follow logistic rules according to this hypothesis; they should optimize the operational features of storage.

1. Efficient Logistics

Logistics and warehousing improved rapidly during the Second World War and the subsequent decades. Practitioners learned to stock up accessories, materials, feedstock, liquid and other products according to precise and efficient criteria (Langfor 2006).

The progress of Logistics yielded three empirical principles for the design of storehouses.

1. First Principle

The structure of storage has to be *functional for users*. Experts mould the form of a warehouse that must offer efficient, friendly services to operators. E.g. a super-market tenders self-service goods that lie in low and open racks so that a consumer reaches out his hand and picks a product. E.g. a forecourt is designed in favor of cars ready to exit and to be sold. E.g. a reservoir holds water and distributes this water to surrounding area in the dry season through prearranged channels.

2. Second Principle

A modern store does not stock scattered and spread items, instead those items are kept inside special holders which have identical shape and size. *Modularity* is a basic feature for modern stores that normally consist of *store-units*. For example a plant seals the products into *pallets*. E.g. a harbor organization places commodities into *containers*. E.g. a library keeps books on *bookshelves*. Containers, pallets and bookshelves are familiar store-units.

3. Third Principle

The capabilities of a depot rely upon available space. Space may be small or large in the trivial sense that the depot can hold few or many items.

Space may be small or large even in the sense that *space develops in one, in two or in three directions*. The *dimensions* of the space allocated for storage heavily impacts the organization of the store, in that the dimensions facilitate or otherwise limit access to the store units. Items allocated in one-dimension space are accessible in a sole way, instead an agent is capable of accessing three-dimension storage along three directions. For example containers form a queue along the loading dock of a harbor. Docks are one-direction stores and one must cover all the dock to access the last container. E.g. bookshelves offer two-direction space to store books and one may move horizontally along a tier or otherwise vertically on the bookshelf.

2. DIGITAL MEMORIES

If we accept the parallel between storing data and storing goods, archives should be designed in accordance to criteria 1, 2 and 3 afore introduced.

There is a wide assortment of memories in a digital system and the complete examination goes beyond the scopes of the present book. I restrict attention to traditional mass storages serving structured programs notably written in Cobol, Basic, RPQ etc. This limit is not severe because structured programs make a very large segment in the modern software market.

1. Serviceability

Serviceability is intended to intimate that experts design an archive in relation to the services this archive must provide. Normally data storages serve algorithms – note how this books uses the terms *programs* and *algorithms* as synonyms even if these words have slightly diverging significance (Rapaport (2005)) – in fact computer archives involve software programs even when humans access stored data. An archive combines with programs and one deduces two possible employments; an archive should attend:

i) A predefined group of algorithms,
ii) A group of algorithms that cannot be foreseen.

That is to say a data organization serves a defined logic or otherwise serves unpredictable logic. Because of this pair of duties, one reasonably concludes that there should be two basic data organizations from the theoretical perspective.

Facts confirm this reasoning is true. Computer experts usually install the following archives that methodically correspond to the foregoing points:

i) Files,
ii) Databases.

Some writers hold that a database is *domain-independent* to underline the DB capability of supporting any logic; a file is said *domain-specific* due to its narrows objectives and contents (Sonenberg et al. 1988).

2. Modularity

The principle of modularity is intended to intimate that files and databases should be modular.

In fact every piece of information is contained in a portion of memory, called *data-field* just introduced in Chapter 4. A sequence of fields makes the *record* which is the store-unit of files; the *table* is the store-unit of databases.

3. Accessibility

Principle 3 indicates that the performances of storing depend on the available spatial dimensions. Media such as tapes and printouts have a linear form and the access is necessarily unidirectional. One has to start at the beginning and sequentially reads all the data until it gets to desired information. Instead optical disks and magnetic disks extend into two and three dimensions respectively. Their physical structure allows for the random access to information. Notably one goes directly to the desired track to access in a multi-dimension medium.

We briefly comment on the various decisions made to solve technical problems by digital experts.

3. FILES

We have assumed that the file is a collection of information allocated in favor of a specific group of programs, and thus it may be defined as such:

A data file adheres to a precise logic. [6.2]

Hereupon a file has the following properties.

A. Record Format

Suppose the file Y works for the defined family of algorithms y, experts conform to Principles 1 and 2 and fix the storage unit in accordance to the services required by y (Hanson 1982). Normally an algorithm moves a block of data in input and/or in output, thus this block constitutes the store-unit of the file called *record*. Software analysts usually draw the *record format* which contains information accessed by the intended algorithms.

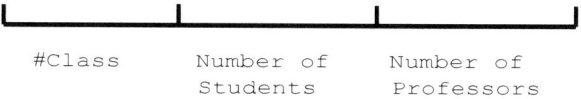

Figure 6.1. Record format of Classes.

E.g. a payroll program needs employees' details such as `Name`, `Surname`, `Address`, `Title`, `Seniority` and other qualifications necessary for salary computation, thus these fields make up the record of Employee Registry. E.g. a statistical survey computes the number of students and the number of professors per class, thus the output-file Classes includes #Class and the related numbers.

B. File Rigidity

Experts shape a file in accordance to the served algorithms and this direct relation entails that a file constitutes a rather rigid organization. The principle of serviceability throws this practical consequence: if the logic of the software algorithm varies, the record format must change, and the file is to be reinstalled. Notably the record and file do not evolve, but experts have to create a new file.

C. Files and Storage Media

A *mono-direction* storage medium hosts exclusively *sequential files* that allow only sequential access. *Non-sequential files* – called *direct* and *random* – are usually allocated on a 3-dimension physical support that allows for access from different spatial directions.

In short *multi-dimension storage media* enable any form of file, instead a sequential file can occupy only a *sequential medium*.

File Organization	Mono-dimension Medium	Multi-dimension Medium
Sequential	X	X
Direct	-	X
Indexed	-	X

Figure 6.2.

A sequential file may be stored even on a disk, but a record can only be retrieved sequentially, even though the medium potentially allows for direct access.

D. Non-Sequential Files

It seems necessary to add a few comments on non-sequential files which are less intuitive concepts than the sequential file (Roberts 1972).

One can access a record in *direct files* and *indexed files* thanks to the *record key* which labels all the data in each record. A computer program can read/write a specific record by means of the key of the intended record. To exemplify `#Class` guides the access to each record of Classes (Figure 6.1).

In practice specialists allocate formatted space on disk. Each section of this formatted space has an *address* (or a *displacement*). The location in this space is related to the record key, so that the record x with the key value k_x will be located in the section h_x. In this way the disc-driver can reach the record x at the displacement h_x using the key value k_x.

There are two principal methods to associate the key k_x and the address h_x. One can employ either a function or a table.

1. Direct Organization

With *Direct File* organization experts assign the relative displacement h in the medium based on a formula known as *hashing algorithm*. The *module functions* (or *division remainder functions*) constitute the most important class of *hashing functions*. For example the following function divides the record key k by the constant M, which may be any, and uses the reminder plus one to obtain the address h

$$h(k) = k \bmod M + 1 \tag{6.1}$$

The goal of a hash function is to uniformly disperse records in the accessible space. In particular experts must avoid *collisions* that occur when two keys have the same location in the medium. The keys k_a and k_b with the same address h are called *synonyms* and cause data overlapping.

2. Indexed Organization

An *Indexed File* includes a table that relates the generic record key k_x to the location h_x where the record x takes place. This table is just like the table of contents in a book where each topic has a page number. Each group of key-values has a pointer to the storage location where the group of records is stored. For example the table in Figure 6.3 points to key-records from 1 to 10 in track 3 of cylinder 1, records from 11 to 20 in track 5 of cylinder 3 etc.

10	Cyl 1 Track 3
20	Cyl 3 Track 5
30	Cyl 2 Track 7
40	Cyl 1 Track 4
...	... ...

Figure 6.3. Indexing records in an Indexed File.

When the indexed file is large, each entry in the primary table does not refer to a block of records, instead it points to a secondary table which in turn points to the records. *Primary* and *secondary indexes* accelerate the search for data in a very large indexed file.

3. Pros and Cons

Once established the algorithm (or group of compatible algorithms) to be served, the designers discuss the most effective file organization for the designated programs. Software analysts often evaluate pros and cons of each organization and select the appropriate file for the software program to install. Experts ponder the different features of the sequential file, of the direct file and the indexed file.

Processing a sequential file presents disadvantages because to access the specific record *x*, all records preceding *x* must first be processed. Suppose that a file contains 1 million records. On average 500,000 accesses are required to find a record in this sequential file. Instead if an indexed file has 1 million records and the index contains 1000 entries, it will take on average 500 accesses to find the key, followed by 500 accesses in the main file; in conclusion 1000 accesses in all: evident access saving.

It is even more demanding to update (add and/or delete records) a sequential file, since a computer program needs to rewrite the old file to obtain a new one that includes the desired modifications. On the other hand the sequential file is the most efficient form of organization when the entire file, or most of it, must be processed.

Software analysts consider other sides of the file organization besides the amount of processed records. They frequently weigh with thoroughness:

- *Data volatility* that is the frequency of adding and deleting records. As the volatility increases, indexed file organization becomes more suitable.
- *File activity* that is the percentage of records actually accessed during any one run. When the activity rate is around 60% or higher, namely 60% or more of the records in the file is accessed at any one time, sequential should be considered.
- *File query* involves speedy, real-time operations, for instance automatic teller machines launch fast transactions on files. When information must be retrieved very quickly, a form of direct organization should be used.
- *Data currency* may be told as timeliness of data. If data needs to be delivered up-to-the-minute, then direct file organization is counseled.

4. DATABASES

The record format includes a limited amount of information that comes out inadequate for those users who need versatile and exhaustive information in a variety of situations. It is evident how the narrow mission of a file dedicated to a specific logic is found wanting in many environments (Pyle 1999). The *relational data base* (DB) is the answer to the problems. In particular DB is the exhaustive collection of information accessible to any gender of operators, to present and to future software programs, thus we obtain the following definition:

A database is complete with contents and in keeping with differing and unpredictable algorithms. [6.3]

The adjective '*complete*' means that DB must be exhaustive, and the clause '*unpredictable algorithms*' implies that DB has a flexible structure. Definition [6.3] yields the following features that are necessary for a database.

1. Flexibility

DB responds to unpredictable logic and *is capable of serving a huge amount of software programs including unforeseen and future programs.*

When a computer operator seeks out a piece of news he moves without any rule inside the database and does not follow a predefined path. His inquiry does not have a predefined logic and one can conclude that DB fits with searching purposes. *The relational database is suitable for inquiries and for trying unforeseeable discoveries.*

2. Exhaustiveness

A database collects all the news regarding a precise matter. By way of illustration, a business installs Selling DB and Production DB; a school owns Classes DB; a geographic institute has Earthquakes DB. These collections include numerical and verbal information, along with photos, pictures, videos etc. A database holds all data of the DB owner and is exhaustive within the limits of the owner faculties.

Direct confrontation should enlighten the different capabilities of conveying information. For ease the file Customer Registry includes customers' details required to compute the invoices; instead the table Customer in a DB includes all the attributes of the customers in the hands of the company: Customer ID, Customer Name, Customer Address, City, Zip Code, list of Phone Numbers at which customer can be reached, and also Logo if customers are companies or Picture if they are individuals.

A. Structure of the Relational Database

The above commented features – flexibility and exhaustiveness – suggest the structure of the relational database in this way.

A database handles all the data related to a *predefined wide topic or subject matter* such as Selling, Production, Travels, Flights, and Earthquakes. Each subject matter includes a finite set of *subtopics* or *entities* or *subjects*.

To exemplify Selling covers the following subtopics in a business:

1. Company *customers*,
2. Customer purchase *orders*,
3. Company *products*,
4. Company *agents*.

A table collects all the attributes of each entity notably the tables constitute the store-units of a database in accordance to the principle of modularity. To exemplify Selling DB embraces the entities from 1 to 4 and contains the tables Orders, Products, Agents and Customers.

Each table refers to a special subject and provides a separate view thus the tables are to be linked in order to offer the entire illustration of the broad topic typical of the designated DB. Connected tables allow an operator (or a program) to obtain complete information, to pass from one subject to another subject and to conduct cross searches (McFadden et al 1988). For example the tables of Selling DB are connected as in Figure 6.4 and one can cross-refer columns and lines of various tables. E.g. an operator looks for the agents who have conducted best business, and relates Agents to Orders through Customers.

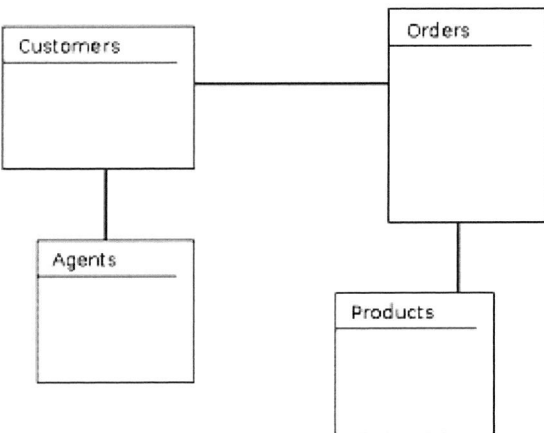

Figure 6.4. Entities and relationships in Selling DB.

The interconnected tables respond to the typical needs of users who want exhaustive information (Alagić 1986). The links enable the complete exploration of the database, which is driven without predefined restrictions.

B. DB Manipulation

The entity-relationship structure denies the flexibility discussed in previous Subsection 1 unless one can modify this structure. A static set of tables cannot serve whichever logic and one concludes that a database should be repeatedly modified through suitable operations.

This logical reasoning finds confirmation in the practice as a user or an algorithm can manipulate the database by means of special instructions and create new tables. An ever-new logic can identify new subjects and can take advantage from the renewed data source.

The operations to handle a DB are: *join, select, project, union, intersection* and *difference*. An agent obtains original tables through the above listed instructions for manipulation (Stephens et al 2000).

Dictionaries define the entry '*base*' as '*the premise or the starting point from which a reasoning process is begun*', namely the term '*base*' clarifies the pliable nature of DB whose initial structure will vary several times by time passing.

5. DESIGN OF DATA ORGANIZATIONS

The file organization derives from one or more algorithms on the theoretical plane, hence on the practical plane experts use a specific group of programs that provide all the details pertaining to the file to be designed. Analysts deduce the record format and all the other features the file must have from the assigned programs. The theoretical origin of a file summed up in [6.2] and the professional methods are fully consistent; both of them start with the programs **P** and go toward the result. It may be said that the design of a file turns out to be rather manageable.

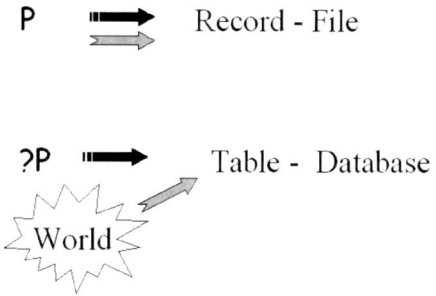

Figure 6.5.

Theoretical definition [6.3] holds that databases operate in favor of unpredictable logic, thus an analyst cannot derive the DB blueprint from algorithms because the algorithms to serve are undefined and analysts are forced to take another way: they get going from the experimental reality (Hoberman 2005). This method entails that DB design and the validation of the DB blueprint are somewhat demanding.

A. Entity Relationship Diagram

A relational DB holds information regarding a predefined wide topic – say **Selling** – and software analysts explore this wide topic in the world. They find out all the subjects pertaining to the intended topic in the physical reality – say **Customers, Agents, Products, Orders** – and place the subjects discovered in the world into the *Entity Relationship Diagram* (ERD) (Pin-Shan 1988).

Normally a noun labels one entity in ERD and a verb labels one relationship. Nouns and verbs combine sentences along the edges of ERD. To exemplify: '*customers place orders*'; '*agents call on customers*'. The sentences show the realism of the graph, and in such a way the DB designers check whether the diagram is in line with the physical reality.

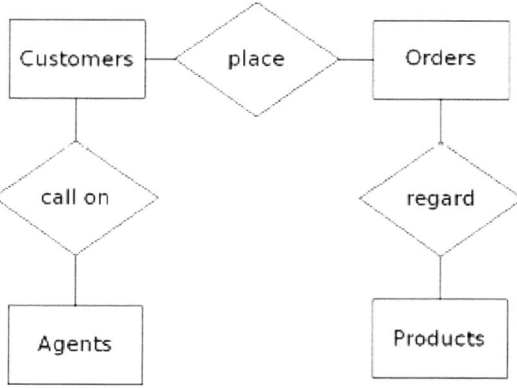

Figure 6.6. ERD of Selling DB.

B. Normalization

In the second stage experts fill the tables with attributes fitting the table label. For example they place all the data dealing with customers into the table **Customers**. Each attribute must be contained in the appropriate table, but database experts gather a wealth of information and risk placing a column inside a table whereas the column does not pertain to this table. Details may be assigned to an improper container. Misplaced information turns out to be hidden and thwarts inquiries. The whole database goes out of control if columns mismatch with the table label.

DB designers are called to check if each table has consistent contents, but this control is complicated. The problem of establishing the consistency of an attribute with the assigned table appears somewhat tricky, because judgments may depend on personal feelings, and two distinct experts easily provide two opposing answers about the location of a detail within the database.

In the seventies, Edgar Richard Cobb devised an objective procedure to confront the problem for sure. This method, popularized as *normalization* brought to an end questions which could not be scaled otherwise due to subjective interferences (Teorey 1999).

Functional dependency provides the logical basis to normalization and establishes that *all the attributes (or columns) of a table must be functionally dependent upon the table key*. That is to say each attribute must be *coherent* to the key of the table. 'Coherent' means that the *meanings of data* in each row must be pertinent to the key-value, thus the functional dependency may be also called *semantic dependency*.

A three-step rule puts into action the concept of functional or semantic dependency. Experts execute three subsequent validation actions of the DB design and at last release the correct version of the blueprint. In practice a designer checks out that each column value matches *bi-univocally* with the key value. Secondly each column value has to match with *the whole key value* and not only with a part of the key when the key is a compound word. Third, each value in a column must *directly* fit with the key value.

In the event that a column does not comply with any of the foregoing normalization rules, the column is removed from the table and placed in another pre-assigned table or an entirely new table. At the end of the normalization process, every table in the DB includes attributes whose meanings are absolutely coherent with the key and provides contents having logical precise relevance to the subject matter of that table.

Books

Book ID	Author	Book Title	Publisher	Year
001	Yudof John	Human Knowledge	J & K	1988
001	Yudof John	Human Knowledge	Momy	1990
001	Yudof John	Human Knowledge	Hartler	2000
Book ID	Author	Book Title	Publisher	Year
002	Berdahl Frank	The Prussian	Smith	1976
003	Cunning Bob	Daisies in Spring	Hartler	1964
003	Cunning Bob	Daisies in Spring	Waley	2003

As an example suppose the table **Books** includes the authors, the book titles, the publishers and publishing years. Book-ID is the table key which bi-univocally should determine each column value according to the first normalization rule. Each attribute must depend on Book-ID instead we find Book-ID=001 defines a precise author and title, but does not determine a precise publisher and publishing year. Also Book-ID=003 does not show bi-univocal functional dependence.

The pair of columns on the right does not pertain to **Books** because these columns violate the bi-univocal correspondence rule. One pulls these columns out of **Books** and makes the new table Editions.

Books

Book ID	Author	Book Title
001	Yudof John	Human Knowledge
002	Berdahl Frank	The Prussian
003	Cunning Bob	Daisies in Spring

Editions

Edition ID	Publisher	Year	Book ID
S-B	J & K	1988	001
A-A	Momy	1990	001
S-L	Hartler	2000	001
G-J	Smith	1976	002
G-G	Hartler	1964	003
R-U	Waley	2003	003

Note how the final contents of each table have significance strictly pertain to the labels '*books*' and '*editions*' respectively.

Normalization goes on in a systematic manner. The whole database gets corrected as long as each table contains data strictly related to the table-key and in turn to the table-name namely each table has attributes solely significant to table's subject (Codd 1985). The control of the DB design is complete and objective.

6. CONCLUDING REMARKS

The present chapter aims at pointing out how digital engineers conform to logistic and semantic principles. Designers employ operational criteria which have nothing to do with discretization, the Boolean algebra and other typical topics of the digital paradigm. Information is conveyed and stored through channels and memories which comply with criteria that in turn are followed by other transport and storage resources.

We have seen how each technical detail answers a special logistic problem, namely the decisions made by experts have been solicited by operational necessities and semantic status.

A. Annotations on Current Literature

Undoubtedly *Operational Research* (OR) (Keys 1991) stands as the most significant domain of studies that teaches people how to optimize stocks and warehouses. A noteworthy amount of inquiries on OR matured the minds of specialists upon storing (Carter et al. 2000).

The semantic properties of files and databases prove to play a central role. The present pages share the theoretical perspective grounded upon Semantics which was opened in the past decade and progressively emerged in the DB sector (Hull 1997).

On the other hand I cannot dodge quoting the majority of writers who deal with computer storage and prefer abstract tenets: tables are *arrays*, records are *vectors*, and the *relational algebra* works out the operations necessary to manipulate DB. The discussion on the data structures revolves around the properties of *abstract types*.

Abstraction dominates over the present field and commentators have no concern for relating the solutions to problems. By definition an abstract study detaches a problem from its physical root-causes, hence files and databases are not seen as resources answering special practical needs. Minute technical features are not justified from the down-to-earth perspective and hereupon software practitioners do not learn to use perfectly efficient methods. It may be said that software specialists strive to do their best because they are not fully aware of the significance of the various components pertaining to files and databases.

B. Future Expansion

Analog solutions, ineffective and weak in many respects, cannot be placed apart. The analog paradigm declines in certain areas – e.g. tools, circuits and systems – but faces great challenges in three areas discussed in the last three chapters respectively. The intervention of the analog paradigm cannot be replaced in the following strategic areas:

1. Transducers,
2. Channels,
3. Memories.

The success of the digital revolution is multifaceted; it results in the phasing-out of some analog applications and in the phasing-in of equipment 1, 2 and 3. The grand total is positive, in the sense that the expansion of converters, channels and storages appears astonishing.

For the future one may forecast two great challenges.

On one hand researchers will discover more cost-effective technologies with respect to current electronic equipment. We have seen bio-technologies and quantum-technologies at the horizon.

On the other hand scientists will find more effective units 1, 2 and 3. For the present *LCD* and *plasma screens* may be quoted as a new generation of components 1; *optical fibers* and *satellites for transmissions* for point 2; *integrated memories*, *digital versatile disc* (*DVD*) and *high-density magnetic disks* for 3.

The advance of circuits appears predefined, in the sense that new chips will be measured in terms of speed, miniaturization and costs. By contrast one cannot forecast what experts could invent in the analog areas 1, 2 and 3. Innovative transducers, channels and memories cannot be foreseen and new disclosures in this field are presently indiscernible. In spite of this ignorance we are sure that future discoveries will shoulder economies as they will form essential components of computer systems and ICT infrastructures.

The reader can see how the discussion upon what is analog and digital is not a matter as easy as comparing the adjectives 'artificial/natural' or 'discrete/continuous'. The scenario is richer in details and we shall further explore this argument.

BIBLIOGRAPHY

Alagić S. (1986) - *Relational Database Technology* - Springer.
Carter M.C., Price C.C. (2000) - *Operations Research: A Practical Introduction* - CRC Press.
Codd, E.F. (1985) - Is Your DBMS Really Relational? - *Computerworld*, Part 1: October 14; Part 2: October 21.
Hanson O. (1982) - *Design of Computer Data Files* - Computer Science Press.
Hoberman S. (2005) - *Data Modeling Made Simple: A Practical Guide for Business & Information Technology Professionals* - Technics Publications, LLC.
Hull R. (1997) - Managing Semantic Heterogeneity in Databases: A Theoretical Perspective - *Proc. Sixteenth Symposium on Principles of Database Systems*, pp. 51-61.
Keys P. (1991) - *Operational Research and Systems: The Systemic Nature of Operational Research* - Springer.
Langford J.W. (2006) - Logistics: Principles and Applications - McGraw-Hill Professional.
McFadden F.R., Hoffer J.A. (1988) - *Data Base Management* - Benjamin-Cummings Publishing Co.
Pin-Shan Chen P. (1988) - The Entity-Relationship Model: Toward a Unified View of Data - *Readings in Database Systems*, Morgan Kaufmann Publishers Inc, pp. 374-387.
Pyle D. (1999) - *Data Preparation for Data Mining* - Morgan Kaufmann.
Rapaport W.J. (2005) - Philosophy of Computer Science: An Introductory Course - *Teaching Philosophy*, 28(4), pp. 319-341.
Roberts D.C. (1972) - File Organization Techniques - in *Advances in Computers*, Alt F.L. (ed), Academic Press, vol 12, pp. 115-174.
Sonenberg E.A., Topor R.W. (1988) - On Domain Independent Disjunctive Database - *Proc. 2nd Intl. Conf. on Database Theory*, pp.281-291
Stephens R., Plew R. (2000) - *Database Design* - Sams Publishing.
Teorey T.J. (1999) - *Database Modeling & Design* - Morgan Kaufmann.

Chapter 7

EFFICIENT STRATEGY

The physical nature of signs has suggested a number of parallels with Logistics, Operational Research and Physics in the previous pages. Here the concept of signifier yields other intriguing inferences.

Goods face special risks when they are stored and moved. Products may be stolen by thefts; merchandise may waste after transportation and commodities may involve cumbersome volumes to hold. Because signifiers are concrete items one should deduce that messages, documents, news, notices, pictures and so forth encounter critical situations when they are archived and moved.

Let us seek elements to prove whether this reasoning is true.

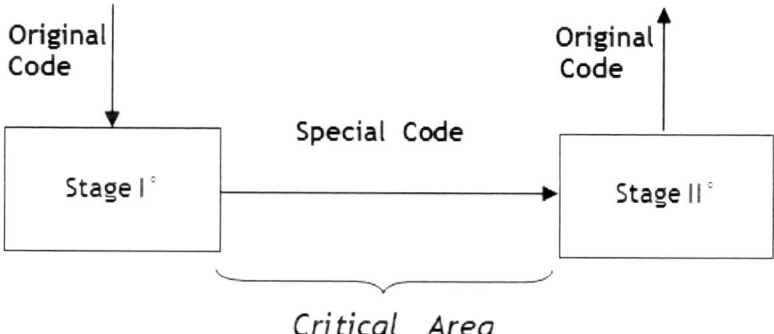

Figure 7.1. Protective setup.

Computer users and customers fear crucial hazards during transmission and storing and demand special assistance from technicians. As a matter of facts storing and telecommunications constitute two critical areas and experts attend to these areas in a special manner. They pay great attention to the problems of computer operators and investigate extensively three pressing questions:

1) How to reduce the volumes of data,
2) How to shelter data from theft,
3) How to make more robust data.

Digital experts implement special shields against the listed threats during critical events, in particular they compress data to overcome risks 1; they encipher texts and make redundant signals against 2 and 3 respectively.

It is interesting to note how digital experts implement distinct corrective measures but apply a sole strategy. All the defense systems work in the following manner: a special code takes the place of the regular code before possible crisis and risks, notably before storing and transmission. The initial pieces of information transmute and are restored at the end of the hazard range.

Hardware and software components apply these tactics using coupled algorithms: an algorithm runs in I° and a second algorithm, which restores the initial situation, runs in II°. For example an algorithm enciphers a text against menace 2 in I° and the deciphering algorithm gives back the transparent text in II°. This strategy operates just within the area of risk and is not invasive, its confined intervention proves to be inexpensive and does not cause collateral damage. Algorithms are implemented in hardware and/or in software according to pragmatic evaluations. The unique strategy in favor of targets 1, 2 and 3 brings further evidence of the style typical of digital experts who optimize the solutions to operational problems.

Several heterogeneous and creative measures embody the digital plan and I believe it is necessary to pinpoint a number of details to verify the foregoing scheme that involves points 1, 2 and 3.

1. COMPRESSION

Many computer users require large volumes for pictures, movies and songs, and the number of such applications constantly increases. Compression looks to be the best way for storing and transferring massive amount of data; compressed messages improve the effectiveness of operations and reduce costs.

In practice a compression algorithm converts the data to a smaller number of bits while preserving the information content in post I°. Data returns to the original volume for human uses in post II°.

The theoretical foundations of data compression were laid by Claude Shannon – see also (7.5) in this chapter – who established the minimum length for a set of messages (Hankerson et al. 2003). Theorists discovered significant algorithms for compression such as *Run-length coding, Dynamic Markov compression, Elias gamma coding, Discrete cosine transform, Lempel-Ziv (LZ) methods* and *Fractal compression*. These methods lie at the base of the major families of products for compression (Bell et al. 1990).

In the first period scientists designed *lossless* algorithms, in which all of the information in the original stream is preserved, and the stream of bits is recovered in a form identical to its initial form in the stage II°. Soon after scientists contrived *lossy* compression, in which some of the information in the original stream is lost, and decompression results in a data form slightly different from the original.

A. Lossless and Lossy Compressions

Lossless compression provides final outcomes that are identical to the input stream. This service turns out to be necessary for programming, for handling documents and technical parameters. Compressed files have usually zip, gzip, winzip or other formats which adopt the LZ methods, and may be reduced up to 50% of their original size.

Lossy algorithms do not restore information to its precise form in point II°. This technique is frequently used in reducing the size of audio and video files, where the slight differences in the original data and the data recovered after lossy compression may be imperceptible to the human eye and ear. For example, *Joint Photographic Experts Group* (JPEG) enables to compress pictures and graphics; *Motion Picture Experts Group* (MPEG) is used to compress video.

Lossy compressions work with a set of calculations which ranges from very simple equations to intricate mathematical functions (e.g. discrete cosine transform). Lossy techniques provide high reduction of space, e.g. 5:1, 6:1 or more and the operator can determine this ratio. For example when a user creates a jpg or converts an image from another format to a jpg, he is asked to specify the quality of image he wants. Since the highest quality results in the largest file, a user makes a trade-off between image quality and file size (Salomon 2004).

2. ENCRYPTION

Speaking at large, owners of goods protect their properties against the risk of theft and also owners of documents shield these special goods from thieves using normal measures such as safes and strongboxes. In addition information owners resort to the ensuing tactic exclusive to digital paradigm.

Suppose a confidential document printed on paper has an extraordinary economic value, by contrast this document has insignificant value from the physical viewpoint in that the signifier is a thin film of ink that has a negligible price. Thus the owner allows the document to be stolen provided that the content of the document has become unintelligible.

This trick stratagem can run thanks to the arbitrariness principle. In fact people communicate exclusively on the basis of a semantic convention, and if the owner of a document breaks this semantic agreement and establishes a new semantic rule, that document cannot be interpreted. In addition the new significance cannot be discovered by chance in the digital territory because of the potential monster-quantity of codewords produced by the exponential law.

The word *encryption* comes from the Greek term '*kryptos*', which means '*hidden*' and tells how this technique hides the content of news. The origins of cryptography date back to Julius Caesar, who created a system in which each character in his message was replaced by a character k positions ahead of it in the Latin alphabet.

```
ABCDEFGHILMNOPQRSTUVZ
 ↓           ↓ ↓   ↓
ABCDEFGHILMNOPQRSTUVZABC
```

ROME ⇒ URPH

Figure 7.2. Shifting encryption ($k = 3$).

For centuries cryptography protected military and diplomatic secrets (Budiansky 2002), (Kahn 1996).

The ability to securely transfer sensitive information has proved a critical factor in the Internet and cryptography has turned into a front-line of defense. Nowadays encryption is the most widely employed method for providing confidential data over an insecure medium (Whitfield 2007).

A. Secret-Key Encryption

In the living environment, the encryption process transforms intelligible plain texts into obscure ciphered texts in stage I° (Figure 7.1). If an unauthorized person detects the encrypted message, he/she cannot comprehend its content between I° and II°. After the critical interval, the receiver uses the inverse operation to recover the clear text from the cipher text. Only the intended recipient of the message can decrypt the message whose meaning is concealed to everybody else. This tactic is particularly important when multiple people have access to sensitive information. Encryption allows for secure communication channels and for secure stores when the underlying infrastructure is insecure.

There are several couples of algorithms for enciphering and deciphering in stages I° and II°. The most known techniques operate through a *keyword*, a secret parameter which impacts substantially on the enciphering process with the constraint that the same key must be used for decryption.

Data Encryption Standard (DES), devised in the early seventies, is one of the best-known methods to encipher documents using a secret key. DES has been superseded by the Advanced Encryption Standard (AES), using the Rijndael algorithm, which operates with 64-bit keys. Triple DES reinforces the operations of DES. It takes three 64-bit keys, for an overall key length of 192 bits. The procedure for encryption is exactly the same as regular DES, but it is repeated three times (Curtin 2005).

B. Public-Key Encryption

Generation, transmission and storage of private keys make consistent duties, because all the keys in a secret-key cryptosystem must remain hidden. Secret-key cryptography often has difficulty providing secure key management, especially in an open environment with a large number of users. The transmission of private keywords appears the weak spot in modern ICT infrastructures and scientists set up *public-key encryption systems* which overcome those difficulties.

Whitefield Diffie and Martin Hellman discovered the first algorithm to avoid the secret transmission of keys (Diffie et al. 1976). Ronald Rivest, Adi Shamir and Leonard Adleman contrived a more effective method in 1977. Their article *"A Method for Obtaining Digital Signatures and Public-Key Cryptosystems"* learns how to encipher a message using prime numbers. Prime numbers including hundreds of bits are special keywords that may be openly delivered (Rivest et al. 1978). Obviousley the public-key encryption stimulated mathematical inquiries on the prime numbers. Theorists investigate the largest prime numbers, their distribution and other possible properties in order to evaluate the reliability of public-key encryption systems.

Quantum cryptography is another valuable trend of research. The extraordinary property of quantum cryptography is the ability of the two communicating users to detect the presence of any third party trying to gain knowledge of the secret key.

3. REDUNDANCY

Redundancy is a powerful weapon in science and engineering, whose importance goes beyond the purposes summed up in point 3). Redundancy crosses different areas of theoretical and applied fields.

Logicians argue about the essential conditions to express a true sentence. I remind the *theory of redundancy* and the subsequent *deflationary theory of truth* that scrutinize the necessary contents to convey the truth by means of a sentence (Grupt et al. 1993).

One finds several definitions of redundancy in the technical domain.

➤ Claude Shannon (1949) verbally suggests the following definition of redundancy and provides the equations to reduce the redundancy of a data source to the minimum:

➤ "The ratio of the entropy of a source to the maximum value it could have while still restricted to the same symbols will be called its relative entropy. (…) One minus the relative entropy is the *redundancy*".

➤ We have seen how the most reliable net is a complete graph (Chapter 5, Paragraph 3). The ability of a network to maintain or restore an acceptable level of performance during a failure relies on *redundant connections*. A mesh has the possibility in responding to a knockout by means of the use of alternative routes within the network.

➤ In robotics the *kinematic redundancy* is defined as the ability of a device to imitate human sophisticated movements and is calculated by the Jacobian function.

➤ In *reliability theory* a machine becomes more robust by *the provision of multiple interchangeable components to perform a single function* in order to cope with failures and errors.

Technical definitions of redundancy seem to have nothing in common, but this suspect has no ground. Mathematical formulas appear incompatible at first glance instead they are consistent and may be treated using a unified approach which I began to illustrate in (Rocchi 2007). In the present book I mean to put forward a comprehensive way to address redundant applications in the information sector.

A. A Definition of Redundancy

Dictionaries suggest a good starting point. The term '*redundant*' stands for something '*abundant, plentiful, and more than required*'; and I am prone to deduce a mathematical expression from this verbal definition.

Suppose the system S is equipped with n *modules* (or *components*) that achieve m functions. Redundancy means abundance hence I find it reasonable to define the redundancy of S as the surplus of active modules with respect to the fulfilled duties

$$R = (n - m) \qquad (7.1)$$

If the system has just m components to bring forth m jobs – that is to say $n=m$ – than R equals zero and the system is not redundant. If the number of components exceeds the number of functions to execute – namely $n>m$ – the parameter R is positive and S is redundant. For example, a leg is sufficient to sustain a table. When carpenters make four legs, there are 4 units to perform one function and a common table is a redundant device

$$R = 4 - 1 = 3 > 0$$

In fact a table still stands if a leg breaks down.

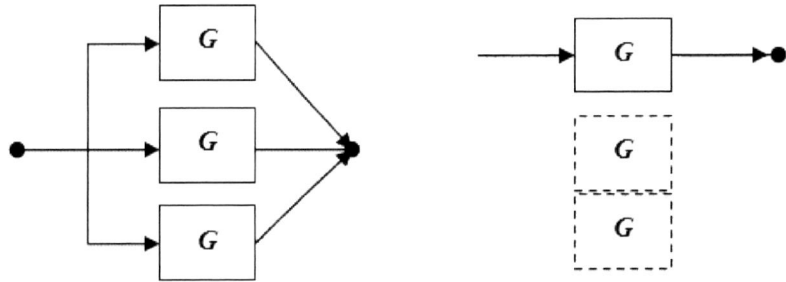

Figure 7.3. Active units and stand-by units.

A redundant system – namely $n>m$ – proves to be expensive since n contemporary running devices absorb more energy and resources than necessary. Engineers adopt stand-by devices that are cheaper than the devices working in parallel.

Suppose k modules execute a sole function, practitioners prompt one module while $(k-1)$ modules are idle and ready to start in case of failure. Reserve components are available but operate on-demand (Zio 2007). In conclusion designers arrange the system S with:

- *Active redundancy* when k modules are contemporary running,
- *Passive redundancy* when one module works and (k − 1) modules are ready to intervene in case the active module breaks down.

Figure 7.4.

B. Active Redundancy in Human Communication

The practical hypothesis assumed in the inception of this book allows us to draw a straight line connecting appliances and pieces of news. One can reasonably derive precise conclusions from the ensuing essential features of signifiers introduced in Chapter 1:

(1) *A signifier has a physical basis,*
(2) *A signifier stands for something.*

A signifier is a physical module due to property (1). Secondly one can infer from (2) that a signifier is an active element and does its own job. In particular signifiers are components specialized in executing semantic functions and operate like working machines, because they convey information. To exemplify **CHICAGO** is a physical item that represents a town in Illinois (USA). The four signifiers **CHICAGO CHICAGO CHICAGO CHICAGO** repeat the same job four times, and are similar to four devices running in parallel. The redundancy of the previous list including four identical nouns is

$$R = 4 - 1 = 3 > 0$$

The definition of R is useful to quantify the active redundancy of written texts and even of mixed expressions. A message including different signs that convey the same information makes a redundant system. For instance modern advertising is frequently based on presenting and representing a sole content under a variety of forms. Take the banner, the image and the final slogan that promote the sunglasses (Figure 7.4). In substance the manufacturer of sunglasses means to repeat three times the same message extolling the exceptional qualities of sunglasses and the advertising poster is redundant

$$R = 3 - 1 = 2 > 0$$

Generous levels of active redundancy are crucial to human communications, because of the numerous ways in which a message might be degraded: faulty transmission, lack of clarity in the text, lack of attention on the part of listeners, noise and so forth.

People are bombarded by advertising and marketing messages daily: on television and radio, by product placement in films, ads on the underground, posters in the streets, people handing out fliers, pop ups when we browse the Internet, junk mail sent to our homes and spam to our email, cards left under the windscreen wipers of our cars; it goes on and on. According to social surveys, we receive several thousand marketing messages every day which demonstrate how businessmen want to neutralize the problems emerging in human communications.

As doubled components in a machine are more reliable, so doubled signifiers increase the chance that their subject matter will be received correctly and reduce the possibilities that contents will be missed or misinterpreted. Repeated messages convey the same notice several times, and make a more dependable communication system.

Redundancy makes persuasion more effective, also distracted listeners or those who have difficulty understanding, grasp repeated notices. Doubled messages become intelligible despite the possibilities of misinterpretation; they increase mind retention when simultaneous presentations of multiple signals have the same significance.

Everyday private communication manifests redundant shapes. Even unschooled people choose repetitive messages as a conversational strategy to bolster their communicative effectiveness. They fill a discourse with repetitious signals and doubled sentences. In some instances redundancy is a reflex, an unaware habit.

Grammars generate active redundancies. A breadth of grammatical rules makes phrases redundant and in turn makes it easier to control a sentence. Take for example the following expression

"Where did you buy that car?"

Four signs denote the interrogative meaning in the sentence. As first it is signaled by the question-word **where**, by the addition verb **did**, and by the inversion of that auxiliary verb and its subject, and finally by the question mark. All of them together express the interrogative significance of the sentence. Four items convey the same information and redundancy is greater than zero

$$R = 4 - 1 = 3 > 0$$

As we speak or write, we are all carrying along a load of redundant elements without being aware of it (Hampe 2002).

C. Active Redundancy with Digits

Telecommunications and storages constitute critical areas, and data corruption has a variety of causes. For example the interruption of connection causes information loss between the transmitter and the receiver. Wire networks are susceptible to interference from the environment, for ease a thunderstorm can block the signal conveyance. Data may be lost during storage after a hardware or software failure, for example head crashes of a magnetic disk disrupt all the stored data in the disk.

Engineers scale to all those problems using a preventive measure. They make input messages redundant in the first stage (Figure 7.1), repeated pieces of news increase the probability that the receiver gets one correct message at least. The receiver recovers the normal form of messages in II°.

Duplicate messages increase the costs of exercise, they delay transmission and need large memories, and thus engineers accomplish moderate forms of redundancy in order to reduce this negative impact. Modern storage and especially telecommunication nets switch low-redundant data for sure communications. Experts tune up active redundancy at the minimum in point I°. The control located in point II° takes immediate corrective actions in case of errors.

Various researchers contributed to design minimal forms of redundancy from the fifties onward. Richard Hamming devised the first codes that allow the receiver to detect and even to correct errors without any retransmission. The *Bose-Chaudhuri-Hocquenghem (BCH) code* and the *Reed-Salomon code* further enhanced the effectiveness of transmission (Pohlmann 2005).

Low-redundant coding causes a light increase of volumes as a counterpart of data control. For instance a Hamming codeword is 11% to 38% longer than a minimal word. Technicians assess the risks and make a precise trade-off between the increased volumes and the improved reliability produced by the redundancy.

By way of illustration, suppose a transmitter does not double the number **17543** but adds two checksum digits located on the far right of this block: **1754320**. If the summation of the first five figures mismatches the number at the far right, the receiver detects an error. What are the measures for this moderate redundancy?

The above written block includes three signifiers that convey two values. The item **17543** represents the decimal value 17543; the item **20** means 20; last **17543** stands for 20 by means of calculus.

$$E_1 = \mathbf{17543} \quad \rightarrow \quad NE_1 = 17543$$
$$E_2 = \mathbf{20} \quad \rightarrow \quad NE_2 = 20$$
$$E_3 = (1+7+5+4+3) \quad \rightarrow \quad NE_2 = 20$$

The items E_2 and E_3 have identical significance and we obtain the following result

$$R = 2 - 1 = 1 > 0$$

The number **1754320** is two digits longer than the normal number **17543** and R increases the volume by 40%.

D. Passive Redundancy with Digits

The *passive redundancy* is an intriguing form of redundancy exclusive to the digital field. Passive redundancy overlaps and mixes with other forms of redundancy in several solutions, thus I mean to delve into this topic.

A coder uses the base B and the fixed length L, and obtains the grand total of the codewords at disposal

$$N = B^L \tag{7.2}$$

As a case, suppose a coder adopts the binary base. He has $N=2^2=4$ words in hand to which he assigns the following meanings

00	Pear
01	Apple
10	Peach
11	Cherry

These codewords work like four modules that are active at the same time. Now suppose another coder uses the previous codewords to mark the sex

00	Male
01	Female
10	-
11	-

The first pair of words is in use while the remnants stay apart.

As a matter of fact **10** or **11** is written in the place of **00** or **01** by error. The addressee recognizes that an error has occurred when he gets one of them, that is to say the signifier **10** or **11** says: "Error" (or something like) to the reader. The spare words **10** and **11** become active in the event of a fault and behave like stand-by units which run in the place of a regular unit. In other terms **10** and **11** act as reserve words that occasionally get out of the stand-by state and exhibit a message.

Suppose a coder does not employ all the N words at disposal. He assigns significance to m codewords – namely $N > m$ – and leaves aside the remaining words. Definition (7.1) leads to an easy conclusion: the same codewords left over by the coder make this solution redundant

$$R = (n - m) = (N - m) > 0 \tag{7.3}$$

Eqn. (7.3) is the cornerstone of the passive redundancy which although cannot be applied outside the digital territory. The passive redundancy of messages is exclusive to encoding.

Spare codewords spontaneously cause the passive redundancy that is frequently obtained without will. As an example suppose to codify the figures **0,1,2,...9** using bits. From the exponential law (7.2) one obtains the *minimal length* L_m necessary to codify ten figures

$$L_m = \log_B m = \log_2 10 = 3.32 \text{ bits}$$

It is impossible to use 3.32 bits because L_m is decimal and a coder must round L_m to four bits and constructs a code with 16 binary codewords. Ten words out of sixteen will symbolize **0,1,2,…9**, and the residual six words make this solution inevitably redundant.

Passive redundancy emerges in natural languages to a massive degree. Spoken and written alphabets produce a very abundant amount of words respect to the needs of a social group. In Chapter 2 we have seen how the written Latin alphabet generates:

- 26 monograms
- 676 bigrams
- 17,576 trigrams
- 456,976 quadrigrams.

But no modern language runs out of all of the available words. A natural language uses a small amount of the words at disposal and automatically the unused words cause heavy passive redundancy. When you read the following bigrams in English:

aa, bb, cc, dd, …, zz

You are instantly aware that an error occurred. The passive redundancy allows for spontaneous forms of control. People check an error when an unexploited string of letters emerges in a text. This natural redundancy, exclusive to the digital paradigm, casts further light on the force and effectiveness of the digital methodology that people sometime exploit without being wholly conscious.

One works out the minimal length necessary to encode m words using this expression derived from the exponential law

$$L_m = \log_B m \qquad (7.4)$$

However this equation overlooks the statistical distribution of codewords. Shannon (1949) perfects the calculation of L_m introducing the effects due to the statistical distribution of the signs and obtains the *optimal length* L_{mo} from the entropy

$$H = \sum_i^m 1/p_i \log(p_i) = L_{mo} \qquad (7.5)$$

The argument upon the consistency of (7.5) with the present logical framework goes beyond the scopes of the present book.

4. CONCLUDING REMARKS

Chapters from 4 to 7 illustrate six significant applications arranged by digital engineers in the working environment: the *architecture of systems, networking, storing, compression, encryption* and *redundant coding*. All the solutions show how digital experts never lose their typical rational style and in a way these solutions complete Chapters 2 and 3 which examine the digital paradigm from a static stance. Digital authors keep their principle-based approach when they work inside companies, factories and laboratories.

A. Annotations on Current Literature

Current literature expands on technical details which pertain to compressed files, encrypted data and redundant codes. Writers spell out several techniques but do not explain – to the best of my knowledge – how those different techniques have common roots and exhibit significant, unified properties. Only when one makes the various solutions into a unit, these solutions reveal the intelligent strategy of the digital designers.

Redundancy, adopted in many areas of engineering and research, proves to be a powerful and flexible weapon, however this topic sounds somewhat messy in literature in that each redundant solution appears unrelated to the others. Humanists and engineers often debate over topics which seem to be incongruent instead those topics are fully consistent.

Shannon's work dominates as the principal theoretical contribution in ICT but some facets of redundant information are unexplored such as passive redundancy which appears still confusing.

BIBLIOGRAPHY

Bell T.C., Cleary J.G., Witten I.H. (1990) - *Text Compression* - Prentice Hall.
Budiansky S. (2002) - *Battle of Wits: The Complete Story of Codebreaking in World War II* - Free Press.
Curtin M. (2005) - *Brute Force: Cracking the Data Encryption Standard* - Springer.
Diffie W., Hellman M.E. (1976) - New Directions in Cryptography - *IEEE Transactions on Information Theory*, 6, 644-654.
Grupt A., Belnap N. (1993) - *The Revision Theory of Truth* - MIT Press.
Hampe B. (2002) - *Superlative Verbs: A Corpus-based Study of Semantic Redundancy in English* - Gunter Narr Verlag.
Hankerson D.R., Harris G.A., Johnson P.D. (2003) - *Introduction to Information Theory and Data Compression* - CRC Press.
Kahn D. (1996) - *The Codebreakers: The Comprehensive History of Secret Communication from Ancient Times to the Internet* - Scribner Publisher.
Pohlmann K.C. (2005) - *Principles of Digital Audio* - McGraw Hill
Rivest R.L., Shamir A., Adleman L.M. (1978) - A Method for Obtaining Digital Signatures and Public-Key Cryptosystems - *Communications of the ACM*, 21(2),120-126.
Shannon C., Weaver W. (1949) - *The Mathematical Theory of Communication* - University Illinois Press.
Rocchi P. (2007) - Redundancy: A Measurement Crossing Cutting-Edge Technologies - in *Informatics in Control, Automation and Robotics,* J.Filipe, J.L.Ferrier, J.A.Cetto, M.Carvalho (eds.), vol 2, Springer, pp. 11-16.

Salomon D. (2004) - *Data Compression: The Complete Reference* - Springer.

Whitfield D. (2007) - *Privacy on the Line: The Politics of Wiretapping and Encryption* - MIT Press.

Zio E. (2007) - *An Introduction to the Basics of Reliability and Risk Analysis* - World Scientific Publishing Co.

Chapter 8

ADAPT FOR SURVIVAL

As a matter of fact digital computers have the property of being programmable. This class of machines cannot work without the support of a software program thus I am obliged to go ahead in my analysis. I must switch from the hardware to the software to conclude the present discussion on digital methods.

1. SOFTWARE PROGRAMMING

In the early thirties Alan Mathison Turing became involved with the *decidability problem* – in German *Entscheidungsproblem* – posted by Hilbert shortly before. The question concerned the existence, at least in principle, of a definite method or process by which all mathematical questions could be decided. Turing put forward an answer to the decidability problem introducing a conceptual system controlled by a work-program written through a suitable alphabet. In his article: "*On Computable Numbers, with an Application to the Entscheidungsproblem*" Turing imagines not a mechanical process, but a person who executes deterministic mechanical rules slavishly.

A. The Essential Feature of the Software Technology

Turing (1936) described an abstract method controlled by means of instructions and firmly established the basic lineaments of a programmable system. In particular from Turing's seminal paper it follows that a computing machine is guided by means of *a script which may be punched, written, or typeset*. Each operation is fully determined by a finite set of elementary instructions and I am inclined to fix the following statement:

A software program consists of symbols. [8.1]

This property is so strongly inherent to a computing machine that a system not controlled by symbolic instructions cannot be catalogued as a modern computer.

In the late nineteenth century calculators, tabulators, sorters and card punchers – expanding in companies, banks and institutes in those years – were controlled by panels whereby the operator selected the operations to be executed. The panel and the pluggable cables, very like a telephone switchboard, determined the operations achieved by those machines. Wired-switching was the early form of work-program for calculating machines that – as they did not involve the use of a script – were not classified as software-programmable computers by commentators (Swedin et al 2007).

Characters and symbols for control purposes mark the difference between calculating machines constructed in the pioneering years and classical computers. *Colossus*, built to decrypt the Nazi messages during the Second World War, provides an intriguing case. Colossus – installed in 1943 at Bletchley Park, London – ran intricate cross-correlation algorithms, but the specialists used a combination of telephone jack-plugs, cords and switches to set up this system. Colossus ran effectively and fast thanks to being switch-programmed, and this technique excludes that it was an authentic computer (Copeland 2006).

The first computer doer was Konrad Zuse who on May 12, 1941 presented the *Z3* to an audience of technicians in Berlin. Science historians agree that the model *Z3* – developed after the prototypes *Z1* and *Z2* – is the earliest real modern computer due to the control based on symbolic commands (Slater 1989). In particular Zuse utilized a recycled movie film to punch the work program for *Z3* and put in practice [8.1].

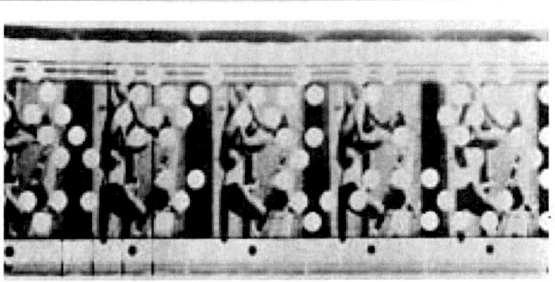

Figure 8.1. A piece of Zuse's program.
Punched on recycled motion picture film

Zuse's model used an external tape to store the software program, the *Small-Scale Experimental Machine*, even known as *Baby*, was the first computer to run a program stored in an electronic memory. Baby – designed and built at the University of Manchester, England – was a little and rather incomplete system that rolled as an experiment. The instruction set included less than ten operations.

The *Electronic Delay Storage Automatic Calculator* (EDSAC) was designed and completed by Maurice Wilkes at Cambridge University, England in 1949. EDSAC was over, two years before EDVAC thus EDSAC became the first stored-program computer in general use and not a prototype (Stern 1981).

By the way, the state of being first has a purely moral value for Europeans. English and German inventors did not make money with those machines as did their American more commercially oriented counterparts who produced brilliant economic successes.

B. Points of Question

Symbolic programs prove to be essential to digital systems, no matter if those programs are registered in a magnetic tape, punched in a strip, stored in a disc memory, or over another support. The indispensable support of software calls for the appeasement of the intellectual curiosity of readers who perhaps pose questions such as:

Why must digital systems be programmable?
Why does a work program consist of symbols?
Can we imagine another method beyond the software technology?

By bad luck modern thinkers and engineers do not pay much attention to the previous points of question. They are inclined to avoid inquiries on the root-causes of software programming. I have found generic convictions in literature which may be related in a few lines.

Logicians are inclined to assume a program as a collection of logical assertions that define the solution to a problem and thus software programming is an application of mind (Dohlen 1999). Programming is pure thinking in accordance to Turing's lesson and the above listed questions are rather nonsensical from the logical stance.

A circle of engineers and economists sees software programming from an empirical viewpoint. They are aware that the computer was born to automate calculus and to obtain results at cheaper conditions hence software programming appears the most effective tool to achieve computations. A computer system can be reconfigured to solve multiple problems, that is, to answer many different questions. A tremendous number of electronic circuits should execute an elaborate calculation unless software programming, which engages a unique set of physical circuits, reduces hardware resources dramatically. Software programs cut down the hardware components to the essential, and the software is a prerequisite for reasons of economy.

The economical benefits resulting from the software technology appear unquestionable but could not be completely convincing to establish the superiority of the software technology. One may object that also the panels and the pluggable cables adopted in ancient calculators repeatedly use a hardware circuit. The same may be said for the *firmware technology* which turns out to be cheaper than plugged networks. Instead the code written to the read-only memory is not so popular and experts go ahead with the software technology.

One reasonably imagines that significant facts give an edge to the software over the firmware. One suspects that a substantial advantage or necessity – which should be scrutinized – sustains the massive use of software programming.

2. ADAPTATION

Logicians follow Turing's thought who inquired over the essence of programming and drew a fascinating parallel between the computing machine and the human mind. The English mathematician anticipated many ideas now central to AI in the article: *"Computing Machinery and Intelligence"* (Turing 1950).

The idea that the essence of computing is tied to human intelligence and logic acquires non-trivial consensus in the scientific community. Literature talks over the intriguing relations between the mind and programming, and I agree with this perspective but am not inclined to assume these connections are linear. Because of the complexity of the nervous system I suspect the relationships tying biological and artificial systems cannot be direct. The argument in favor of the analogy between a computer and a human brain should include some stages and should take a long route.

In particular the concept of *adaptation* drew my attention long since and I assumed this concept as a trusty key to address the question points posited in the previous section.

A. Mechanisms for Adaptation

Charles Darwin introduced the earliest idea of *adaptation*. He came to understand that any population consists of individuals that are all slightly different from one another. Those individuals having a variation that gives them an advantage in staying alive long enough to successfully reproduce are the ones that pass on their traits more frequently to the next generation. Subsequently, their traits become more common and the population evolves. *Evolutionary adaptation* is the winning process by which favorable heritable traits become more common in successive generations of the population, and unfavorable heritable traits become less common. *Natural selection* results in adaptation during long arch of time as a consequence of increased fitness. Selection means evolution with gradual modification: describing how species arose from ancestors through a sequence of intermediate stages.

Besides the evolutionary adaptation, researchers have found an ample set of biological mechanisms that operate locally and adjust a living being to its habitat. Different organs bring forth *specialist adaptation* such as the hormonal system, the warm/cool adaptation, and the water regulation system.

Specialist adaptation does not cross generations and generally provides answers in a short while. For example, when a human moves to a higher altitude, respiration and physical exertion become a problem, but after spending a short time in high altitude conditions one acclimatizes to the pressure and no longer notices the change.

Least animals – including humans – have a third system of adaptation that is *based on the use of the neural system*. They determine the best conduct in the context by means of complex strategies and interfere with several aspects of life. *Intelligent adaptation* adjusts the behavior of an individual within the environment which elicits creative responses in an individual in order to survive. The mind generates decisions that solve specific problems like finding food, avoiding predators, making alliances, attracting mates, and raising cubs. Individuals – especially humans – differ from one another in their ability to adapt effectively to the environment, to learn from experience, to engage in various forms of reasoning, to overcome obstacles by taking thought (Ridley 1998).

B. Intelligence and Adaptation

Various thinkers have given many actual definitions of intelligence frequently far differing from one another, in fact defining intelligence is subjective, value laden and culturally relative.

In broad strokes there are two trends in the *theory of intelligence*: those who believe intelligence is a single ability and those who believe in many differing intelligences.

The first group ranges from the French psychologist Alfred Binet, to Charles Spearman (1904), and to his disciples Richard J. Herrnstein and Charles Murray. This psychology school proposes quantitative methods and contrived various *intelligence quotient* (IQ) tests. Spearman credits that all tests of intelligence have positive correlations, and calls *general intelligence factor* 'g' what is common to the scores of all the intelligence tests. IQ tests serve organizations and companies well but also raise objections; test-outcomes are precise but narrow, operationally neat but dangerously myopic.

The proponents of pluralist intelligence make a more ample group, however their theories do not seem to converge toward a uniform view. L. L. Thurstone posits seven vectors of the mind; J. P. Guilford discerns 150 factors of the intellect. Howard Gardner (1983) proposes a view based on seven relatively independent intelligences. Those intelligences are logical-mathematical, linguistic, musical, spatial, bodily-kinesthetic, interpersonal, and intrapersonal. John Horn has developed a theory of intelligence that specifies two basic factors, fluid abilities and crystallized abilities, along with numerous specific factors that support the general ones. Robert Sternberg's (1985) theory of intelligence has three components: analytic intelligence, creative intelligence, and practical intelligence. Undoubtley the various theories cast light on intelligence: a prismatic talent capable of managing varied and evolving contexts.

The pluralist schools do not exclude the possibility of unifying the different facets of the mental activities and the concept of *intelligent adaptation* progressively gains space.

The developmental psychologist Piaget emerges as one of the most profound advocates of this perspective. Piaget (1963) comes to believe that intelligence is a form of adaptation, wherein knowledge is constructed by each individual through the two complementary processes of *assimilation* and *accommodation*.

Assimilation and accommodation work like pendulum swings at advancing our understanding of the world and our competency in it. According to Piaget (1999), assimilation and accommodation are directed at a balance between the structure of the mind and the environment, at a certain congruency between the two. Piaget notes that there are periods where assimilation dominates, periods where accommodation dominates, and periods of relative equilibrium.

If one accepts the idea that intelligence essentially is the application of an adaptation process, he/she sums up all the strategies and tactics to live into the adaptive process, and concludes that intelligent adaptation is a multifaceted capability which includes the abilities of learning, speaking, abstract reasoning, problem solving, memorizing and decision making.

The interpretation of intelligence as adaptation is most popular amongst researchers in AI and systems. They focus on *adaptive systems* whose behavior changes according to the system's experience. An adaptive machine attempts to improve its performance in carrying out the tasks under the assumption that future experiences will be similar to past experiences.

The concept of adaptation casts light over the coupled tenets intelligence/efficiency which frequently overlap in engineering. Wang (2006) tells about this topic:

> "What is unintelligent?
> If everything is intelligent, then this concept is empty. If every computer system is intelligent, it is better to stay with the theory of computation. (…) According to the working definition of intelligence introduced previously, an unintelligent system is one that does not adapt to its environment. Especially in artificial systems, an unintelligent

system is one that is designed under the assumption that it only works on problems for which the system has sufficient knowledge and resources. An intelligent system is not always 'better' than an unintelligent system for practical purposes. (…) As Hofstadter said, for tasks like adding two numbers, a 'reliable but mindless' system is better than an 'intelligent but fallible' system".

The effectiveness of the intelligent adaptation process comes out as a critical feature to argue over. The problem is uneasy to tackle and I find that two disciplines offer significant aid. Zoology and Botany furnish intriguing clues to decipher the origins of the success which smiles on human intellect and even the origins of the tragic limits of the human brain. The direct confrontation between vegetal and animal species turns out to be very telling in my opinion.

C. Animals and Vegetables

Animals utilize complex substances – e.g. proteins and fats – that the digestive organs decompose to gain energy; instead vegetables synthesize elementary substances such as carbon dioxide and water so as to subsist.

Animals must take organic molecules from biological beings. Only living entities contain carbohydrates, proteins etc. hence they graze and hunt in order to feed. All beasts and men effectively act as serial killers which systematically slaughter other living beings. Also vegetarian species share this murderous lifestyle since they deprive grasses and plants of life.

Once an individual has eaten a living being to subsist, that individual has destroyed its source of life and must search for another prey and roams around of necessity. Mobility is the obligatory habit of animals which hereupon have to cope with random events and actors in order to stay alive. Think for example about the urgent needs to detect preys, to circumvent barriers encountered during a travel, to escape from a predator. The multifaceted fast-changing habitat determined by movement cannot be managed by means of the evolutionary and specialist adaptation processes just seen. Intelligent adaptation is indispensable to control endless, heterogeneous occurrences. The nervous system – typical of the animals, from the most elementary species up to Man – is responsible for this task.

Intelligent adaptation marks the animal lifestyle and especially the human way to existence. Hominids proved to be so inclined to exploit this distinctive capability that the brain increased in volume and this character became an inherited trait. The growth of the nervous system had a reciprocal influence with the size and movement of the body (Aiello et al 1990). The evolutionary package including upright walking, modified dentition, rich communication, ample experience, and sharper intelligence marked the progress of mankind (Bellman et al 1984). The combination of intelligent and evolutionary adaptations enhanced the mental functions of hominids who enlarged their dominions. The logic of this mutual enrichment may be seen in (Williams 1966) who gives the basis of modern evolutionary psychology

Animals are said to be *heterotrophic* since they need to dispose of an available food supply that they have to procure or to hunt. Vegetables are *autotrophic*: they do not search for nutrition but produce and get all that they need from the air and the soil on which they are located (Bell et al 2000). Vegetation acquires inorganic molecules from the air and soil – say calcium, carbon dioxide, nitrogen, oxygen (Webber 1947). Vegetables make use of materials that are abundant in Nature and that may be absorbed everywhere through the leaves and the roots, hence a plant does not need to walk and clings to a steady context. Vegetation has no concern with the fast-variable world, in the sense that it is enough for a plant to conform to the weather typical of each season. The specialist adaptation offers support to react to a dry period of time, to pruning and to other events and do not need to be aware of the context minute by minute. Plants do not move and intelligent adaptation turns out to be unnecessary for them. As a matter of facts vegetables do not possess the nervous system.

The direct comparison of vegetal and animal living beings shows how intelligence is the requisite to survive through changing relationships with the environment. The nervous system may be defined as the organ specialized in attacking the problems arising from mutable contexts.

D. Time Constraints

There are three kinds of adaptation: *evolutionary, specialist* and *intelligent adaptation*, and all of them operate within time limits. The first process carries on significant upgrades but spans over a series of generations and is somewhat tardy. The second adaptation process runs fast but is narrow in scopes. A biological feedback loop usually handles a special parameter and does not manage the entire life of an individual.

Adaptation	Scopes	Time-constraints
Evolutionary	Broad	Long
Specialist	Narrow	Short
Intelligent	Broad/Narrow	Severe

Table 8.1.

Intelligent adaptation pursues minute and broad scopes as well and may be called to manage even rapid-changing occurrences. Intelligence administers the life of an individual and decisions should be made in advance of deadlines determined by the events to control. Results must be produced within time limits that often are scarcely flexible: time is the supreme measure of intelligence.

Intelligence is usually assessed by the intelligence quotient, a score derived from one of several different standardized tests. Each IQ test must be assessed within precise temporal limits in that time constraints erect as the fundamental, severe boundaries for human intelligence.

The nervous system must make an individual suited to a special situation until the time limit expires. If the modification process is too late or comes to an end beyond the temporal line necessary for a man/woman to survive, the adaptation process does not work out the expected way. For example a doctor finds the correct cure for a patient and the disease is over. But the patient risks death when doctor's intervention delays.

Time can cause serious repercussions for operations. The temporal constraints are so demanding that intelligent adaptation is solicited to intervene in advance of an occurrence. Well-known modern strategies adopted by professionals working in various fields are called:

Anticipatory countermeasures,
Prevenient acts,
Proactive decisions,
Political deterrence,
Preventive medicine, etc.

Machiavelli (2003) emphasizes the need of timely countermeasures and suggests initiating change rather than reacting to events. A fine reference to proactive intervention may be found in "*The Prince*" where Machiavelli explains how a political leader must prevent conflicts that will spread over the nation if not dealt with early enough, and likens this strategy to a doctor's behavior:

"In the beginning the malady is easy to cure but difficult to detect, but in the course of time, not having been either recognized or treated in the beginning, it becomes easy to detect but difficult to cure. Thus it happens in affairs of state, for when the evils that arise have been foreseen (which it is only given to a wise man to see), they can be quickly redressed, but when, through not having been foreseen, they have been permitted to grow in a way that every one can see them. There is no longer a remedy."

Direct connections come out of intelligence, effective answers, information management and time limits. These topics inevitably should throw some consequences on the structure of digital equipment as we shall argue later.

E. Open Systems

In advance of any discussion on computing machines, we need the suitable terminology to cross various boundaries. The definitions provided by Ludwing von Bertalanffy (1950) and his school tend to unify the views on living systems and machines, and the tenets from the *general system theory* fits the needs. I quote a few tenets which are enough to go on in the present account.

1. Dynamical Open Systems

The *dynamical* or *operational system* OS is a set of working elements pursuing the same scope; say OS is a machine, a biological organism, or a work organization.

OS carries on its operations within *the environment* EV – e.g. the habitat, the markets, the political society, the scientific community, and national economies – which spontaneously evolves due to unpredictable reasons within itself.

By the way the same system OS can contribute to change EV, but this topic does not matter the present account.

Environmental modifications provoke consequences over OS which we assume to be an *open system*. The actions over OS are positive and negative as well and may reach a noteworthy degree of weight. Obstacles may be so insurmountable as to impede the survival of the operational system. On the other hand, the universe can offer brilliant chances and pushes OS to smart living. EV is able to press so that OS goes toward the end or otherwise springs toward the full success. Sometimes the compulsion is so evident that a single system dies or boosts while the competitors go on their way.

2. Shortcoming

An open system presents an evident heavy defect in the face of the random conduct of EV. By definition, OS is a pure operational compound and is incapable of perceiving its landscape. This severe shortcoming prevents OS from releasing all its latent capabilities and from proceeding to live in the new situation. The incapability of perceiving and handling information keeps OS from correcting itself in accordance to the surrounding trends.

The installation of the *information system* (IS) is the mandatory remedy to the shortage of OS and lastly one obtains the *general system* S equipped with two essential components. Suppose IS and OS are subsets in the set space, the following formal expression sums up the structure of the overall system

$$S = (OS \cup IS) \qquad (8.1)$$

The information system has the fundamental mission to adjust a dynamical system to the different circumstances by means of sharp strategies. *IS works as the agent of intelligent adaptation in favor of OS.*

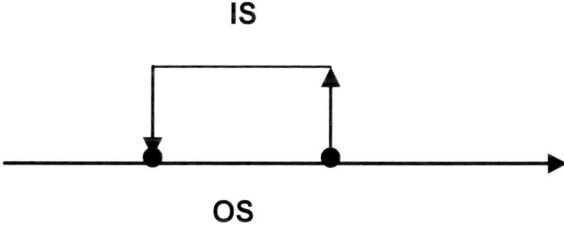

Figure 8.2. Feedback loop.

We find complex IS such as the nervous system that acts in favor of the survival of the single individual OS. At an intermediate degree of complexity one can place the accounting apparatus that sustains the sales and makes the company successful. Analog regulators offer the most straightforward examples of IS, such as the Watt regulator quoted in Chapter 3. Amongst modern simple solutions there is the thermo-regulator of common refrigerators, the carburetor float in a car, the gyrocompass in aircrafts, mechanical stabilizers for vehicles. Such devices guide the conduct of OS through linear procedures. The *feedback loop* and the *feed forward loop* are two classical patterns for those automatic devices.

Modern literature associates the *feedback loop* and the *feed forward loop* to Cybernetics and to the seminal book by Norbert Wiener (1961). The Greek name of the steersman inspired Wiener who coined the word '*cybernetics*' to denote "the entire field of control and communication theory, whether in the machine or in the animal". The emblematic image of the skipper summarizes topics such as: information, communication, adaptation, control, natural and artificial systems. The naval master of a ship or the helmsman is a vivid metaphor for *IS*.

The concept of *information system* infiltrated the circle of software engineers in the eighties and in the beginning was mostly related to clerical organizations that use computer systems. By time passing thinkers found out the multifaceted significance of *IS* which applies to a variety of contexts. Philosophical discussions upon this argument may be found in the article (Finkelstein 1998) and the essay (Hirschheim et al. 1995).

3. WORK ORGANIZATIONS

Controllers and regulators fall into the group of information systems because they manipulate quantities – such as temperature, luminance, or voltage – which are distinct and comply with the sharpness principle. Though analog regulators constitute the simplest information systems and sound as somewhat trivial cases.

The problems for fast adaptation become serious challenges in complex organizations thus I mean to draw attention to work organizations whose information systems are compounds that manage and fulfill complex duties. *IS* handles information the carriers of which can be personal, social or technical units. Intelligent adaptation emerges as a faint concept within automatic control appliances instead intelligent adaptation turns out to be a keen key to scrutinize huge systems.

In modern economies, common information systems are bureaucratic apparatuses and executive teams, statistical staffs and accounting offices, Web sites, libraries, research teams, schools, mass media and many others. An information system comprises one person, a single department or a large coordination where humans and equipment collaborate for the same purposes. From the present stance the whole scientific community may be seen as a unique global information system that assists a broad assortment of active organizations. Normally *IS* includes managers and employees, leaders and operational workers. Information systems exhibit uncountable forms and different structures within firms and institutions. *IS* assumes endless shapes to the extent that the full survey is unachievable so far.

A. The Brain of an Organization

Since prehistory men mobilize their physical abilities to achieve great outcomes. In the Stone Age people began to hunt together, to raise crops and to cooperate in other jobs. People pooled their muscle power together and the intelligence of their brains. The communications amongst hunters embodied the early information systems. Thenceforth the information systems escorted mankind during its eventful history and progressively took advantage from science and technology. In the start *IS* was exclusively based on manual operations – in the sense that will be discussed in Chapter 10 – lastly fully mechanized processes brought benefit to *IS*.

By definition an information system detects signals, stores news and provides counsel in order to adjust *OS* according to the circumstances, in such a way that the former compensates the deficiencies of the latter. An information system is *intelligence at work*, in fact it puts in practice the profound essential nature of intelligence seen in the previous pages. This fundamental property is more visible in human organizations than in simple self-controlled machines.

The concept that an information system is the '*brain of a company*' became popular since authors began to investigate organizations and the interactions within them and the context from the systemic/cybernetic perspective. Anthony Stafford Beer – the first to apply cybernetics to management – emerges among the world's most creative and profound thinkers on the subject of management. In 1971 Beer defined '*business management*' as the "science of effective organization" and developed an account of the firm based upon insights derived from the study of the human nervous system. He opened the way to interpret the behavior of the whole system through modeling the dynamical feedback process going on within it. Beer's *theory of viable systems* is an extension and accomplishment of his pioneering works (Beer 1981).

Banks, industries, trades, transport companies and other businesses have the vital, urgent and daily problem of coping with the environmental dynamics. These may be market trends, consumer fashions, government directives or renewed contracts with trade unions, scientific discoveries or competitor initiatives. Human organizations cannot escape the dominant influence of surrounding occurrences and *IS* provides vital relief to *S*. The brain of the company surveys novel events; it collects indications from several sources and provides guidelines to proceed successfully. An enormous amount of books and articles analyses and develops this argument; I restrict myself to quoting the fault-finding article by Charles Oppenheim (1997) and the fascinating book by Barnett (2008). I cite also Richard House (2009) who recently has highlighted how 'corporate evolution' has become a sort of modern 'management rhetoric' in current literature.

B. Precautionary Tactics

The mission of *IS* consists in guiding *OS*, and each information process closes with a decision which determines the appropriate line of conduct for *OS*. The essence of making decisions is recognizing patterns in vast amounts of data, sorting through choices and options, and responding quickly and accurately.

It was not until Jacob Marschak (1974) that a systematic account of the role of information in business was discussed. He approaches information systems and the concept of information itself from a decision theory perspective. This is very useful because an '*economic man*' is basically a decision maker, the full analysis of companies should consider the impact of information on decisions at every level. This perspective yields that information is an asset and better information leads to better determination (Kriebel et al. 1982). Right conclusions lead, in turn, to better use of resources, and to higher success (Casson 2001). The enormous number of articles and books in this field makes the survey of current literature rather tricky and outsized for the present book.

1. Crucial Decisions

Unhappily *decision making* is the climax and the crucial activity of *IS* at the same time. Nobody has the key to secure success as we have seen how intelligent adaptation does not guarantee benefits for sure. "Nothing is more difficult and more precious than to be able to make the right decision" – said Napoleon. Threats and lucky opportunities take ever-new forms, and no rule is valid for ever. Nobody owns the secrets for successful decision making and is capable of unraveling the conundrum in favor of the right conduct of *OS* for sure.

Successful decisions and effective lines of conduct are at hand when *IS* restricts its range of action or anyway focuses on a short section of *EV*. We have seen how regulators are always able to make the right decision every minute since they handle situations which are fully predictable. Decisions are handy for such limited information systems.

2. Gathering Information

Speaking at large, the mission of an information system is absolutely risky and presses people to search for an aid and to size up precautionary tactics. A common proactive measure for *IS* consists in gathering a large amount of information ahead of time. The more information decision makers own, the more they hope to be successful. Standard procedures pile up copious amounts of data in companies which in addition invest money to monitor the trends of prices, incomes, savings and credits along with many other business parameters that will likely assist managers or at least will facilitate their tasks.

Decision makers could find information rather useless when information has not the appropriate format, thus *IS* extracts significant correlations, it brings forth summaries, reports, simulations and so forth using information just collected. In particular *IS* tries to foresee future scenarios and to calculate the best countermeasures in advance so that decision makers are not caught off-guard. People esteem it is better to foresee a decision early than to improvise, in this way they temper short time deadlines.

Naturally all the gathered pieces of news are stored with care. Information systems tend to archive a high number of data even if a very small part will be accessed. Managers do not mind the efforts for this investment in that the assistance of an archived document may become vital. The huge amount of scientific publications stored in traditional and electronic repositories provides a telling case. Solely a minority of research reports sparks the interest of readers and an even lower percentage really impacts on life, however the potential effects of stored information are so influential as to make the investment worthwhile.

Files offer even other advantages. Stored information helps to surmount obstacles and even wards off dangers. Documents in archives avert possible attacks and intrigues. For instance, copied invoices are capable of deterring fraudulent attempts because they bring undeniable evidence in favor of the commercial operator in case of dispute.

In conclusion precautionary tactics significantly strengthen modern information systems. The tragic blemish of the information system whose services are unique and vital, and cannot be replaced, stimulate the reinforcement of the *IS* structure to enhance the probability of successful decisions.

C. The Growth of Information Systems

The amount of activities dealing with information has enormously increased in institutions and companies. For example, in the twenties a staff of nearly ten individuals managed a company producing mechanical items with 1,400 workers (authentic data in Italy). Nowadays, the staff leading a similar business doubles, in addition it has the support of dozens of computers and of external teams – e.g. trading associations, professional societies. Other cases are even more evident. Over 95% of a bank's activities are information based, a negligible minority of activities executes physical operations such as the transport of money. The rates nearly inverted in the past. In the Renaissance, a Florentine money-broker spent most of his time to open the shop, to place the counter, to arrange the coins, to verify those genuine, to put them in the safe etc. while data management was grounded on straightforward accounting operations.

In recent decades companies have stepped up the number of collaborators who fulfill information duties. Top managers and middle managers, employees, secretaries, accountants, file clerks, writers, programmers, analysts etc. make wide *IS*. Also workers, who in the past were exclusively devoted to manual operations, dedicate part of their time to data handling. It may be said that a modern information system infiltrates every corner inside a work organization (Blattberg 1994).

Information production is mounting to the extent that some information systems constitute autonomous business. I quote randomly: news media, education, public utilities, consulting, radio, television, and movies. Specific enterprises are devoted to the manipulation and the production of information with a high degree of specialization. These companies constitute the so called *service sector* or even the *tertiary sector* (Stonier 1983).

D. Humans and Machines

The human position is prominent inside an information system. People cannot be replaced in the decisional layers but show to be somewhat imprecise and unreliable in doing repetitive tasks. Men/women tend to work rather tardily and sometimes do not produce results on time. Inaccuracy, low performances, non-specialized tasks and clumsiness emerge as common shortcomings that have weighty impacts due to the principle of precision that regulates the mechanical and manual activities of *IS*. Speed and accuracy should be the distinguished qualities of those who are called to manipulate information.

In the beginning computers emerged as the best substitutes of humans for non-creative jobs. Computing machines were first employed as vicarious of employees; they performed humdrum tasks in less time than an unaided human could accomplish. Progressively computers conquered ever wider spaces. Managers are inclined to delegate a machine when the rules for decision-making are wholly foretold. At any moment managers are capable of revoking the delegation to computing machines and can keep the events under control. Flexibility and economical characters turn out to be valuable to the extent that computing machines fulfill a noteworthy amount of operations at every level in *IS* on the top, in the middle and at the lower levels.

Nowadays the digital paradigm plays an essential role. Digital devices assist companies, institutes or a single individual to survive current accidents or to grasp a chance in time.

Present challenges would be totally impossible to win by means of exclusive manual information handling. Digital systems have invaded all countries and have ushered in a worldwide movement.

E. Post-Industrial Revolution

Experts recognize how advanced economies have followed a developmental progression that took them from a heavy reliance on agriculture, toward the expansion of industry – e.g. automobiles, textiles, shipbuilding, steel, and mining – and finally toward a more service based structure. Computing machines have had such a broad impact on the planet that they have steered the course of history. Ample literature comments on the *post-industrial revolution*: the radical shifts originated by ICT (Bell 1976).

In history, the *industrial revolution* started around the eighteenth century with powerful production systems which evolved from artisan standard to industry. The first economy to follow this path in the modern world was the United Kingdom; other countries followed its example decades later.

In the course of decades industrial manufacturing revealed some defects, for ease sometime production proved to be cumbersome. Industrial plants overran and customers refused tons of useless products. Manufacturing lines turned out to be somewhat rigid and rather unbalanced with respect to the market demand. The post-industrial revolution has gone beyond this stage promoting intelligent planning. Flexible and light systems commeasure the production of goods to the market demands. Corporations learnt to respond to sudden and articulated orders coming from everywhere in the world. Companies contended for q*uantity* in the industrial revolution; nowadays they prefer to compete for *quality* and *promptness*. They operate just in time thanks to fast and precise input data that exclusively computer systems can handle.

The speed at which economies have made the transition to service-based ones has accelerated over time thanks to the substantial support of electronic devices that sustain this colossal expansion and act as lead actors in the present scenario (Landes 1969).

Post-industrial revolution is seen as the successor to industrial revolution, closely related concepts are *information revolution* and even *knowledge society*, *telematic society*, *information society* in which manufacturing and commercial life is critically dependent on information (Castells 1996). News has become the major product or anyway the essential component of any product, with recognition that an organization's success depends on the ability to exploit innovation and novelties (Grossman et al. 1991). In modern economies most people's wealth depends on the information flows. Individual and social welfare relies on computerized processes in a special manner; specific to this kind of society is the central position ICT has in production and business.

The human race has proved to be the most inclined species to take advantage from intelligence with respect to other animal species. The current post-industrial revolution sustained by computer systems appears as the most recent and astonishing application of human propensity for brightness. Men and women have always favored their own intellect since prehistory and nowadays they expand the ICT infrastructures as a support of their distinguished capability.

4. PROGRAMMABLE SYSTEMS

The above colossal phenomena cannot avoid affecting technology, and I mean to reach a number of conclusions relating to digital systems.

A. Two Stages, Two Technologies

The context has a random influence over *OS* and in turn has an influence on *IS* which assists and guides the organization. The unstable and unpredictable behavior of *EV* gives origin to the mutable operations of *IS*, and in turn to variable computing processes. An information system modifies its actions due to the incostant context *EV*. The restless and mutable pressures coming from the universe cause a computer to achieve jobs subjected to variation. It is evident how digital systems cannot cut themselves off from the invasive and variable dynamics of *EV* since these systems sustain a large part of *IS*. On the theoretical plane I am inclined to conclude that a just implemented computing machine is able to respond to today's problems correctly, but in a few days this machine will have to fulfill a new duty that is unforeseeable now.

It seems obvious in the present framework how a digital system cannot be initiated and completed in a single phase since nobody is able to assign the definitive jobs to the machine equipped with the peripherals and the central unit in the plant. The mutable context forbids the implementation of a computing machine according to the classical methods of construction. It seems reasonable that the design and the manufacture of computing machines begin inside the industrial warehouses of necessity but the artifacts cannot be brought to fruition. A second stage should refine the hardware appliance. A computing machine should be brought to finish in the face of the sudden events caused by *EV*.

The concept of intelligent adaptation leads me to define two engineering sectors that prepare the computer system in succession and in this way suggests a reply to the riddles expressed in the inception of the present chapter.

Figure 8.3. Punched program to control the Jacquard loom.

Common experience brings evidence that the present reasoning is correct.

Electronic manufacturers produce digital appliances which however are incapable of executing a precise job. Software practitioners assign a program of work to the hardware machine and make this machine able to operate. In other words the software technology completes the preparation of computer systems. Software specialists make the refinements of the appliances that hardware producers have released as incapable of working. The hardware and the software technologies intervene one after the other. *These technologies present far differing theoretical contents and methods of work but pursue a common goal.* The software together with the hardware enables a computer to carry on a precise job.

B. Efficient Stratagem

Two expert teams, specialized in different technologies, work in tandem even outside the computer sector. Several designers adopt the above described stratagem and sustain my previous inferential reasoning in various fields. Normally the manufacture, which serves unpredictable requirements, splits into two separate stages; both stages pursue the same duty but adopt disparate technologies. For ease, civil engineers design the structure of the skyscraper and supervise the raw building prepared with concrete, steel and glass. Later an interior designer refines the premises according to the owner's preferences. The first stage offers a generic product that cannot be used as is; instead the second stage suits the product to precise purposes. The profession of the interior architect resembles the programmers' activity, which perfects the hardware units.

A large class of machines cannot be entirely produced in factories since nobody knows what precise activity those machines will carry out in the future. For instance modern industrial production lines and advanced control equipment are programmable systems because they must modify their actions from time to time. Also ordinary devices – such as household appliances – are to be programmed when they are requested to fulfill variable duties. The washing machine offers a very familiar example.

Historians of Computing cite looms and pianolas as ancient predecessors of card driven devices (Koetsier 2001). Those musical instruments could not be finished in the factories due to the variety of entertainments they had to perform in favor of the spectators. Pianola-makers do not arrange leisure events, and a mechanical piano is necessarily supplied with punched cards to play the pieces of music selected by the organizers of each party.

Historians also quote the Frenchman Joseph Jacquard who invented specially punched bands to control the production of textiles in the early nineteenth century. This method was a prerequisite to allow for various levels of complexity in the patterns according to the fashions and clients' variable taste.

Textile looms, musical instruments, washing machines, industrial production lines *are required to deliver unpredictable and variable services*: this is the unique feature they have in common with computers. And the aphorism written by Shawn A. Bohner (1996) summarizes the present argument in a fair manner:

"Software is supposed to change - otherwise software functions would be implemented in hardware!"

The technical split – hardware and software – is caused by the random actions of *EV*. Conversely if *EV* steadies, the behavior of the digital system may be forecast and entirely determined in a manufactory; software programming proves to be non-essential in this event. Engineers implement all the functions in hardware. The present logical frame provides an answer around the emergence of the software and even around the absence of the software.

One may object that frequently a stable system is implemented in software. E.g. an embedded system has the control of traffic lights even if this control process follows fixed rules. This fact seems to disprove the present argument.

The answer is easy.

Frequently a programmed system is far cheaper than ad hoc hardware equipment. The market of microprocessors offers chips at low costs, and a programmer assigns the intended job to a microprocessor spending a reasonable amount of time. Experts adopt a programmable device because this device is more economical than a plugged solution.

C. Excellence of the Software

The random behavior of the universe entails that a digital system cannot be produced *en bloc*. Traditional methods of construction are unavailable and two subsequent stages of operations must intervene in order to complete a computer. The former begins the computing machine and the latter tunes up that machine by means of programming. Now we can argue over the last query in the initial paragraph:

Why do software programs instead of other programming techniques steer computers?

I put up the following reasoning.

An intelligent adaptation process must bring forth adequate answers in time. The operations must be terminated by precise deadlines. This undisputable premise entails that the technology accountable for the final setting up of computing machines should conform to present-day fast events. Sudden and light adjustment of the hardware devices is the severe prerequisite for program development and maintenance. Quick changes in the world suggest the use of signifiers for programming in that signifiers emerge as the most lightweight substance handled by humans and machines. Programmers should reconfigure a digital system at speed rate using signs.

Do the facts prove this reasoning?

A software program consists of a sequence of symbols that give an edge to the software with respect to programming technologies based on switches, buttons, pluggable circuits and other elements that require weighty muscular actions and complex operations. Past programmers who reworked a computing machine by means of mechanical instruments wasted a lot of time.

Software programmers handle signs, which constitute the lightest elements available for control purposes. A script is quickly written and rewritten, it may be erased and updated at ease. The edge of writing over hardware switching appears remarkable from the present practical perspective. The 'soft' manipulation of symbols is the fundamental feature of present-day programming which ensures superior services and higher performances.

Signifiers may be manipulated time and time again thanks to their lightweight essence and to speedy instruments. *Firmware* – a comparable technology – is grounded on the use of signifiers but a code registered in read-only memory (ROM) is ready after an industrial process that wants raw materials, the assistance of workers etc. Also programming processes of EPROM and flash EEPROM are comparatively slow, they do not permit full access to individual memory locations and thus are generally infrequent.

As a matter of facts, the agile way to rework digital systems is the best visible attribute of software programming with respect to concurrent methodologies.

Several analog computers were experienced from the fifties up to the seventies. Usually the performances of those electronic systems were higher than the performances of the corresponding digital systems. The response-time of the former was even 10^3 times faster than the latter. Alexander K. Dewdney (1984) provides a colorful discussion of the speedup that can be achieved through analog computation. However an analog system required weeks of work to be tuned up, instead a digital system was made ready to run using a few lines written in Fortran.

There was no alternative way to assign a job to an analog computer in that one cannot control a continuous system through a finite set of commands. Conversely a software programmer can arrange whatsoever plan of work using a finite list of instructions because digital computers are finite state machines. Engineers, who prepare an analog computer for a predefined job, make an intricate mesh of hardware components; this job is time consuming and limited in scope.

In conclusion experts deemed negligible the high speed of analog circuits with respect to the efficient services offered by a software program. Software technology conveyed substantial advantage in favor of the digital paradigm which won out over the analog paradigm in the working environment.

5. CONCLUDING REMARKS

The dynamical system *S* is capable of adapting itself and surviving with success thanks to the support of the information system which responds to positive and negative effects coming from various sources. The dependency of *IS* on the random behavior of *EV* implies that the functions achieved by a digital system vary over and over again and are to be programmed.

The software technology proves to be the nimblest and the lightest method to refine the hardware systems. In addition software programming results in economical advantages due to the reuse of the hardware circuits.

Software programming strengthens the theory-based profile typical of the digital paradigm. The rational behavior of digital designers emerges even in the software territory.

A. Annotations on Current Literature

The software technology casts further light on the intriguing similarity emerging between the human mind and the digital computer. The united study of hardware and software supports the ideas introduced by Alan Turing half a century ago.

Unluckily current literature tends to treat the hardware and the software technologies one apart from the other. This gap mirrors the tendency of theorists who work in narrow fields and do not spend much time to go beyond their own boundaries, and are not prone to investigate the relations between the hardware and the software. This idle attitude does not contribute to enhance our knowledge on Computing and even does not improve the methods of work. Partial views harm the practitioners in the field and places misconstruction in the living environment.

By way of illustration a significant case may be quoted.

All the software professionals – analysts, system engineers, data managers etc. – rarely take measures; they hardly ever gauge the software elements that they prepare or use. They appear somewhat reluctant to support their duties with numbers, even if most of them have a scientific-mathematical extraction. When they make a numerical estimate, this value is often rough or generic. Take for example the crude evaluations of storage, the average runtimes of programs. The slow advance of *software metrics*, still under scrutiny, reinforces the idea that measures play an ancillary role in the software environment (Kan 2003).

However even a layman is aware that engineers need measures and calculations to build up something and the allergic attitude of software experts seems undoubtedly paradoxical. Software specialists give the impression of working as extravagant engineers and raise more doubts about *software engineering*: a field which has not got satisfactory illustrations so far. A number of authors are skeptical about the real essence of software engineering. I quote the article by Fred Brooks (1987) which examines the said situation in the field.

The methods of software engineering go beyond the scopes of the present book, though an answer may be suggested for the paradoxical behavior of software specialists.

I help myself comparing two groups of professionals in order to offer a key to interpret the foregoing original facts. I mean to correlate hardware engineers to civil engineers on one hand, and software developers to interior designers on the other hand

Civil engineers – and electronic engineers too – use measures all day long. Civil engineers calculate the structure of a building; they work out the extension of floors, and several other particulars. In parallel hardware designers establish the characteristics of chips and devices on the basis of numeric values.

At the other hand interior designers customize the rooms for the purchasers and rarely calculate or measure physical quantities. When an interior architect serves his customer, he discusses the organization of the apartment, the forms of the details and the liveability of the environment, he selects the colors with care. In a similar manner a software analyst listens to customer requests and tailors a software application. The project is not grounded upon calculations since a software analyst deals with clients' will who focus on qualitative chooses and personal preferences especially in companies, businesses and institutions. The details can rarely be translated into numbers. This habit is particularly evident in the enterprise software sector due to the vivid interactions between customers and technicians.

In conclusion the infrequent measures achieved by software engineers are consistent with the role of those experts who refine hardware systems.

BIBLIOGRAPHY

Aiello L.C., Dean C. (1990) - *An Introduction to Human Evolutionary Anatomy* - Academic Press London.

Barnett W.P. (2008) - *The Red Queen among Organizations: How Competitiveness Evolves* - Princeton University Press.

Beer S. (1981) - *Brain of the Firm* - Wiley

Bell D. (1976) - *The Coming of Post-Industrial Society: A Venture in Social Forecasting* - Basic Books.

Bell P.R., Hemsley A.R. (2000) - *Green Plants: Their Origin and Diversity* - Cambridge University Press.

Bellman K.L., Goldberg L.J. (1984) - Common Origin of Linguistic and Movement Abilities - *American J. of Regulatory Integrative Comp Physiology,* 246 (6915-921), pp. 1-21.

Bertalanffy von L. (1950) - The Theory of Open Systems in Physics and Biology - *Science*, 111, pp. 23-29.

Blattberg R.C., Glazer R., Little J.D.C. (eds) (1994) - *The Marketing Information Revolution* - Harvard Business School Press.

Bohner A.S. (1996) - Impact Analysis in the Software Change Process: A Year 2000 Perspective - *Proc. Intl. Conf. on Software Maintenance*, pp. 42-51.

Brooks F.P. (1987) - No Silver Bullet: Essence and Accidents of Software Engineering - *Computer*, 20(4), pp. 10-19.

Casson M. (2001) - *Information and Organization: A New Perspective on the Theory of the Firm* - Oxford Univ. Press

Castells M. (1996) - *The Rise of the Network Society* - Blackwell Publishers.

Copeland B.J. (2006) - *Colossus: the Secrets of Bletchley Park's Codebreaking Computers* - Oxford University Press.

Dewdney A.K. (1984) - On the Spaghetti Computer and Other Analog Gadgets for Problem Solving - *Scientific American*, 250(6), pp.19-26.

Dohlen von R.F. (1999) - *An Introduction to the Logic of the Computing Sciences: A Contemporary Look at Symbolic Logic* - University Press of America.

Finkelstein L. (1998) - General Systems Theory: An introduction - *European Journal of Information Systems*, 7(1), pp. 75-75

Gardner H. (1983) - *Frames of Mind: The Theory of Multiple Intelligences* - Basic Books.

Grossman G.M., Helpman E. (1991) - *Innovation and Growth in the Global Economy* - MIT Press.

Goldstine H. (1972) - *The Computer from Pascal to von Neumann* - Princeton University Press.

Kan S.H. (2003) - *Metrics and Models in Software Quality Engineering* - Addison Wesley.

Koetsier T. (2001) - On the Prehistory of Programmable Machines: Musical Automata, Looms, Calculators - *Mechanism and Machine Theory,* 36, pp. 590-591.

Kriebel C.H., Moore J.H. (1982) - Economics and management information - *SIGMIS Database* , 14(1), pp. 30-40.

Hirschheim R., Kelin H.K., Lyytinen K. (1995) - *Information Systems Development and Data Modeling: Conceptual and Philosophical Foundations* - Cambridge University Press.

House R. (2009) - Change Agents and Systems Thinking: The Non-Revolution in Management Rhetoric - *Proc. Intl. Professional Communication Conference,* pp. 1-6.

Landes D. (1969) - *The Unbound Prometeus. Technological Change and Industrial Development in Western Europe from 1750 to the Present* - Cambridge University Press.

Machiavelli N. (2003) - *The Prince* - Dante University of America Press, p. 31.

Marschak J. (1974) - *Economic Information, Decision, and Prediction: Selected Essays* - Springer.

Oppenheim C. (1997) - Manager's Use and Handling of Information - *Intl. Journal of Information. Management,* 17(4), pp. 239-48.

Piaget J. (1963) - *Origins of Intelligence in Children* - Norton.

Piaget J. (1999) - *The Psychology of Intelligence* - Routledge

Pinker S. (1994) - *The Language Instinct* - Perennial

Ridley M. (1998) - *The Origins of Virtue: Human Instincts and the Evolution of Cooperation* - Penguin.

Slater R. (1989) - *Portraits in Silicon* - MIT Press.

Spearman C. (1904) - "General Intelligence" Objectively Determined and Measured - *American Journal of Psychology,* 15, pp. 201-293.

Stern N. (1981) - *From ENIAC to UNIVAC, An appraisal of the Eckert-Mauchly Computers* - Digital Press.

Sternberg R.J. (1985) - *Beyond IQ: A Triarchic Theory of Human Intelligence* - Cambridge University Press.

Stonier T. (1983) - *The Wealth of Information: A Profile of the Post-Industrial Economy* - Thames Methuen.

Swedin E.G., Ferro D.L (2007) - *Computers: The Life Story of a Technology* - Johns Hopkins University Press.

Turing A.M. (1936) - On Computable Numbers, with an Application to the Entscheidungsproblem - *Proc. of the London Math. Soc.,* ser. 2. vol. 42, pp. 230-265

Turing A.M. (1950) - Computing Machinery and Intelligence - *Mind,* 49(236), pp. 433–460.

Wang P. (2006) - *Rigid Flexibility: The Logic of Intelligence* - Springer.

Webber I.E. (1947) - *Anywhere in the World: The Story of Plant & Animal Adaptation* - W.R. Scott Inc.

Wiener N. (1961) - *Cybernetics or the Control and Communication in the Animal and the Machine* - 2nd edition, MIT Press and Wiley.

Williams G. (1966) - *Adaptation and Natural Selection* - Princeton University Press.

Chapter 9

THE GALAXY OF PROGRAMS

The information system *IS* works like an *organizational brain*, and has the fundamental mission to adjust the dynamical system to the different circumstances so that *S* can go toward full success. Computers constitute essential parts of the organizational brain and contribute to the intelligent adaptation of *S* with respect to the environment. The fundamental role played by computing machines results in significant consequences on the computer set up: a digital system cannot be built up and completed in a single step. Software experts bring to an end the device which electronic engineers have left incomplete in a previous stage.

This two-step approach is not universal. When a system puts under control a physical parameter or anyway handles situations predictable in a complete manner, this system – no matter if analog or digital – is implemented in hardware. Electronic engineers complete their artwork and do not need the support of software practitioners.

The connections of the software technology with the intelligent performances of *IS* are rather evident. It may be said that smart and sophisticated duties to fulfill require software, whereas trivial and static functions are implemented in hardware directly.

The present analysis perhaps sounds rough to the reader who may object that also a large number of software programs are not involved with mutable contexts.

It is necessary to go deep into this subject and to complement the argument.

1. VARIABLE INFLUENCE OF THE CONTEXT

I have assumed that *S* comprises the *operational system*, which manipulates a variety of objects along with the *information system* which exclusively manipulates information. I rewrite equation (8.1) that sums up the structure of the dynamical system *S*

$$S = (OS \cup IS) \tag{9.1}$$

However this statement appears rather generic on closer scrutiny.

A. Structure of Levels

The information system adapts OS to external changes so that the overall system becomes suitable to a new or special application or situation. IS coordinates the operations OS, and S is a structure of levels due to this hierarchical property

$$\frac{IS}{OS} \quad \begin{array}{l} level\ 1 \\ level\ 2 \end{array}$$

(9.2)

This structure tells that the operations of IS guide the operations of OS.

However subdivision (9.2) is rather rough and incomplete. Commentators – see the nice article by Thomas H. Hammond (1993) – show how the information system is subdivided into levels, where each upper level coordinates a lower level. Hierarchical relations join the sections $IS_1, IS_2, IS_3, \ldots IS_n$, and I expand (9.2) into the following structure of levels

$$\begin{array}{l} IS_1 \\ \hline IS_2 \\ \hline \ldots \\ \hline IS_n \\ \hline OS \end{array} \quad \begin{array}{l} level\ 1 \\ level\ 2 \\ \\ level\ n \\ level\ (n+1) \end{array}$$

(9.3)

This structure enables the accurate scrutiny of how things go.

Senior executives operate under the direct sway of EV, namely they are responsible for the management of the events which act on S. Managers and leaders make decisions and can but manipulate information in a creative way to cope with novel episodes.

The lower levels of IS follow the upper levels, and rarely contend directly with the external entities. When an external occurrence hits an agent at the bottom, he/she has the assistance of the upper levels. The screened influence enables people to follow procedures and to fulfill predefined duties. The hierarchical order spells out how the upper levels cope with the contextual entities, while the lower levels are less affected. It may be said that random and sudden occurrences pour from a height.

One finds computer programs at any of the layers $IS_1, IS_2, \ldots IS_n$, therefore the influence of EV should vary over the software programs running inside an organization. The structure of levels should show how the context results in a range of effects on the software products.

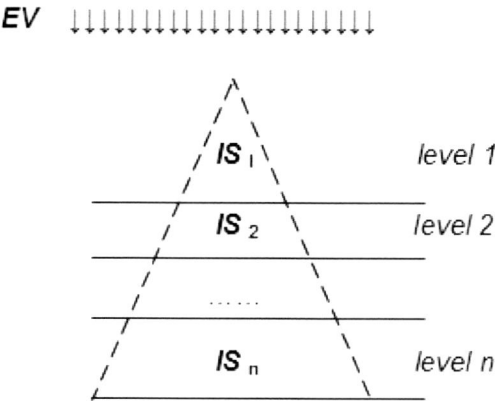

Figure 9.1. Decreasing contextual influence.

B. Multifold Effects

Let us see whether the conclusions in the previous section are true.

1. Predictability

As first one can classify environmental phenomena by predictability:

𝕬) *Foreseeable* occurrences are said the events which can be foretold and described in advance. E.g. the rocket's flight is normally calculated ahead of time.

𝔅) *Unforeseeable* occurrences are said those events which cannot be foretold. E.g. the sales in the next year cannot be calculated in any detail.

This pair of events impacts on *software development and maintenance* (SDM) in different manners.

Software programs influenced by foreseeable occurrences are rather easy to manage. Even if the algorithms are complex, programmers are capable of analyzing and scheduling all the operations for the computer system. Software updates amount to a small number since all programmable operations are known in advance of installation. To exemplify the launch of a satellite raises intricate problems but experts are able to scrutinize all the situations which are regulated by physical laws. The satellite's flight constitutes an advanced topic to be studied but can be completely analyzed thanks to the systematic researches conducted on space navigation during decades.

On the other hand there are environments which cannot be perfectly foreseen even after great efforts and inquiries. Experts become aware of the event 𝔅) day by day or even minute by minute, thus practitioners cannot arrange software development and maintenance at their ease. *Enterprise software* operates in this context because external events and actors turn out to be largely unpredictable. Nobody is able to forecast customer behavior, social conflicts, and political interventions for sure and the algorithms influenced by those events cannot be studied successfully. SDM challenges managers and technicians because of the blurring details or because the functions to be programmed become repeatedly altered. Sometimes the requirements of the software project are modified during the same implementation phases.

2. *Additional Circumstances*

Different circumstances aggravate SDM or conversely put SDM in a better state.

The structure of levels (9.3) implies that a group of algorithms are directly dictated by *EV* or by the upper levels of *IS*. I could say this family of software programs lies in the front-line with respect to the system context and can but have critical effects on SDM. For example the laws of a state determine the administrative fees and regulate the mechanized procedures in a direct way. Other computer programs are influenced by *EV* in a light, indirect way. Take for example the new version of a computer game. This version could enjoy consumers who have relatively little weight on the strategies of the computer game producers.

By definition intelligent adaptation has to intervene within the required time, and *S* must adjust itself with respect to *EV* before a certain deadline. When the adaptation process is too late and goes beyond the timelines, the countermeasures of *IS* prove to be useless and ineffective. It is evident how the time-limit is the supreme constraint for software practitioners. Short deadlines dramatically push over SDM, conversely when the temporal boundary is ample software management becomes more bearable.

Different levels of authority and economic obligations tune the reactions of software practitioners. For example when a top manager or a *golden customer* requests a software change, experts have to accomplish the requirements with great care. Instead when a lower level authority places the order or there are no penalties to pay, practitioners consider the work conditions in more flexible terms.

In conclusion eight major dichotomous paradigms affect software development and management:

- ✓ Predictability/unpredictability,
- ✓ Direct/indirect impact of the context,
- ✓ Short/long deadlines,
- ✓ High/low economic pressing.

2. SPECTRUM OF POSSIBILITIES

The surrounding context acts on software programming in different degrees of severity due to joined effects.

There are durable software packages at one extreme which refer to perfectly described events. It may happen that the actions accomplished by external entities are feeble, and/or the owner of the software program does not exercise tough control and/or there is time to carry out the software implementation.

On the other hand one finds software products influenced by unpredictable events which directly determine algorithms, the owner has a prominent position and/or time lines are short.

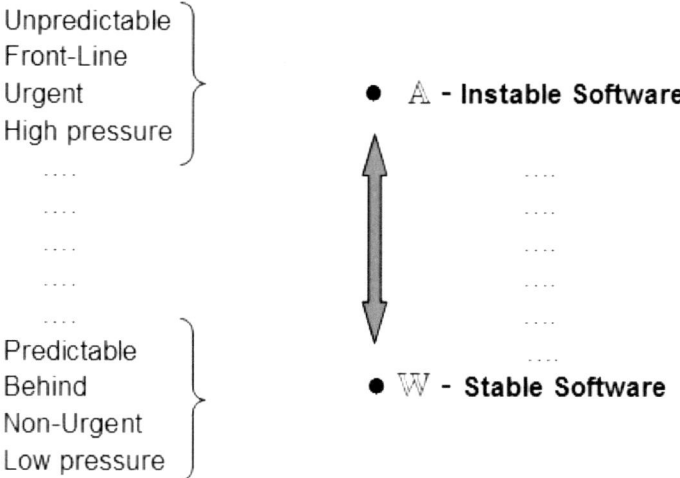

Figure 9.2. Distribution of software programs.

A. Genres of Programs

Three significant groups of software products spell out the continuous distribution from A to W.

Decisions made in businesses and institutions involve *enterprise software* and force it to be changed within strict deadlines. For example a government regulation or the provisions of a law determine the sudden design and implementation of a new *accounting program*. Other enterprise programs lie closely to the end-point A; I quote randomly *billing of merchandise, salary payment, bank account manager, invoicing of sales, preparing classes of students, scheduling courses*, and *statistical surveys*.

A group of programs has been written for the utility of computer users such as: *operating systems, compilers, editors, music players, compressors, programs for backup and restore*. Often these programs are named '*system programs*' to signify these programs are closer to the hardware than to the community needs. People also coined the name '*base programs*' to highlight the vital assistance which they offer to facilitate the use of the computer system. These appellations allude that real events exercise an influence over this group of programs too, but act in a light and rather indirect manner. Basically *system programs* provide essential services and optimize the performances of a computer system, and are not directly involved with the survival of the company day by day.

Dictionaries say that '*abstract*' is "*something potentially related to the world out there*". A large space separates an abstract computation from the world, and mathematical programs constitute the limit case at the point W. Everyday life has no concern with the logic of a mathematical function which is eternal and will never ever change. Researchers have discovered a set of algorithms that solve mathematical problems or problems treatable in abstract terms. These programs are resources at free disposal of scholars and professionals, and are not subjected to change. One finds *arithmetic algorithms, searching algorithms, sorting algorithms, selection algorithms, text algorithms* and many others in the ample account by Eric Grosse (1990), and also in (Sedgewick et al 1995), (Skiena 2008).

B. Flexible Cataloguing

There are no lines between the software programs in Figure 9.2. The spectrum from fast evolving programs to stable programs makes a continuous interval because the classification depends on random, physical interferences which do not create barriers between algorithms.

Professional experience brings evidence that the software products do not fall into fixed boxes and confirms the continuity established by the present framework. One cannot see a border between two different programs since the mix of external effects results in a continuous range. The three levels including business programs, base programs and mathematical programs are to be considered representative and not rigid in Figure 9.3.

A program is not classified by its subject matter but by the external influence acting on that program. For instance a business program can rank the bottom of the spectrum $\mathbb{A}$–$\mathbb{W}$ due to an exceptionally calm environment; and a mathematical package can be modified again and again due to the customers who want sophisticated visualization of the mathematical computation.

In addition a single software program can change place in between the range $\mathbb{A}$–$\mathbb{W}$ since a program may be influenced by a whirly context for a while and later on does not suffer any change. As a case I quote a program which experts repeatedly improve under the influence of test-runs executed by customers. By way of illustration consider a system to play chess. The rules of chess are completely defined and the software programmers can implement the first version of the software package Z. Skilful chess players provide novel suggestions and request changes to the product Z. Finally the software producer releases the version of Z that does not vary for a long while, namely the software program Z shifts from $\mathbb{A}$ toward $\mathbb{W}$.

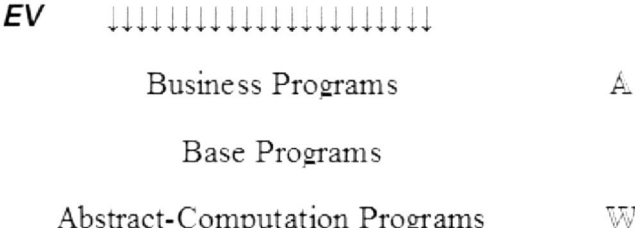

Figure 9.3. Decreasing contextual influence over software programs.

The sharp contrast between the properties of programs $\mathbb{A}$ and programs $\mathbb{W}$ yields conspicuous consequences on the professional practice.

C. Calm and Eventful Management

I have not enough space to scrutinize all the methodical details involved in the software development and management from $\mathbb{A}$ to $\mathbb{W}$. We can restrict our attention to the extremes for the sake of simplicity.

- Exact and accurate methods involve specialists dealing with the software projects that are not heavily pushed by *EV*. In principle managers are capable of scheduling the implementation of products $\mathbb{W}$ and allocating the resources sufficient to design good solutions. The requirements of the project are clear or anyway there is sufficient time to make them clear. Designers can excogitate brilliant ideas; they even have time to optimize the algorithms after the initial and provisional design. Software specialists take care of the project documentation which supports the subsequent rare changes, often scheduled. The software offering may be illustrated to the customers and have time to penetrate through the market.
- Feverish races against time involve software experts working with products $\mathbb{A}$. Unforeseen occurrences generate software updates which catch practitioners. External sudden evolution works strongly against effective and efficient SDM. Sometimes the owners of the software application express the requirements in generic terms, the software designers struggle to clarify what the customer really needs and does not specify due to hurry. Practitioners are forced to accept fast disposals because of short deadlines. Experts have to change direction even during the initial phases of SDM. Software specialists cannot waste time on massive script, and must adopt agile methods for documentation. After the delivery of the software product, the maintenance phase persists as a very heavy concern and interventions are fulfilled from time to time (Thayer et al. 1997).

Clashing differences emerge between the working environments which manage the software products $\mathbb{A}$ and $\mathbb{W}$. Objective difficulties spoil SDM, in particular developers of programs $\mathbb{A}$ have encountered several obstacles so far.

3. CONCLUDING REMARKS

The present chapter casts light on the complete spectrum of software products: from the most enduring algorithms to the fast evolving enterprise algorithms. The various programs advocate somewhat opposed strategies for the management of people and resources.

A. Annotations on Current Literature

The range of programs from $\mathbb{A}$ to $\mathbb{W}$ matches with the studies conducted by Meir Manny Lehman perhaps the most eminent author in the field. He formulated the *Laws of Software Evolution* together with his colleague Laszlo Belady (Lehman et al 2002). Lehman derived eight laws from experience obtained when working on the development of operating systems and other types of software packages. Lehman concludes his work with the description of three types of programs:

E-type programs mechanize human or societal activities, namely operate or address a problem or activity in the real world [**E** means '*embedded in the real world*'].

P-type programs make solutions to limited problems which cannot be described completely on a formal level. The problem is simplified and continuously improved [**P** stands '*for problem solving*'].

S-type programs address a problem with a computational solution in abstract and are rather close to the mathematical domain [**S** symbolizes '*specifiable*'].

It may be said that E-type programs rank the top within the spectrum $\mathbb{A}-\mathbb{W}$, S-type lies at the bottom and P-type takes an intermediate place.

The assortment of programs from $\mathbb{A}$ to $\mathbb{W}$ requires different techniques for software updating, and the present discussion consists with Bennet P. Lientz and E. Burton Swanson who in 1980 devised four categories of maintenance:

- *Corrective maintenance*: Reactive modification of a software product performed after delivery to correct discovered problems;
- *Adaptive maintenance*: Modification of a software product performed after delivery to keep a software product usable in a changed or changing environment;
- *Perfective maintenance*: Modification of a software product after delivery to improve performance or maintainability. These three groups of updates take place when there is a known requirement for change, by contrast next modifications are preventive;
- *Preventive maintenance*: Modification of a software product after delivery to detect and correct latent faults in the software product before defects become effective faults. (Lientz et al. 1979).

This catalogue was supplemented by many authors but the ISO/IEC International Standard has kept the basic four categories.

The three types of programs and the four categories of maintenance go far beyond the static interpretation of the software based on the abstract Turing model and advance the knowledge on software techniques. Lehman, Lientz, Swanson and other researchers who follow the empirical approach provide realistic views on the field. Recent contributions clarify software development and maintenance in tangible terms. Practical cases bring evidences that the static view of software programming is outdated, that the pioneer theories are surpassed in a way.

Pragmatic studies provide precious suggestions to software experts however they have not modified the culture in the field so far and have not eradicated the problems arising in the working environment that are worth examining.

B. Abstract Culture

Clear surveys exhibit disruptions of services in business software development and maintenance. Researchers provide deep insights into this wide phenomenon with documentary evidence (Flowers 1996), (Hatton 1997). The articles by Robert Glass who commented on computer calamities in *Communications of the ACM* and in *IEEE Software* for years are illuminating. Glass has recounted many episodes and probably stages as the best publicist of these modern disasters that harm companies and institutes so far (Glass et al. 1998).

Flops take a large variety of forms, they arise from endless causes and provoke significant deficits. Fritz L. Bauer coined the term '*software crisis*' at the first NATO Software Engineering Conference held at Garmisch (Germany) in 1968. The multiform software crisis in companies may be summed up in the following terms (Gibbs 1994):

- ✓ Projects running over-budget,
- ✓ Projects running over-time,
- ✓ Software is inefficient and of low quality,
- ✓ Software often does not meet requirements,
- ✓ Projects are unmanageable and code difficult to maintain,
- ✓ Software is never delivered.

Economic losses have such an ample extension that a number of managers consider these failures out of control (Radice 2004).

The sad state of fast evolving programs appears stunning with respect to the healthy state of other software sectors. Mathematical programming seldom meets technical catastrophes during the software lifecycle. Important emergencies do not crop up during the development and the maintenance of scientific packages. Shortcomings – if they emerge – are dissimilar to the acute troubles encountered by enterprise software developers (Wilson 2002).

The gap emerging between the business programming sector and scientific programming appears rather paradoxical because the algorithms in the first area are less demanding. *Commercial mathematics* does not present problems as serious as the problems confronted in the scientific field. It seems that software programmers plain sail over knotty areas, they solve advanced problems, instead they wreck during the production and the maintenance of trivial algorithms. It seems as if a group of geniuses is operating on one hand, while a group of bunglers are operating on the other hand.

This astonishing and somewhat absurd gap emerges everywhere: in the South and in the North of the world, in Western countries and in emerging countries. I can but believe that a systematic error obstructs the way and a non-trivial knot rises up:

What are the origins of such curious professional performances?

Software experts of various areas attend different courses of specialization, although all education curricula stem from joint roots. Labor specialization requires learning appropriate topics, but the introduction to software programming is unique for all the students and adopts the same style world-wide.

All the schools introduce Computing through Logic and Mathematics in the five continents and this pair of disciplines provides the eyeglasses through which software specialists will view the pieces of work, the working methods and the technical questions all their life long. The culture of the software practitioners comes to light on the abstract plane and systematically resorts to abstract tenets. The idea that software technology assists a company to survive in a variable environment appears somewhat remote to students, and the pressing requirements arising in businesses and institutions overtake software practitioners who are compelled to search a remedy day by day. Extemporaneous corrections and temporary patches can but fall short of the expectations. Customers inevitably find wanting solutions.

The behavior of software specialists comes from the matters and the methods taught in the courses of Informatics that mirror the mathematical way of reasoning (ACM/IEEE-CS 2008) and this tuition brings about that a practitioner is better prepared for scientific software programming than for enterprise software programming. Managers, analysts and developers are familiar with the complexity of algorithms, with optimization techniques, with dynamic programming and with other advanced topics; whereas the daily evolving context *EV*, which dictates the shape of the software programs, has little to do with their cultural background. Practitioners obviously underestimate the consequences of the pressing dynamics that affect the software technology and frequently make mistakes.

Why do teachers introduce a static and partial view on software programming?

The answer is easy.

The vast majority of reference books on programming shares the static approach to computing inherited from the past and teachers can but follow this way. Authors overlook the sudden and unforeseeable actions that digital systems undergo from outside and determine the very existence of the software, hence partial interpretations of the software technology infiltrate courses, lessons, and instruction.

Since the invention of the computer, it has been accepted with little question that the theoretical foundations of Computer Science lie in abstract Logic and in Mathematics. The difficulties encountered by practitioners have been attributed to the inherent complexity of computation, which can only be overcome with disciplined methodology.

I am not sure this conclusion can orientate software technicians and managers toward the full professional success. Abstraction tends to keep practitioners unaware of the urging methods required in the eventful environment typical of programs $\mathbb{A}$. The mathematical culture induces people not to comprehend or to underestimate the efforts necessary to develop and to update fast evolving programs.

Sometimes subtle arguments lead software experts toward a rather deformed view of practical questions. For instance practitioners-to-be become acquainted with the *decidability of computing* – the famous problem posed by Hilbert and solved by Turing – and are unaware of the *predictability of computing* – see the criteria A and B – that dramatically affects software development and maintenance. The decidability and the predictability of computing are parallel questions since these questions deal with the possibility of defining an algorithm in a rigorous manner, but the former question is a problem of pure logic whereas the predictability of computing – discussed in the previous section – influences enterprise programmers in draconian terms.

I find a support for my analysis in the survey conducted by Timothy C. Lethbridge (2000) of the Ottawa University that exhibits the effects of current training on professional practice. He asked software developers and managers from around the world what they think about a number of educational topics. The replies concur that some widely taught topics – most of them mathematical – have little impact on an everyday job, while coverage of other topics – mostly technical – are insufficient and should be increased. The knowledge they were taught in their formal Computing education does not always match the knowledge they need to apply to their daily work. Lethbridge concludes:

"Mathematics, especially calculus, is extensively taught in computing programs. (...) On the other hand, relatively little mathematics turns out to be important for software engineers in practice and it tends to be forgotten. If we are to continue to teach the amount and type of mathematics [that we presently teach], we must justify it by other means than by saying it is important to a software developer's work: our data show that is normally not the case."

I am prone to believe that serious cultural shortcomings materialize in the mind of those who associate the program design to the solution of a mathematical problem and tend to see the software changes as incidents. They take the mathematical problem as the universal model for a software program; thus methodologies, recommendations and advices put forward to manage rapidly changing software have little effect on the present cultural confusion. I quote the recent *Agile Methods* for software documentation (Aguanno 2005) which do not succeed in bringing about expected advantages.

C. Exhaustive Studies

In a recent book Karl Fant (2007) holds how Mathematics and Computing pursue fundamentally different aims. He claims that the abstract foundations of Computer Science are a primary source of unnecessary complexity and mess. I partially share this severe judgment in the sense that mathematical concepts become a source of confusion because they are good but insufficient to assist experts. Commentators on software programming should integrate past theories dealing with static algorithms with appropriate formulations dealing with evolving algorithms. Students should apprehend the full spectrum which comprises programs from $\mathbb{A}$ to $\mathbb{W}$. The entire culture of software experts should advance with respect to the usual methods which work perfectly at the extreme $\mathbb{W}$ but are untrustworthy at $\mathbb{A}$.

The mathematician Turing anticipated the rigorous model of modern computers long before the systems were built up, his seminal lessons still remain as inalienable references. Logicians have invented most algorithms; they proved significant statements such as the *fixed point theorem* (Curry 1942), the *structured programming theorem* (Bohm et al. 1966). I should like to quote even abstract studies such as the *Banach-Mazur computability theory* (Mazur 1963) and the *fractals theory* (Mandelbrot 1982). Eminent theorists have enlightened the advance of software such as Edsger Wybe Dijkstra (1982) who may be quoted as an exemplary reference in the domain of *algorithm design*, *program design* and *distributed processing*.

Successful achievements obtained through abstraction are evident. I do not mean to discredit this solid approach to Computing but to show how this approach should be perfected with innovative theoretical contributions – such as the ideas put forward in these pages – capable of illustrating the properties of fast evolving programs.

In conclusions the digital paradigm shows evident qualities. The solutions derive from solid principles and the whole field emerges as a systematic, theory-based methodology. The principles form a logically consistent network of statements which clarify the principal technical solutions. Rational criteria govern the hardware technologies and the software technologies alike, and guide creators to contrive astonishing devices which have changed the history of the planet.

Faults, omissions and errors emerging in the zone 𝔸 of the software territory result in heavy losses but do not disclaim the qualities of the overall digital mode. In the close of preceding chapters I meant to comment on various intellectual difficulties and practice obstacles deriving from the abstract approach to Computing. The mathematical/logical interpretation of Computing undoubtedly has worked and is still working with success but is unable to serve the entire area of studies and applications. Researchers, students and practitioners should add pragmatic concepts to abstract concepts because the former can answer questions that the latter are unable to explain so far.

In my opinion another substantial reason should solicits researchers to investigate the digital and analog domain.

D. Strategies of Research

Alan Turing (1950) hoped that machines could compete with men in the intellectual field. His influential papers inaugurated an intriguing argument which has stirred up debates so far (Petrol 2008). Scientists, biologists, philosophers, engineers and logicians have broadly discussed the multidisciplinary quests over the intelligence exhibited by natural and artificial systems (Husbands et al. 2008). They reveal the rich network of cross-disciplinary contributions.

The essential features of human consciousness such as working memory, attention, self-reflection, language and so forth seem to be far away from convincing definitions. The human mind is an organ that opposes resistance to scientific and philosophical inquiries as far as now. The conclusions by John Holland (2002) seem shareable:

"Attempts to discover mechanisms that generate thought and consciousness have occupied humankind since the beginning of recorded history. Most psychologists now believe that consciousness is tied to the activity of neurons in the central nervous system, but we still know surprisingly little about the relation between consciousness and neural activity. Unraveling this relation has proved to be notoriously difficult, and I do not expect sudden 'solutions' in the next fifty years."

Anyway the route is not completely closed.

The Artificial Intelligence argument revolves around two major poles: the brain and the digital computer. Nature has given a brain to humans and neurologists do not have the brain's blueprint in hand, instead the schemes of computing machines are absolutely accessible. The system designed and built up by people is undoubtedly the most manageable side of the AI conundrum. If researchers want to apply an economical plan of work, the most efficient strategy should attack the problem from this side. The accurate scrutiny of computers should bring forth a number of positive consequences. Researchers could claim that half the job has been done once the principles of computers are put to light.

Thinkers could establish a solid point of reference and could clarify the architecture of the mind through similarities and dissimilarities. Physicians normally follow this way when they illustrate the body organs using a device as comparison term: the heart resembles a pump, the kidneys work like filters of liquids, veins and arteries are pipes and so forth. The term of comparison does not act as an artistic metaphor in sciences; it does not provide a vivid image but suggests the properties and the criteria to decipher the intended biological organ. Notably the compared device works as an essential element of knowledge which enhances the scientific progress.

One could believe that the potential benefits coming from a research on the principles of the analog and the digital technologies should have triggered a wealth of cultural initiatives. Scientists would have strained every nerve to define the general tenets that regulate computer systems.

Instead things did not take this course. Turing's lessons did not encourage researchers to dissect the computing machines and the related technologies. The discussion upon the digital/analog concepts did not meet with the favor of numerous thinkers and still nowadays the scientific community does not spend too much effort to address this argument and other similar topics. My annotations on current literature at the end of various chapters pinpoint a number of consequences which derive from the distracted conduct of theorists.

The fundamentals of the technologies that revolutionize the world do not appear as a challenging area of interest, and sometimes those who declare interest in basic topics on Computing, really pursue other scopes. For example the *Technical Committee on Foundations of Computer Science* of the *International Federation for Information Processing* (*IFIP*) states formally to unify the development of "frontiers, laws and limits of information processing". One perhaps imagines that this team inquires into some broad properties of Computing, instead this team focuses on *continuous algorithms, computational learning theory, cellular automata and machines, concurrency theory* and other themes narrower in scope with respect to its proclaimed purposes (Anonymous 2009).

An invention occurs after systematic investigations or it may even be involuntary. Sometimes a discovery comes about through a mistake. Take the case of Alexander Fleming, the Scottish bacteriologist who came upon penicillin by chance while working with a bacterial culture in 1928.

In the history of sciences one sees how scientists systematically search for the full understanding of each discovery regardless of the course pursued by inventors. The time elapsed before reaching the full knowledge of findings was ample in the past centuries; this period of time has been greatly shortened in modern times. Scholars often become fully aware of a breakthrough in a few years. It may be said that pragmatic discoveries and theoretical explanations walk arm in arm. For example in 1887 Albert Michelson and Edward Morley recognized that the speed of light is a physical constant using an interferometer. Albert Einstein provided the interpretation of this paradoxical result by his first paper on the relativity in 1905: only eighteen years after the Michelson-Morley experiment.

The case of digital technologies marks a noteworthy exception with respect to the common trends emerging in the scientific community and I am inclined to believe that computer scientists are strongly influenced by utilitarian fashions. Researchers are prone to judge each result by its usefulness in bringing about immediate tangible advantages. Economic utilitarianism stresses computer theorists who will even focus on a small trivial effect in the hope this effect brings profits.

Sometimes researchers doubt that a study covering an ample domain absorbs a lot of resources and does not bring forth return-of-investment for the long period of work. They are oriented to denying any convenient fall-out from the foundations of Computer Science.

But this negative impression admits some doubt.

As an example the present book discusses the principles of the digital and analog paradigms and in addition has highlighted the problems and the methods necessary for business software development and maintenance (Rocchi 2008a). Forms of redundancy ignored so far have been unearthed (Rocchi 2007). The validation of database design has been pointed out (Rocchi 2010). Deductive educational methods have been successfully experienced (Rocchi 2008b). Practical suggestions for the design of software programs have been proposed (Rocchi et al. 2003).

BIBLIOGRAPHY

ACM/IEEE-CS Joint Curriculum Task Force (2008) - *Computer Science Curriculum 2008* - ACM Press and IEEE CS Press.

Aguanno K. (2005) - *Managing Agile Projects* - Multi-Media Publications.

Anonymous (2009) - *Information Bulletin of IFIP* - 39, Springer.

Bohm C., Jacopini G. (1966) - Flow Diagrams, Turing Machines and Languages with Only Two Formation Rules - *Comm. of the ACM,* 9(5), pp. 366–371.

Curry H. (1942) - The Inconsistency of Certain Formal Logics - *J. of Symbolic Logic*, 7, pp. 115-117.

Dijkstra E.W. (1982) - *Selected Writings on Computing: A Personal Perspective* - Springer-Verlag Berlin and Heidelberg GmbH & Co.

Fant K.M. (2007) - *Computer Science Reconsidered: The Invocation Model of Process Expression* - Wiley Interscience.

Flowers S. (1996) - *Software Failure: Management Failure Amazing Stories and Cautionary Tales* - John Wiley & Sons.

Gibbs W.W. (1994) - Software's Chronic Crisis - *Scientific American*, 9, pp. 86-92.

Glass R.L., Vessey I. (1998) - Focusing on the Application Domain: Everyone Agrees It's Vital, But Who's Doing Anything About It? - *Proceedings of the Thirty-First Hawaii International Conference on System Sciences*, 3, pp.187-196.

Grosse E. (1990) - A Catalogue of Algorithms for Approximation - in J. Mason, M. Cox (eds) *Algorithms for Approximation II*, Chapman-Hall, pp. 479-514.

Hammond T.H. (1993) - Toward a General Theory of Hierarchy: Books, Bureaucrats, Basketball Tournaments, and the Administrative Structure of the Nation-State - *J. of Public Administration Research and Theory*, 3(1), pp.120-145.

Hatton L. (1997) - Software Failures, Follies and Fallacies - *IEE Review*, 43(2), pp. 49-52.

Holland J. (2002) - What is to Come and How to Predict It - in *The Next Fifty Years: science in the first half of the twenty-first century*, J. Brockman (ed). Vintage Books, pp. 170-182.

Husbands P., Holland O., Wheeler M. (eds.) (2008) - *The Mechanical Mind in History* - MIT Press.

Lehman M.M., Ramil J.F. (2002) - Software Evolution - in *Encyclopedia of Software Engineering*, Marciniak J. (ed.), Wiley.

Lethbridge T.C. (2000) - Priorities for the Education and Training of Software Engineers - *J. Systems and Software*, 53(1), pp. 53-71.

Lientz B.P., Swanson E.B. (1979) - Software Maintenance: A User/Management Tug-of-War - *Data Management*, 17(4).

Mandelbrot B.B. (1982) - *The Fractal Geometry of Nature* - W.H. Freeman and Company.

Mazur S. (1963) - Computable Analysis - Grzegorczyk A., Rasiowa H. (ed.) *Rozprawy Mat.*, 33, pp. 1-110.

Petrol C. (2008) - *The Annotated Turing: A Guided Tour Through Alan Turing's Historic Paper on Computability and the Turing Machine* - Wiley.

Radice R.A. (2004) - *High Quality Low Cost Software Inspections* - Paradoxicon Publishing.

Rocchi P., Haag A. (2003) - An Operational Approach to Program Design - *J. on Computers, Systems and Signals*, 4(2), pp. 3-10.

Rocchi P. (2007) - How 'Unused' Codewords Make a Redundant Code - *Proc. 45th ACM Southeast Conference*, pp. 407-412.

Rocchi P. (2008a) - Intelligent Adaptation and the Nature of the Software Changes - *Proc. 7th IEEE Intl. Conf. on Cognitive Informatics*, pp. 138-143.

Rocchi P. (2008b) - Lectures on CS Taught to Introduce Students with Different Background - *Proc. Informatics Education Europe III*, pp. 115-124.

Rocchi P. (2010) - A Method to Validate the Relational Database Design - in *Relational Databases and Open Source Software Developments*, J.R. Taylor (ed), Nova Science Publishers.

Sedgewick R., Flajolet P. (1995) - *An Introduction to the Analysis of Algorithms* - Addison-Wesley.

Skiena S.S. (2008) - *The Algorithm Design* - Springer.

Thayer R.H., Yourdon E. (1997) - *Software Engineering Project Management* - Wiley-IEEE Computer Society.

Turing A.M. (1950) - Computing Machinery and Intelligence - *Mind*, 49(236), pp. 433-460.

Wilson D.A. (2002) - *Managing Information: IT for Business Processes* - Butterworth-Heinemann.

Part 3

Chapter 10

PEOPLE LIKE TO COMMUNICATE

There is a large number of studies on the effects of Computing on culture and society. Thinkers argue over the galloping evolution of electronic technologies and voice their doubts. They question if appliances contribute not only to a higher standard of living but even to what life is worth living. They reflect on the contribution of sciences to the real happiness of mankind. Philosophers discuss the consequences of the technological wave and fear the menace of misconception and opposition appearing between Man and machines (Winner 1978), (Hughes 2005), (Herrera 2007), (Shneiderman 2002).

I have prevalently seen the analog and the digital paradigms in relation to appliances so far; probably I contributed to reinforce the controversy between Computing and social sciences.

In the closing of this book I mean to override those feelings of mistrust and add a few pages so as to carefully examine how the analog/digital modes interfered in the past and still interfere with human factors nowadays.

1. HUMAN WORK

Broadly speaking there are three possible ways of production: people create an item using exclusively their muscles; machines bring forth products through an automatic process; and thirdly a mixed approach consists of human actions and mechanical operations. In parallel there are three ways to follow in the information sector which I sum up in the ensuing manner:

- α) **Muscular Approach** – Body organs such as vocal cords and gestures offer the direct way to build up pieces of information. Professionals such as TV commentators and speakers make money thanks to the performances of their vocal organs. I call this approach to ICT '*muscular*', since this approach is symmetrical to the muscular work of blue collars.
- β) **Instrumental Approach** – People enjoy the support of special instruments and machines to prepare information: such as a typewriter or a telephone device. The present approach includes different elements: part manual and part mechanical and is placed in the intermediate position between points α and γ.

γ) **Mechanical Approach** – This way consists of the exclusive intervention of automatic machines. Electronic computers complete an entire cycle of work without any human aid. Systems provide sophisticated astonishing outcomes because computing machines handle minute items of information that turns out to be uneconomical when this job is executed by individuals.

The foregoing approaches – muscular, instrumental and mechanical – exhaust the interventions of people and machines in the information sector. The factual ways devoted to the construction of information rank levels of progressive complexity. The previous chapters focus preferably on γ), in the next pages I go into the points α) and β) more thoroughly.

2. POOR AND RICH LANGUAGES

Hominids inaugurated the Muscular Approach producing sounds and gestures in a very spontaneous way.

Vocal languages consist of acoustic waves. The disposition of the human limbs together with facial expressions, manual acts etc. make up the gestural language (Riggio et al 2005). Unfortunately we have no evidence of those languages in the Prehistoric Eras – tape-recorders were not invented alas! – but Charles Darwin offers a chance to the discussion.

A. Initial Grunts

The *theory on the origins of the species* holds that Man derives from anthropomorphic apes (Leakey 1994). And this hypothesis – accepted in various scientific environments– offers a support to argue on the earliest human communication. If we agree on the idea that apes are the ancient forefathers of humans, we reasonably deduce that the intermediate species between monkeys and men – located in the dawn of the Paleolithic era, say about two million years ago – exchanged sounds and gestures very similar to the signals taken on by chimps nowadays. It seems rather logical that our progenitors used to cry, to emit guttural sounds, to hop, to clap, to hoot, to beat their breast, to show their organs as a sexual appeal and so forth, in a manner very close to apes (King 1999).

Note how the single gesture is a non-trivial signifier and can deliver a profound message. For example a cry expresses pain, a twinge, or fury; a dance means joy, or happiness; the beaten breast signifies power, social position, aggression; facial expressions may communicate surprise, malevolence and other feelings. Pain, fury, joy etc. make consequential information for listeners but monkeys and humanoids do not describe the details of their feelings. Grunts and gesticulations do not refer thorough accounts. Primitive languages do not provide minute descriptions and for this reason one definitively says that the earliest languages of hominids were *poor*.

	Range of Variation (cm³)	Average Volume (cm³)
Chimpanzees	320-480	393
Gorillas	340-685	497
Australopithecines	450-750	576
Pre-Neanderthal men	1070-1280	1.175
Classic Neanderthal men	1300-1610	1.438
Modern Homo sapiens	1010-2000	(1.345)

Figure 10.1. Comparison of cranial capacities (Source: Washburn op.cit. p. 215).

Neither should one believe those signs were equivocal or fuzzy. Scientific observations – see for example the renowned inquiries of Dian Fossey within the mountain gorilla groups (Maple 1982) – bring evidence that an ape's message is clear and manifest to the listeners. I barely underline how primitive communication delivered by humanoids was non-analytical. Primitive languages imparted succinct information and did not provide details. Authors did not explicate the fibers of their soul, or any subtle reasoning (Corballis 2002).

Because primitive languages were not analytical one cannot say whether those languages complied with the digital or otherwise the analog paradigm. Crude forms do not allow for technical analysis and therefore I refrain from any conclusion.

B. Brain Evolution

Paleontologists agree that the human brain gradually increased its volume in the prehistory. The size of the cranium continued to rise in a punctuated evolutionary pattern. There apparently was a period of comparative stasis beginning around 1.8 million years ago but, by 800,000-600,000 years ago, human brain size began to grow very rapidly. This uprising trend continued until around 100,000 years ago or a bit earlier.

People needed a non-negligible amount of signals to express the progressively expanding thought process. Human intellect directed toward analytical communication, and the physiology of the vocal apparatus perfected to serve the mind appropriately (Lieberman 1988). Since the early twentieth century – see the pioneering works by Victor Ewings Negus (1949) – anthropologists are aware that some of the characteristics of the larynx reflect the adaptations that enhanced human speech. In fact apes have a larynx positioned high in the throat which enables them to breathe and to gulp down at the same time, yet limits the gamut of emitted sounds. Man has the unique characteristic of having the larynx in the lower position. For that reason it is impossible for him to breathe and gulp down at the same time without risking of stifle, but he can utter a larger gamut of sounds. The evolved vocal tract was able to create an ample gamut of sounds and humans proceeded from poor to rich vocal communication.

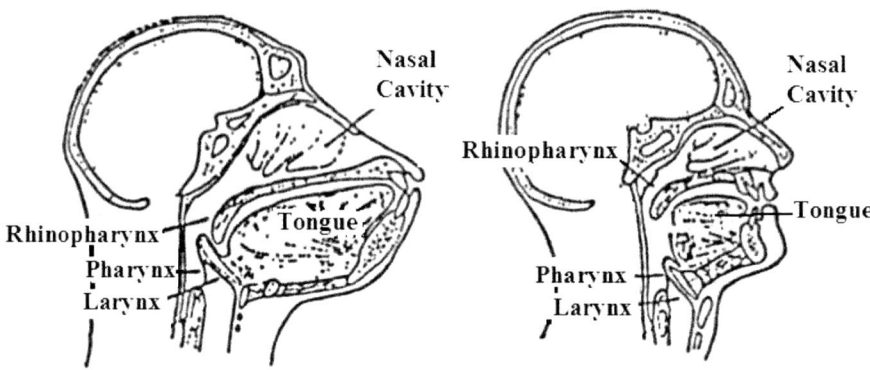

Figure 10.2. Comparison between vocal apparatus of chimpanzee and man. (Adapted from: Lieberman op. cit.)

C. Digital Emergence

People instinctively tend to imitate Nature and are strongly inclined to adopt a realistic style when they prepare a piece of information in order to be easily understood. The icon E reveals immediately the intended significance NE and this property gives an important edge to the analog approach.

Unfortunately a very small set of objects and events may be characterized by distinguished sounds. The vast majority of entities in the real world are mute or anyway do not have a distinctive sonorous mark. Hominids could describe a few items using onomatopoeic criteria and were forced to introduce the digital paradigm. The scarce number of sonorous entities to imitate pushed people toward digital methods of necessity. People were unconsciously driven to reduce the number of sonorous elements and to scramble those elements (Mac Whinney 1999). It was sufficient to combine a few sounds to make a lot of different words. Social groups migrated from the earliest guttural languages and from onomatopoeic-analog tongues toward digitalization.

Communication evolved toward an ample vocabulary of words through the digital revolution adopted beyond specific awareness. The exponential law is so powerful that even unschooled people sensed the solution to their communicative problems in the Stone Age. The possibility of expressing abundant contents was obtained by means of exchanging the order of sounds independent from whatsoever aesthetical relation with the reality. Digitalization supported humans in the preparation of words, phrases and discourses.

The independence of the digital signifier E from the signified NE conforms to abstract reasoning and hominids found it easy to pass from the representation of the object NE_X present in the world to the representation of the concept NE_Y related to NE_X but placed inside the mind. The digital symbols can signify abstract concepts in a perfect manner due to the principle of arbitrariness. Sophisticated spoken languages whose distinct trait is symbolism and massive intervention of the superior functions of the brain progressively sustained human relations.

Years	Period	Anthropological Evolution
3,000	Neolithic	
8,000	Mesolithic	
10,000	Upper Paleolithic	
40,000	Middle Paleolithic	
100,000	Lower Paleolithic	Homo Sapiens
		Homo Erectus
2,000,000		Homo Habilis

Figure 10.3. Subdivision of the Prehistoric Era (Years are out of scale).

3. NO WORRY FOR INFORMATION TECHNIQUES

Besides the Muscular Approach we bring attention to the Instrumental Approach which has abundant archeological evidences.

A. Lithic Industry

Anthropologists agree that Homo Habilis, living in the Lower Paleolithic over two millions years ago, had a craftsman's talent and began to shape pebble tools. Massive amounts of objects show the development of a stone-age lithic industry in the various continents (Mellars 1991)

No one can doubt the importance that pebble tools hold in the history of Mankind's development. They enabled the earliest humans to butcher animals for their meat. Vegetables, fruit, fish along with meat made for rich and varied nourishment which allowed humans to survive and to flourish to one day populate and dominate the earth (Seth 1993).

The lithic industry is characterized by crude cores from which splinters were removed with blows from a hammerstone. Both the flaked cores and the flakes themselves were employed as tools for a variety of tasks.

Materials in use were determined by available local stone types. Flint is most often associated with the deposits discovered in Western Europe; in Africa sedimentary and igneous rock such as mudstone and basalt were most widely worked.

Primitives progressively shaped more refined cobbles having effective cutting edges. Tool types found in the Paleolithic sites include cleavers, retouched flakes, scrapers, hand-axes, and segmental chopping tools. A hard hammerstone would first be used to rough out the shape of the tool from the stone by removing large flakes. These large flakes might be re-used to create tools. The tool maker would work around the circumference of the remaining stone core, removing smaller flakes alternately from each face.

It is rather evident how pebble culture required non-trivial skills in primitives.

B. Fine Arts

There is no evidence of the information technology during the Lower Paleolithic. Life did not remain easy for those people. Pressed by the survival struggle, hominids probably did not find time to apply themselves to ICT; they confined themselves to the use of the vocal and the gestural languages. The most ancient signs stretch back to the Middle Paleolithic around 100,000 years BC.

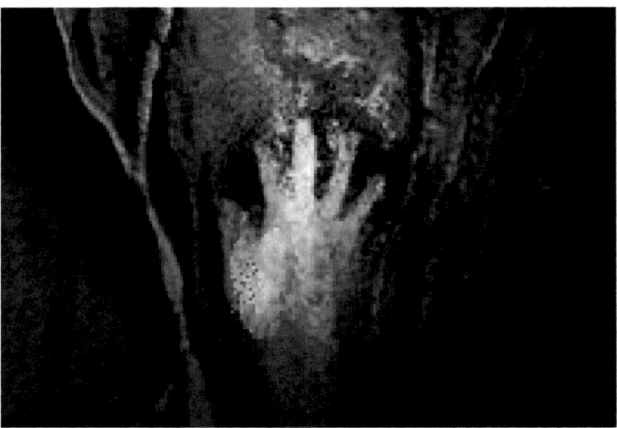

Figure 10.4. Handprint at Chauvet Cave (~ 32,000 years ago).

Whereas the lithic industry implied evident manual ability, selection of appropriate stones and hard work, the earliest evidence shows how information artifacts, rough and simple, were not gained by special study or skills. In fact the sharpness principle implies that a signifier does not require special materials and craft to become distinguishable. It was enough to score, to engrave or to smudge a surface to make signs at will. Hominids also exploited ready supports such as special unevenness in the stones to obtain a silhouette.

Hominids created figures all around: over transportable supports such as stones, bones and shells, and over fixed bases such as the cave walls.

Primitives found it very easy to connote a number or a thought as a linear scrap, a dark spot or a circle, and the symbolic communication was at hand. Anthropologists are convinced of the symbolic meaning of the earliest signs made by a cobble. Denise Schmandt-Besserat brings evidence as to how tally came in advance of writing. Abstract accounting tokens were introduced in Neolithic farming communities and those tokens show the presence of abstract numbering (Schmandt 1997).

Later on hominids joined coloring techniques to the lithic techniques.

Chemical analyses show how men found colors on the ground: ochre varying from yellow to red. Ferric oxide (limonite, haematite) provided the shades of brown; manganese dioxide and vegetal carbon were used as dark black; chalk made the white color. Most of those substances were ground up by means of two pieces of stone. Natural excipients such as resin, grease, fish-glue, and even blood gave cohesion and solidity to the pigments. Authors spread those pulps by means of their fingers. Some painted signs were obtained by footprints over clay or by the outline of a hand over a stone.

Figure 10.5. Graffiti at Lascaux Cave (~ 18,000 years ago).

Great difficulties emerged when people became concerned with rendering the link between carved-pictured signifiers and the events in the world transparent, namely when people migrated from the earliest techniques, which I am unable to catalogue, toward the analog paradigm. Homo sapiens began to reproduce the natural aspects of objects, animals and their environment, as they actually were as long ago as 30,000 years BC.

In a first period figures had a geometric, simplified aspect, sufficiently clear to identify the subject. In the closing period of the Paleolithic era humans depicted analytical images encompassing several subjects. Images have a spatial disposition and hint at the idea of movement. Graffiti tell a story or represent some types of events such as hunting scenes. Those art works show how anonymous authors became capable of developing pictures rich in details. They reproduced vivid particulars: animals, weapons and humans, and celebrated the glorious birth of the analog paradigm in ICT.

In conclusion the Muscular Approach evolved from the analog-onomatopoeic paradigm toward the digital. The Instrumental Approach took a diverging course: from rough signs toward the analog-iconic paradigm. Vocal and pictorial languages follow independent ways. But history did not come to an end and other episodes interfere with mankind's history.

4. ONE SIGN ONE SOUND

Volatility is the evident defect of a vocal tongue and the disappearance of sonorous information threatened ancient social relations and business. In the early Neolithic period people felt the need of storing information and strove to tackle the problem by using the pictorial language. Analog signifiers seemed suitable for the purpose of fixing volatile vocal communication.

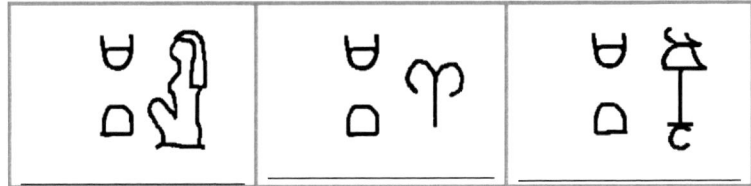

Figure 10.6. Ideograms of a woman, a cow and fine arts (Adapted from: Soravia op. cit.).

A. Ideograms and Letters

People supposed realistic graffiti were adequate to report events, persons and other items which in advance were exclusively described by means of the voice. People introduced *logograms* or *ideograms* between 8,000 and 3,000 years ago in the various areas of the world.

Ideograms appear rather close to the pictorial-analog approach (Liungman 1995). For example the Egyptian hieroglyphics in Figure 10.6 signify a woman, a cow and the arts, in fact the first ideogram exhibits a woman's silhouette at the right side, the second a cow horn, and the last an artistic object (Soravia 1976).

The earliest scripts look like graffiti or frescos but this impression is false: a single ideogram does not coincide with a realistic picture, but illustrates something standard. Each part belongs to a prearranged *set of graphical elements*. This means that ideograms were not joined together in accordance to esthetical rules but according to the modular combination of parts. An author obtained several messages by drawing together different ideograms or giving a different order to the same group of ideograms. An aggregation of ideograms complies with the exponential law and this means that ideograms do not make a realistic painting even if each one keeps an analogical shape. Ideograms are standard units which provide information through the encoding technique. In conclusion *ideographic writing is dualist: it is part analog and part digital.* A single ideogram is iconic and the overall script is digital.

Figure 10.7. Egyptian hieroglyphics over a stone.

However this approach approximately matches up with oral communication which was digital and writing progressed along three lines of development.

Early writers placed ideograms in open order. Sometimes they attempted to depict a realistic scene even if they used standard elements. By contrast vocal expressions flow through the time and constitute a linear process. This basic property of speech forced writers to place symbols in line. Words and texts began to take the form of strings. In various languages graphical symbols are threaded together and located horizontally from left to right as well as from right to left, or even vertically from top to bottom in columns. Writing complies with the linear order typical of speech regardless the adopted direction.

Over time people felt how the realism of logograms was contrasting against vocal expressions in the sense that the pictorial qualities of ideograms thwarted reading in that a sign did not correspond to a sound. Persons began to simplify the shapes of ideograms which lost the most evident iconic characters.

Thirdly the modules of script sought to denote single parts of the vocal language instead of complex ideas.

The prolonged progress of writing led to *alphabetic symbols* that conform as much as possible to the vocal discretization. Written alphabets perfected the attempts to simplify the symbols, to refer symbols to sounds and to place the symbols in line. Alphabets facilitated the methods to relate writing to speech and to store information that otherwise became lost. Written alphabets sustained the evolution from the poor languages exchanged amongst hominids to the rich modern communication (Taylor 2003).

B. Obstacles and Defects in the Alphabetic Project

Alphabetic writing tends toward *the principle one sign/one sound* in order to pursue the supposed initial objectives that were to faithfully keep vocal messages. Alphabets are oriented toward the *segmental phoneme principle* which means that an elementary graphic signifier – called *grapheme* – has to correspond to an elementary vocal signifier – called *phoneme*.

Many facts contribute to missing this target with absolute precision. I summarize the problems by saying that graphemes and phonemes are largely imperfect digital elements and add a few comments on the various deviations.

1. Script

Chinese Calligraphic Styles	Years Ago
Jia Gu Wen	3,400
Jin Wen	3,100
Small Seal	2,200
Administrative	2,100
Exemplar	1,700
Cursive	1,800

Figure 10.8. Birth-date of the principal Chinese calligraphic styles.

As first one should remind that alphabets have not gained universal consensus. Ideograms are in use still today and their popularity is not negligible. Chinese, one of the largest populations in the world, ignore the alphabet. Chinese like *calligraphy*, the art of handwriting, very much (Jackson 1981). The pictorial qualities of scripts amuse the Chinese people and calligraphers are held in high reputation.

Chinese writing did not evolve toward an effective alphabet due to the esthetical love of the Chinese for calligraphy. They also influenced close Asian people such as Japanese.

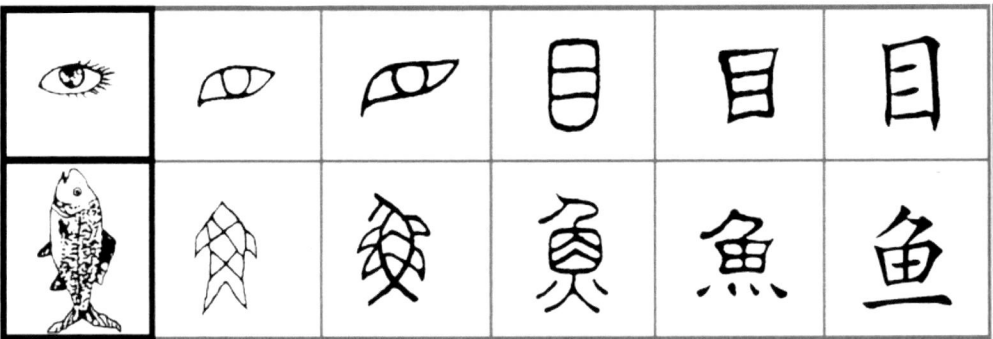

Figure 10.9. Evolution of the Chinese ideograms *mù* (eye) and *yǔ* (fish) crossing different calligraphic styles. (Adapted from: Huaqing op.cit.).

A Chinese student in calligraphy learns the procedures for the perfect execution of traits and even becomes aware of the origin and evolution of each ideogram. He apprehends the calligraphic styles introduced in the arc of centuries that brought novel ideograms into use in successive stages.

Each Chinese sign stands for a concept and in consequence common people are obliged to learn several ideograms. By way of illustration no less that 100 ideograms are necessary to grasp about 40% of everyday scripts, and 1,000 ideograms cover nearly 80% of common texts (Zein 2003). A good calligrapher is familiar with 16,000-18,000 ideograms, a subset of the whole set of orthographic forms of Chinese characters that are estimated to be about 50,000. This datum is enough to grasp the great deal of work on using non-alphabetic writing.

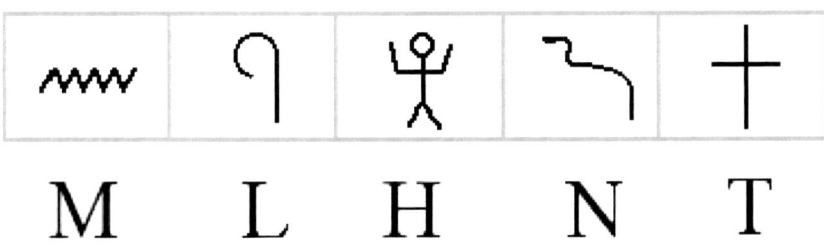

Figure 10.10. Proto-Sinaitic signs and modern Latin characters.

Men invented alphabetic writing at different ages in different parts of the world, and writing advanced at different speeds. The routes leading to efficient alphabets were more or less tortuous in various areas. For example Egyptian script evolved through intricate rules.

Each hieroglyphic in Figure 10.7 exhibits a couple of symbols at the left side that have phonetic values. These symbols signify the consonants '*htm*' which specify the pronunciation of the hieroglyphic 'woman', 'cow' and 'art' respectively. Phonetic, morphemic and determinative symbols were included in a unique ideogram. As a further example, authors of Semitic alphabets considered the symbols to represent vowels as inessential elements of writing.

Residual pictorial aspects remain in the written symbols that maintain a certain artistic profile still nowadays. Many letters are stylized portraits of physical objects. For instance some researchers claim that the proto-Sinaitic alphabets bring evidence of the iconic origins of the Latin letters.

Ideograms and hieroglyphs require special manual skills, and people learnt to employ simplified letters in order to help an individual to write. But notwithstanding this facility, handwriting does not come up to precise outcomes. The manual preparation of a script does not guarantee the results that one could have expected. A device prints a letter that is always identical to itself due to the principle of precision discussed in Chapter 3, conversely scribes deform the letters of the alphabet to speed up handwriting. Penmen give form to signs in an expressive manner that constitutes a defect from the technical perspective because each letter should keep its shape and should be independent from the manual author in accordance to issue [3.1].

Handwriting is so spontaneous and in contrast with the principle of precision that a manually written text mirrors the psychological profile of the author (Saudek 2003). Personal tracts are so apparent that graphologists are able to recognize authors' temperaments and nowadays *Graphology* is a mature discipline grounded upon fundamental principles, methods and laws. Magistrates doubting about uncertain authorship usually request the assistance of a graphological expert who acts as a witness before the court (McNichol et al. 1994).

2. Speech

When people felt the need of recording information and began to find a written alphabet through an empirical approach, they were absolutely unaware of the widespread knotty problem they had just addressed. They attempted to translate the sonorous alphabet into a finite set of written symbols so that each sound might be approximately represented by a graphical tract. The project seems manageable in principle, but turned out to be an enormous conundrum in practice (Diringer 1968).

Hominids found that a few elementary sounds are enough to make up a huge number of words, when they began to employ the coding technique, and spontaneously simplified vocalization. Digitalization involves less complicated phonation than onomatopoeic sounds; humans restricted the gamut of sounds and enjoyed creating uncountable signifiers. I believe the simplification inherent to the digital paradigm swindled the earliest alphabet inventors. Sonorous simplification deceived individuals who first tried to prepare a written alphabet (Logan 1986). The sizes of alphabets – commented on Chapter 2, Paragraph 5 – bring evidence that creators of written alphabets supposed that about two or three dozens of symbols were enough to represent all the phonemes.

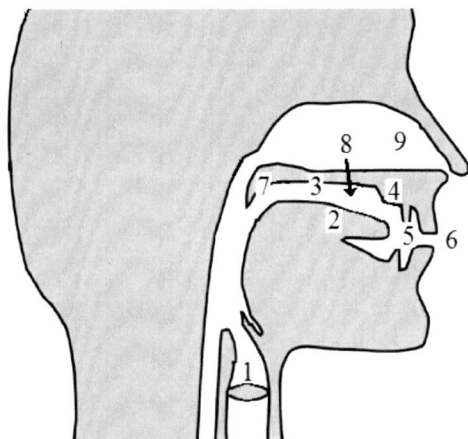

Figure 10.11. Organs of phonation. 1 larynx including vocal cords or glottis, 2 tongue, 3 palate, 4 alveolar ridge, 5 teeth, 6 lips, 7 velum, 8 oral cavity, 9 nasal cavity.

The simplified view on vocal tongues emerges in the earliest treatises on *Phonetics* whose authors operated under ear impressions and related simplified accounts. Ancient credited the sound-elements of speech as belonging either to the 'sonority' group – the *vowels* – or to the 'noise' group – the *consonants*. Modern researchers introduced suitable acoustic instruments in Phonetics, they made photographic records of the shapes of sound waves and progressively discovered an unimaginable variety of forms in the vocal communication. Nowadays specialists recognize thousands of phonemes and investigations have not yet come to an end. As a case, ancient authors identified five vowels whereas modern authors classify 28 different vowels and hundreds of consonants, and inquiries are still in progress (Ladefoged 1996).

Why does the definition of a satisfactory spoken alphabet not seem to be at hand?

The vocal apparatus is equipped with different organs that work together in a continuous way. Persons emit flows of sonorous waves and do not output separate sounds. This phonetic apparatus is somewhat close to the analog mode and does not turn out to be suitable for the digital paradigm.

The vocal organs cooperate in modulating the human voice along with the lungs and result in sophisticated sonorous effects. I quote the *consonant,* a speech sound that is articulated with complete or partial closure of the upper vocal tract. A consonant depends on several parameters: the manner of articulation, the place of articulation, the position of the tongue etc. For example a consonant may be pronounced by placing the tongue to the fore of the mouth (*dental consonant*), in the middle (*alveolar consonant*) or in the back of the mouth (*velar consonant*).

Recently researchers discovered other consonants. Many southern African languages use consonants not obtained by the emission of air from the lungs, but are created by introducing air into the lungs and are called *clicks consonants.*

The *vowel,* a sound pronounced with an open vocal tract should be univocal instead the vocal cords emit a sound having a fundamental wave and a large number of harmonics. The cavities are able to echo and to reinforce a number of waves. When these waves pass through the throat, the mouth, and the nasal cavities the resonant frequencies of these cavities are radiated into the air very magnified and determine the final utterance which may hardly be catalogued into predetermined boxes.

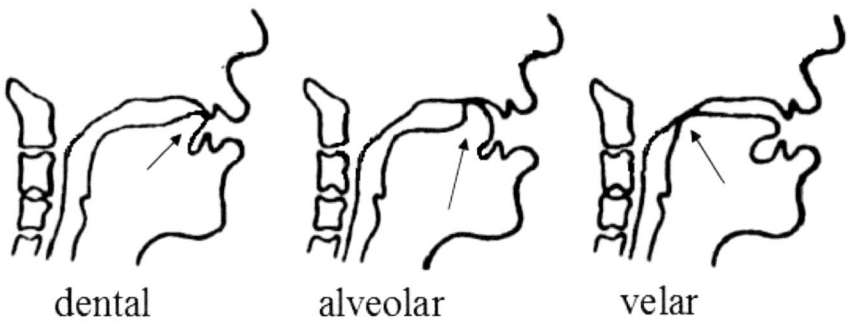

Figure 10.12. Articulation of dental, alveolar and velar consonants (Adapted from: King op. cit.).

Moreover a number of sonorous effects interfere with human speech (Tohkura 1992).

Tones are pitch variations which are used in short stretches of syllable length. Tone is a phonological trait which may be seized to distinguish words. The vast majority of Chinese spoken words are monosyllabic words which convey a variety of significance through voice intonation. For this reason, many words with the same sound express different meanings depending on the tone of the sound.

Tonal patterns vary widely across languages. In English, one or more syllables are given an *accent*, which can consist of a loud stress, a lengthened vowel, and a high pitch, or any combination of these. In French, no syllable is stressed or lengthened, but the final or penultimate syllable has a higher pitch.

The *intonation of voice* is used for emphasis, to convey surprise or irony, or even to pose a question. Intonation is rising when the pitch of the voice increases over time; and is falling when the pitch decreases with time.

Spoken languages present such an ample variety of expressions and lack of discipline that researches can neither define the boundaries of the problems so far. The variances and the discrepancies of a spoken alphabet constitute an open scientific challenge. Thousands and thousands of languages spoken world-wide render the matter merely immense.

Graphemes and phonemes draw away from the parallelism which should be necessary from the digital viewpoint. The speech to-text correspondence that appears indispensable for a perfect digital system is normally inapplicable. The project for an alphabet that thoroughly represents how a written word is to be pronounced was given up until a group of French and British language teachers, led by Paul Passy, reverted to this idea in 1886. They formed a scientific association with the scope of creating a written alphabet absolutely close to the pronounced words. The *International Phonetic Alphabet* (IPA) is coded and revised from time to time with the contribution of new discoveries (IPA 1999). IPA currently emerges as the most rigorous project for a rigorous written alphabet.

5. HYBRID APPLIANCES

Spoken and written languages constitute the most popular and enduring applications of the digital paradigm ever done notwithstanding the above mentioned failures. Natural languages constitute a technical event that had enormous effects on technologies even if people created blended and approximated alphabets, and adopted methodologies in their own way.

The wide spreading digitalization in languages and in numbering forced past scientists to distort analog appliances so that those appliances brought forth discrete results in a way. Letters and figures caused the birth of *hybrid* solutions since the early beginnings. The vast majority of ancient measurement instruments are not purely analog but hybrid. I quote some hybrid devices in Chapters 2 and 3, for example I detail how the clock needle rotates continuously over the Arabic numerals and this device is part continuous and part discrete.

The class of hybrid devices should not be considered as a corrupt byproduct of the analog paradigm. Mixed solutions automated the management of numerical values and texts, and marked the progress of mankind in a decisive manner. Sometime an analog solution encountered mounting success when it became hybrid and anticipated the effectiveness of the digital mode in a way.

I quote the case of the printing systems.

The printing press was well established using woodblocks in the late Middle Ages. Woodblock printing seems to be derived from Chinese techniques for printing on textiles. The wood block was prepared as a relief matrix, namely the areas to show 'white' were cut away with a chisel, and the surface that showed the intended image was left untouched. A sheet of paper was placed on the inked woodblock and an impression was taken by rubbing. In fact it was only necessary to ink the block and bring it into firm and even contact with the paper to achieve a good printed outcome. Even if tedious and rather ineffective, this method of printing provided significant benefits as it was no longer indispensable to handwrite parchment volumes.

Scribes were typically either monks who copied books for use in monasteries or they were commercial copyists who were hired by readers to produce books. There were numerous problems with the scribal method of making books. It was certainly slow and costly. But the central problem with scribes was that they made mistakes in their copies, and then these copies came into the hands of other scribes, who not only copied the previous mistakes but added more mistakes of their own.

The woodblock technique may be easily classified as an analog approach to printing: the pressmen created a carved matrix identical – namely analog – to the image to print.

In approximately 1436 Johannes Gutenberg introduced the *movable type printing* that may be considered as the evolution of the previous analog method toward the digital paradigm because the printing matrix consists of movable types which are discrete elements. The matrix splits into individual components, such as lower and upper case letters, punctuation marks, ligatures and abbreviations. These individual items are assembled to form words and pages in accordance to the combinatorial qualities of the digital paradigm. Gutenberg created metallic types, more robust than wooden types, and enhanced the flexibility typical of the digital modules that can be reused and modified at ease.

Gutenberg's innovation inaugurated a period of great change. Historians argue that, among other consequences, the Gutenberg printing press contributed to the protestant reformation, the rise of the humanist culture in the Renaissance, and the scientific revolution. The success of Gutenberg's discovery was enormous in Europe, comparable to the development of writing, the invention of the alphabet and the introduction of computers. All of them constitute essential steps toward the rational, effective – say the digital – handling of information.

6. CONCLUDING REMARKS

The present chapter focuses on the early origins of the Muscular and the Instrumental Approaches in the information sector – see points α) and β) in the inception of this chapter – which make two threads of autonomous and somewhat related events.

Unstudied people introduced the digital techniques in spoken languages even if the vocal apparatus does not fit with discretization, and drew the migration from poor communication to sophisticated expressions. The Muscular mode exhibits a rather linear trend.

The progression of the Instrumental Approach, richer in episodes, consists of a series of chained events. People prepared symbols using generic tools in a first stage; then they went toward the realistic representation of the physical world.

In a subsequent period the desire to represent speech emerged with evident analog features, and finally writing evolved from ideograms toward written alphabets closer to vocal languages.

Years	Period	Anthropological Evolution	Trends in the Information Sector	
			Muscular Approach	Instrumental Approach
3,000	Neolithic		Rich Speech (digital)	Alphabets (digital)
				Ideograms (analog-digital)
8,000	Mesolithic			
10,000	Upper Paleolithic			Graffiti (analog)
40,000	Middle Paleolithic			
100,000	Lower Paleolithic	Homo Sapiens	Poor Speech	Rough signs
		Homo Erectus		
2,000,000		Homo Habilis		

Figure 10.13. Trends in the information field (Years are out of scale).

Spoken and written alphabets show many defects from the technical viewpoint so that the project to make a perfect parallel between speech and writing have failed so far.

The digital paradigm saw the light in the dawn of mankind and never left people, nonetheless the digital paradigm still puzzles scientists who seek to decipher the digital and the analog approaches. I guess this book will contribute to the quest.

BIBLIOGRAPHY

Corballis M.C. (2002) - *From Hand to Mouth: The Origins of Language* - Princeton University Press.
Diringer D. (1968) - *The Alphabet: A Key to the History of Mankind* - Hutchinson & Co.
Herrera G.L. (2007) - *Technology and International Transformation: The Railroad, the Atom Bomb, and the Politics of Technological Change* - State University of New York Press.
Huaqing Y. (1993) - *La Scrittura Cinese* - Vaillardi.
Hughes T.P. (2005) - *Human-Built World: How to Think about Technology and* Culture - University of Chicago Press.
IPA (1999) - *Handbook of the International Phonetic Association* - Cambridge University Press
Jackson D. (1981) - *The Story of Writing* - The Calligraphy Centre.
King B.J. (1999) - *The Origins of Language: What Non-human Primates Can Tell Us* - James Currey Publishers, p. 442
Ladefoged P. (1996) - *Elements of Acoustic Phonetics* - University of Chicago Press.
Leakey R. (1994) - *The Origin of Humankind* - Basic Books.
Lieberman P., Blumstein S. (1988) - *Speech Physiology, Speech Perception, and Acoustic Phonetics* - Cambridge University Press.
Liungman C.G. (1995) - *Thought Signs: The Semiotics of Symbols* - IOS Press.
Logan K.L. (1986) - *The Alphabet Effect: The Impact of the Phonetic Alphabet on the Development of Western Civilization* - William Morrow and Co.
McNichol A., Nelson J. (1994) - *Handwriting Analysis : Putting It to Work for You* - McGraw-Hill.
Mac Whinney B. (ed) (1999) - *The Emergence of Language* - Lawrence Erlbaum Associates.
Maple T.L., Hoff M.P. (1982) - *Gorilla Behavior* - Van Nostrand Reinhold Co.
Mellars P. (ed) (1991) - *The Emergence of Modern Humans: An Archaeological Perspective* - Cornell University Press.
Negus V. (1949) - *The Comparative Anatomy and Physiology of the Larynx* - Hafner Press.
Newmeyer F.J. (1988) - *Language: Psychological and Biological Aspects* - Cambridge University Press.
Riggio R.E., Feldman R.F. (2005) - *Applications of Nonverbal Communication* - Routledge.
Saudek R. (2003) - *Psychology of Handwriting* - Kessinger Publishing.
Schmandt-Besserat D. (1997) - *How Writing Came About* - University of Texas Press.
Seth P.K., Seth S. (eds) (1993) - *New Perspectives in Anthropology* - M.D. Publications Pvt. Ltd.
Shneiderman B. (2002) - *Leonardo's Laptop: Human Needs and the New Computing Technologies* - MIT Press.

Soravia G. (1976) - *Storia del Linguaggio* - Garzanti.
Taylor I. (2003) - *History of the Alphabet* - vol 1&2, Kessinger Publishing.
Tohkura Y., Vatikiotis-Bateson E., Sagisaka Y. (1992) - *Speech Perception, Production and Linguistic Structure* - IOS Press.
Washburn S.L. (2004) - *Social Life of Early Man* - Routledge.
Winner L. (1978) - *Autonomous Technology: Technics-out-of-Control as a Theme in Political Thought* - M.I.T. Press.
Zein P.H. (2003) - *The Most Common Chinese Characters in Order of Frequency* - http://www.zein.se/patrick/3000char.html

INDEX

Alphabet	49,72,83,89,229
Analog	
- devices	65,69,122
- signs	45,62
Argument	
- natural/artificial	61
- continuous/discrete	66
Backbone	144
Biological computation	111
Bits	31,65,72,80
Boole algebra	73
Brain evolution	223
Cell	146
Channel	138
Coaxial cable	140
Collapse of wave	37
Compression	168
Consonants	233
Converters	122
Couple relativity	38
Criterion of Rayleigh	34
Data field	128
Data file	155
Data processing	122
Database	158
Decibell	42
Digital signs	68
Distance of Hamming	85
Distinct	
- points	30
- subsets	29
- vectors	30
Encoding	78
Encryption	169

Entity relationship diagram	161
Entropy	38, 177
Error factor	70
Evidences	24
Exponential function	79
Factor of contrast	41
Feedback loop	189
Finite state machine	105
First order system	101
Form	17
Genres of programs	208
Graphs	
- complete	142
- linear	143
Hardware technology	195
Hierarchical net	144
Hosts	147
Hybrid appliances	67, 234
Icons	47
Ideograms	228
Improper channel	141
Impulse function	102
Independency from technology	108
Index	47
Information	
- theories	14
- systems	189
Intelligent adaptation	184
Key of	
- encryption	169
- file	157
Language of signs	23
Law of Weber-Flechner	42
Linear continuous systems	100
Linguistic motivations	47
Linguistic typology	21
Logograms	228
Mean	32
Measurement	51
Media (hot/cold)	22
Medical semiotics	23
Mind	19
Mode	
- client/server	147
- master/slave	149
Model	

- hierarchical	132, 147
- IPO	134
- Radial	131
Monocentric net	147
Normalization	162
Open system	188
Optical fiber	140
Organ of phonation	233
Polycentric net	148
Post-industrial revolution	194
Principle of	
- arbitrariness	43
- causality	13
- excluded middle	70
- precision	104
- sharpness	28
Qubits	112
Quantum computation	112
Redundancy	
- generic	171
- active/passive	173
Reference relativity	36
Relative error	70
Second order system	103
Semantic	
- convention	44
- table	85
- triad	18
Sense maker	18
Signified	17
Signifier	
- artificial	53
- generic	17
- natural	53
Simulation	126
Software	
- technology	195
- development and maintenance	209
Spikes	26
Standard	
- assembly	75
- deviation	32
State transition table	105
Step function	102
Structure of level	204
Symbols	47
Symptoms	24

System-time constant	102
Szilard's engine	25
Telephonic cable	139
Turing machine	181
Type of	
- programs	210
- signs	47
Visual illusion	35
Waveguides	139
Wireless system	145
Word	78,85